The Mystery *of* Suffering *and* Death

BROWN-ROA

A Division of Harcourt Brace & Company

Janie Gustafson, Ph.D.

Nihil Obstat

Rev. Richard L. Schaefer

Imprimatur

✠ Most Rev. Jerome Hanus, OSB
Archbishop of Dubuque
November 13, 1998

The Imprimatur is an official declaration that a book or pamphlet is free of doctrinal or moral error. No implication is contained therein that anyone who granted the Imprimatur agrees with the contents, opinions, or statements expressed.

Copyright © 2000 by BROWN-ROA, a division of Harcourt Brace & Company

The Scripture quotations contained herein are from the New Revised Standard Version Bible: Catholic Edition copyright © 1993 and 1989, by the Division of Christian Education of the National Council of the Churches of Christ in the U.S.A. Used by permission. All rights reserved.

Excerpts from the English translation of the *Catechism of the Catholic Church* for use in the United States of America Copyright © 1994, United States Catholic Conference, Inc.—Libreria Editrice Vaticana. Used with permission.

Excerpts from the English translation of *The Roman Missal* © 1973, International Committee on English in the Liturgy, Inc. (ICEL); excerpts from the English translation of *Dedication of a Church and Altar* © 1978, ICEL; excerpts from the English translation of *Pastoral Care of the Sick* © 1982, ICEL; excerpts from the English translation of *Order of Christian Funerals* © 1985, ICEL; excerpts from the English translation of *Book of Blessings* © 1988, ICEL. All rights reserved.

Excerpts from *Handgun Violence: A Threat to Life* Copyright © 1975 United States Catholic Conference, Inc. (USCC), Washington, DC; *Society and the Aged: Toward Reconciliation* © 1976 USCC; *Pastoral Statement of the United States Bishops on Persons with Disabilities* © 1978; *Health and Health Care* © 1982 USCC; *Statement on Capital Punishment* © 1981 USCC; and *Ethical and Religious Directives for Catholic Health Care Services* © 1995 USCC. Used with permission. All rights reserved.

Printed in the United States of America

ISBN 0-15-950575-5

10 9 8

•Contents•

Preface

It is almost impossible to go an entire day without hearing about death or some type of suffering. Sometimes suffering and death occur in foreign lands; sometimes they strike in our own neighborhoods and homes. Consider these examples:

- The 230 people who died on July 17, 1996, when TWA Flight 800 exploded shortly after take-off.
- The 168 people, including children and babies, who were killed when a terrorist bombed the Alfred P. Murrah Federal Building in Oklahoma City on April 19, 1995.
- The 40 people who lost their lives when tornadoes swept through central Florida in late April 1998.
- The growing numbers of young people who die each year as victims of guns or gang-related violence.

Suffering and death, in one way or another, affects everyone.

The topic of suffering and death arouses as many diverse reactions as there are individual people. Some people seek to avoid suffering and deny death as a fact of life; others fear pain or those who are dead. Some, who philosophically believe that suffering is evil, advocate doctor-assisted suicide. Others, who see death as the ultimate evil, seek all possible means to prolong their lives indefinitely. Catholics, on the other hand, look at the reality of suffering and death with the eyes of religious faith. To those of us who believe in the Paschal mystery—Jesus' passing from death to life—death is the beginning of a new kind of living, a glorified eternal existence.

This textbook examines how suffering and death reach into all aspects of life: philosophical, historical, cultural, psychological, social, financial/legal, moral, and religious. Specifically, the book approaches suffering and death from a Catholic perspective. This perspective takes into account both meanings of the word *catholic*. First, it deals with the universal experience of suffering and death. Second, it considers the specific viewpoint of the Catholic Church.

Basic to this book are the Christian beliefs that suffering can be redemptive and that death is the beginning of new life with the resurrected Christ. Within the framework of these beliefs, you will explore various topics and issues related to the mystery of suffering and death. You will also learn how these beliefs have affected Catholic teaching and practice in such areas as the works of mercy, devotion to the saints, the saying of certain prayers, the feasts of All Saints' Day and All Souls' Day, the Sacraments of Baptism, Eucharist, Reconciliation, and Anointing of the Sick, the celebration of the Easter Triduum, and the revised *Order of Christian Funerals.*

The topic of suffering and death can seem overwhelming; yet dealing with this topic is essential both to a life of faith and to a life that is well-lived. What you do with this course will be up to you. Hopefully, your studies will spur you to continued independent exploration and personal reflection. As you pause for introspection throughout these pages, may you come to understand more fully the meaning of Jesus' words: "I came that they may have life, and have it abundantly" (John 10:10).

I am the resurrection

and the life.

Those who believe in me,

even though they die, will live,

and everyone who

lives and believes in me

will never die.

• John 11: 25-26

The Mystery of Suffering and Death

IN THIS UNIT, YOU WILL

For everything there is a season, . . .

a time to be born, and a time to die . . .

• *Ecclesiastes 3:1–2*

I sought whence suffering comes and

there was no solution.

• *Saint Augustine,* Confessions

- explore the reality of human suffering and death;
- learn why studying about suffering and death is important to Christian faith;
- evaluate traditional answers about why the innocent suffer and why good people sometimes die young;
- identify healthy and unhealthy reactions to suffering and death.

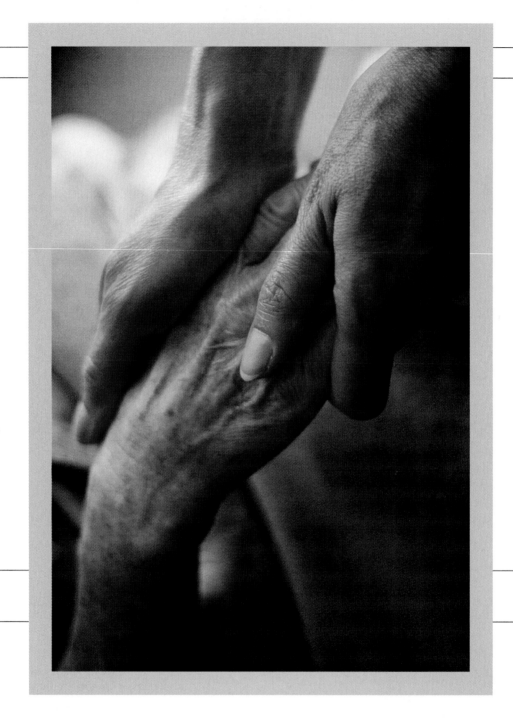

C•H•A•P•T•E•R

1

The Pain *of* Being Human

IN THIS CHAPTER, YOU WILL

- define what suffering is;
- examine different types of pain—physical, psychological, and spiritual;
- study the three major causes of suffering;
- understand why a world with no suffering may not be the best;
- realize how a certain amount of suffering is necessary for the strengthening of human character;
- consider the connection between suffering and love;
- see how belief in the humanity of Jesus can strengthen us in times of suffering;
- evaluate your own ability to face suffering and bounce back from adversity.

Down but Not Out

Of Interest

In 1998, the Arthritis Foundation reported that 2.1 million Americans suffered from rheumatoid arthritis, a progressive, often crippling auto-immune inflammatory disease of the membranes lining the joints. Rheumatoid arthritis results in bone and cartilage damage throughout the body. As yet, there is no cure. Other painful rheumatic diseases include lupus and Lyme disease.

There's nothing worse than chronic, unrelenting pain. Ask 15-year-old Jenna, who is coming to terms with the diagnosis of juvenile rheumatoid arthritis. For her, each moment of the day is an uphill challenge.

It started two years ago. "She complained of pain and fatigue," her mother explained. "But we'd go to the doctor and there was never any explanation for it."

Finally, one morning, Jenna couldn't move. "Her body just shut down and it became obvious what it was when her feet and hands were all swollen," her mother said. "She went from being captain of the pom line in the eighth grade to being almost crippled."

A particularly aggressive and damaging form of juvenile rheumatoid arthritis, one that predominantly strikes teenage girls, had stopped Jenna in her tracks. No more competitive dancing, no more honor roll, no more movies and mall shopping with her friends. "She was in so much pain and so fatigued that she stayed upstairs in her room for five months. I had to lift her so she could sit up in bed," her mother continued.

Now Jenna takes fourteen different medications in the evening and seventeen in the morning. She's on so much Prednisone that it can turn a wonderful person into a monster. But this high school freshman is determined to continue battling arthritis.

"I am the person who can make the biggest difference in my disease," Jenna wrote in an essay for English class. "This disease could easily consume my best efforts to win." But Jenna doesn't intend to let that happen.

"I'm doing everything the doctor says about taking my medication, exercising, and eating properly," she said. "But sometimes it's discouraging and I have to remind myself that it will get better if I just keep going and don't give in to it. I always wanted to be in poms in high school and that's my goal."

Mostly, Jenna craves normalcy. "You take for granted all you can do until you can't do it anymore," she said. "I want my life back. I want to just be me again." ▪

—Adapted from "Poles of pain," © *The Arizona Republic* (February 16, 1998). Article by Linda Helser. Used with permission. Persmission does not imply endorsement.

Discussion

1. Why do you think some people have a great deal of suffering and pain throughout life, while others seem relatively pain-free?
2. If you were in Jenna's shoes, how do you think you would react to the suffering? What would be your feelings? Your thoughts? Your attitudes toward the future?

An Uphill Battle

Many people have memorized the opening sentence of M. Scott Peck's best-selling book *The Road Less Traveled*. The sentence is short and simple but packed with meaning: "Life is difficult." The author could just as well have said, "Life is suffering." Certainly, people like Jenna would agree. Life seems to be a constant, uphill battle. To be alive somehow involves pain.

Most people know from experience what **suffering** is, and yet suffering itself remains a mystery. There is so much about suffering we really don't know or understand. What exactly is suffering? Webster's dictionary says that to suffer means "to endure death, pain, or distress, to sustain loss or damage, to be subject to disability or handicap." According to the International Association for the Study of Pain, "suffering is an unpleasant sensory and emotional experience."

Human suffering has many different causes. For example, natural or human-caused catastrophes—earthquakes, tornadoes, hurricanes, floods, forest fires, car accidents, bombings—are the source of some suffering. Other suffering is caused by loss—the death of a loved one, the theft of one's belongings, the failure to achieve a goal, the break-up of a relationship. Still other suffering is caused by change—moving to a new city, starting a new school year, the divorce of one's parents, the physical and hormonal changes of adolescence. Suffering is also caused by sickness—Alzheimer's disease, multiple sclerosis, AIDS, kidney failure, cancer. Whatever its cause, suffering is real and is not discriminatory. It strikes both the old and the young, the rich and the poor, sinners and saints, and people of all races.

Take some time to reflect on your present attitudes toward and experiences of suffering. Start a notebook specifically for this course. Begin the notebook by writing your responses to the Attitude Survey above. ▪

Attitude Survey	I agree	I disagree	I'm not sure
Suffering and death are evils we must fight against.			
Human sinfulness is the ultimate cause of suffering in the world.			
God sends specific forms of suffering to specific people for a reason.			
I often wonder why God doesn't stop my suffering or the suffering of those I love.			
If our faith is strong enough, we can eradicate worldwide suffering.			

What Is Pain?

Have you ever had the flu, a toothache, a migraine headache, or a sprained ankle? If so, then you know firsthand about different kinds of physical pain. There is the deep, achy pain that accompanies the flu. Every muscle and joint in your body seems to hurt. Another type of pain consists of burning, shooting, or throbbing sensations. Some pain is **acute**, something that is sharp, immediate, and temporary. Other pain is **chronic**; it persists (as in rheumatoid arthritis and cancer).

From a biological perspective, pain is nature's way of telling us something is wrong. We feel pain because we have a central nervous system (a brain and spinal cord) and a peripheral nervous system—a network of fibers known as **nerves** leading to individual nerve cells (**neurons**). Throughout the human body, there are billions of neurons that receive and transmit the electrical and chemical impulses necessary for movement and for sensory function (seeing, tasting, touching, smelling, hearing, and feelings of hot, cold, pleasure, and pain).

suffering *An unpleasant sensory and emotional experience associated with being alive. To suffer means to "to endure death, pain, or distress, to sustain loss or damage, to be subject to disability or handicap."*

acute *Sharp, severe pain that has a sudden onset and lasts only a short time.*

chronic *Long-term pain; suffering that may never be relieved.*

nerve *Fibers of nervous tissue that connect the central nervous system (brain and spinal chord) with neurons throughout the body.*

neuron *A nerve cell; cell that has the ability to receive and transmit electrical and chemical impulses related to motion and sensory perception.*

Journal

1. Have you had any personal experience of suffering? If so, what happened?
2. What are your present feelings about suffering?
3. Why did you sign up for this course?
4. What fears or expectations do you have about this course?
5. What topics and questions do you want to be covered about suffering?

The human brain is the centerpiece of the body's nervous system. It is composed of about one hundred billion neurons and innumerable nerve fibers.

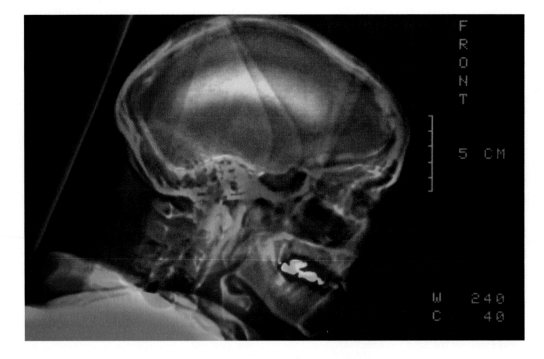

Recently, scientists have discovered different types of nerve fibers. Those associated with pain are called A-delta fibers and C fibers. A-delta fibers have a diameter of 1–5 micrometers and conduct impulses at a medium speed (5–25 meters per second). A-delta fibers register fast, sharp pain. C fibers are smaller and slower. They have a diameter of 1 micrometer and conduct impulses at a rate of about 1 meter per second. They register burning, throbbing pain.

So far, we have no way of measuring how much pain another person is feeling. Nor do we have any clear way of comparing the pain we feel to the pain of someone else with a similar injury or illness. Most likely, the words of the African-American spiritual are true: "Nobody knows the trouble I've seen." No one can really know the pain or trouble we are in. All pain is subjective. Our pain is uniquely ours. That is why it can isolate us from others.

Types of Pain

In general, there are three types of pain—physical, psychological, and spiritual.

Physical Pain

Physical pain can be acute or chronic, sharp and stabbing, or dull and achy. We feel physical pain when the brain's cortex receives impulses from neurons saying, "We have a problem here." Examples of physical pain include serious diseases, the flu, disabilities, broken bones, skinned knees, hurt "funny" bones, toothaches, migraines, sore throats, menstrual cramps, appendicitis attacks, gunshot or knife wounds, painful bruises, and hunger pains. The pain lasts as long as there is a physical problem. Some time after healing takes place, the pain usually stops. (One exception is "phantom limb" pain. Many people who have lost an arm or leg complain about continuing to feel pain in the limb that is missing.)

Of Interest

Doctors once thought babies and young children did not feel the same degree of pain as adults. Now that theory is being contested. To help children between the ages of 3 and 12 express how they are feeling, doctors have developed the Oucher scale. This scale consists of five faces with different expressions ranging from happy to miserable. The results of the test are still subjective. They are not necessarily an accurate measurement of the child's pain.

The Oucher Scale

Psychological Pain

This type of pain includes mental and emotional pain. The pain is "not just in our heads" or imaginary. It is as real as physical pain, although its source may not be physical. Causes of psychological pain include abandonment, rejection, feelings of failure, fear of being hurt, traumatic reactions to violence, fear of "sticking out" or not being "normal," feelings of inadequacy (being too tall, too fat, too ugly, too dumb, and so forth), mental illness, sympathy for the pain of others, helpless feelings, sorrow, anxiety caused by stress, guilt, anger, loneliness, and boredom.

Spiritual Pain

Spiritual pain is connected to our relationship with God and the health of our religious faith. Many saints have talked about spiritual pain in terms of "the dark night of the soul," times of uncertainty and doubt, or experiences of moral blindness. Examples of spiritual pain include doubting that God exists, doubting that God cares for or loves us, a sense of isolation and alienation from God, a loss of hope, rejecting religion because of the scandalous actions of one or several Church members, and the loss of identity, meaning, and purpose. ▪

Causes of Pain

Many people throughout history have considered suffering, pain, and death to be evil. They think these parts of life are opposed to God and are to be fought against continually. Jewish philosopher Moses Maimonides (1135–1204) is among those who label all suffering as evil. In his classic book *The Guide for the Perplexed*, he explains that suffering is caused by three types of evil. ▪

The first type of suffering is caused by evils that exist because humans are subject to birth and death and live in a limited, imperfect world. Such suffering includes sickness, aging, **mortality** (death), tangled emotional involvements, separation from loved ones, childbirth, hunger pangs, and genetic defects. Environmental evils include natural disasters, epidemics, drought, earthquakes, tornadoes, hurricanes, mud slides, and thunderstorms. Biological evils include genetic defects and illness, such as the blindness/deafness experienced by Helen Keller. Accidental evils include the paralysis of actor Christopher Reeve after falling off a horse.

The second type of suffering is caused by evils that people inflict on each other. Such evils include violence, physical and verbal abuse, rape, war, crime, prejudice and discrimination, broken relationships, misunderstandings and fights, gang violence, drive-by shootings, and drunk drivers. Examples of such suffering include the bombing of the Alfred P. Murrah Federal Building in Oklahoma City in 1995, the institution of slavery in early America, the forced imprisonment of Japanese-Americans in the United States during World War II, and the persecution and attempted extermination of Jews and other minorities during the Holocaust of World War II. This type of suffering may be personal—directly aimed at certain people—or it may be impersonal—due to people being in the wrong place at the wrong time, as was the suffering experienced by people who were passengers on the *Titanic*.

mortality *Death; the end of human life.*

Of Interest

Does pain have a color? Children who are asked to draw pictures of their pain overwhelmingly choose the color red.

Activity

In a small group, read one of the following Scripture passages.

- Tobit 10:1–7
- Psalm 22
- Psalm 38
- Psalm 137
- Sirach 37:1–6
- Lamentations 3:1–17

List the types of suffering found in the passage. Then try to categorize each suffering as physical, psychological, or spiritual.

Activity

Work alone or with one or two others to develop a creative description of suffering—either with words, sounds, a picture, or creative dance. Be prepared to share your description with the class.

The third type of suffering is caused by those evils we bring upon ourselves by our own thoughts or actions. Such self-inflicted suffering

*I*f one's futile **hope** for [a happy] **life** is simply to be **unbothered**, then the **happiest** of human beings are in **cemeteries**.

Father William J. O'Malley, *Redemptive Suffering*

may have psychological causes. Today, psychologists define the mental illness of **neurosis** as torture by one's own desires. Neurosis is an unhealthy mental condition in which one is trapped within an endlessly recurring pattern of emotional suffering—anxiety, obsession, self-centeredness, paranoia, fatalism, and so on. Self-inflicted suffering may also have moral causes. We may feel plagued with

guilt feelings because of wrongs we have done. We may be consumed by the desire for retaliation and revenge because we want things we cannot have. Such suffering is demonstrated in the movie *Amadeus*. The envy felt by the Italian musician Antonio Salieri toward Mozart absorbs all his energy. As a result, he never writes the music he is probably capable of composing. ▪ ▪

neurosis *An unhealthy mental condition in which one is trapped within an endlessly recurring pattern of emotional suffering—anxiety, obsession, self-centeredness, paranoia, fatalism, and so on.*

Activity

In a small group, look through a recent newspaper or news magazine. Find three examples of suffering caused by (a) the natural limitations of being human, (b) evil caused by others, and (c) evil caused by oneself. Be prepared to share your examples with the class.

Journal

Think about the suffering you have felt in your life. What percent of that suffering was caused by natural limitations? What percent was caused by others? What percent was caused by yourself? Write about each type of suffering in your own life.

A World with No Suffering

Can you imagine a world without suffering? Many people throughout history have had such thoughts. For example, the authors of the Book of Genesis describe the Garden of Eden as a tropical **paradise**, a heaven on earth in which people walk and talk with God. There are no wars, natural disasters, diseases, sins, or death. Followers of the Buddhist religion seek a release from the world of suffering in a blissful state they call **nirvana**. It, too, is a world without suffering, a situation of perfect happiness and contentment. A number of philosophers, writers, and sociologists—including Plato (*Republic*), Sir Thomas More (*Utopia*), Jonathan Swift (*Gulliver's Travels*), Aldous Huxley (*Brave New World*), George Orwell (*1984*), and Henry David Thoreau (*Walden*)—have described their vision of **utopia**, the ideal society.

The problem with such thinking is its basic premise. The quest for paradise, nirvana, or utopia mistakenly equates human happiness with the absence of suffering. It assumes we can only be happy if there is no sadness, pain, or death. The reality of human existence tells us otherwise. In fact, a certain amount of pain is actually *needed* for a happy human life. Some pain is good! ◼

paradise *A perfect world; a heaven on earth in which people walk and talk with God.*

nirvana *A blissful state of perfect happiness, in which there is no suffering or death.*

utopia *A perfect, or ideal, society.*

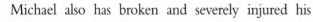

Michael

Several years ago, Michael was diagnosed with congenital sensory neuropathy. What this means is that Michael has no sensation of pain at all. Because of his chronic insensitivity to pain, Michael has been injuring himself repeatedly since infancy. Even walking can be a problem. Michael fails to feel the full impact of his steps and therefore tends to hit the ground far too hard with his feet. So he's broken various bones on both feet about twenty times, to the point where his ankles are disintegrating.

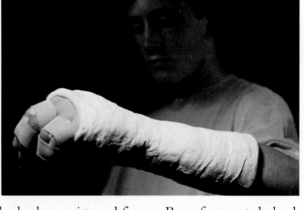

Michael also has broken and severely injured his elbows more than half a dozen times. And there are also the broken wrists and fingers. Bone fragments lodged in and around his elbows have caused him to lose sensation in his fingers.

Because of a painless knee injury that went untreated, infection invaded Michael's body and recently attacked his spine. He didn't feel any pain from infection, so the infection was eating away at his vertebrae. Now Michael has problems with his left leg, too.

The pediatric neurologist who was the first to diagnose Michael's condition nine years ago said the teen's "incredibly rare" malady is the result of recessive genes possessed by both parents. The teen's future is uncertain. "We can't cure him and nobody knows what his life expectancy is."

—Adapted from "Poles of pain," © *The Arizona Republic* (February 16, 1998).
Article by Linda Helser. Used with permission.
Permission does not imply endorsement.

 ### Discussion
Describe your idea of a perfect world or society.

No Pain, No Gain

There is a popular saying, "No pain, no gain." What the saying means is that most of the good things we seek in life require hard work. If we are willing to suffer to reach a goal, then (1) the goal must truly be worthwhile, and (2) we must really want to attain it.

Ask any Olympic athlete about suffering and pain. He or she will tell you about years of self-sacrifice, strenuous exercises, and continuous discipline—all to reach the goal of an Olympic medal. Or ask anyone who has lost fifty pounds or quit smoking. He or she will tell you about the suffering involved in self-denial and will-power—all to reach the goal of a healthier life. Ask a doctor or dentist who recommends surgery to correct a medical problem. After the surgery, the patient may feel worse than before; but in the long run, he or she may be better off.

Most adults will tell you they are happiest when they are busy with worthwhile, meaningful work. Such work may be child care, accounting, nursing, providing social services to those who are poor, building a skyscraper, or driving a bus. The type of work and the amount of money it earns are not nearly as important as the sense of purpose it gives to the worker. Work, however, requires a certain amount of suffering. We give up our

> *I*f I had to **choose** *between* **pain** *and* **no feeling**, *I would choose* **pain**.
>
> William Faulkner

freedom—doing exactly what we want when we feel like doing it—to do what a manager tells us to do or to meet deadlines that a company sets. A certain amount of such suffering is actually good. It contributes to our self-esteem, our sense of accomplishment, and our need "to make a difference."

Working with others (family, parish community, debate squad, sports team, and so forth) also requires a certain amount of suffering. We give up some of our independence when we form a team. Sometimes we may have to curb our feelings and compromise. Other times we may have to keep trying despite few immediate rewards.

Indeed, a certain amount of suffering seems to be necessary for the strengthening of human character. Think about it: If we always lived in a perfect world, we would never have opportunities to be generous, show compassion, display courage, be determined, or exhibit heroism. There would be no need for firefighters, doctors, nurses, social workers, judges, lawyers, pharmacists, soldiers, police, or

A certain amount of suffering is good. It contributes to our self-esteem and our sense of accomplishment and helps us be generous, show compassion, display courage, and be determined.

countless other professionals. In fact, there would really be no need for any one of us. If society were already perfect, we would not be needed at all. There would be no achievements, contributions, inventions, or discoveries we could make. Life would truly be boring! ■

The Drama of Suffering

At the core of every good book or movie—fact or fiction—is the element of suffering. A certain amount of suffering and conflict is needed for drama. Think about any engaging book you have read or any exciting movie you have seen. Chances are, the main character (the protagonist) must struggle to overcome one or more problems. Either the character triumphs or the problem does. ■

Consider the movie *As Good As It Gets*. It is the story of Melvin Udall—a mean and neurotic romance writer who hates people and dogs. He is a **bigot** who puts down Simon, his homosexual artist neighbor, and thinks nothing of tossing Simon's dog, Verdell, down the garbage chute. Melvin is also obsessive-compulsive. He follows the same routine, day in and day out. He takes his own plastic utensils to the same restaurant. He must sit in the same seat at the same booth and be served by the same waitress, Carol Connelly.

At first Melvin treats Carol as he treats everyone else—with contempt and rudeness. But eventually he discovers more about Carol as a person. She is a struggling single mom with a very sick son whose asthma has almost made him an invalid. On her small income, she must endure endless red tape and unsatisfactory medical care. As a result, she is consumed with worry and feelings of helplessness. For some reason, Carol's situation

strikes a chord of compassion in Melvin. He surprisingly pays for a doctor to help the boy.

Meanwhile, Melvin's neighbor Simon is robbed of his most valuable possessions. In addition, he is physically beaten in an assault that leaves him almost dead. Since there is no one else to look after Verdell while Simon is in the hospital, Melvin is "stuck" with the job. Eventually, the dog's antics and companionship affect Melvin. He begins to care about something other than himself.

The transformation of Melvin into a kind and loving human being is not sudden or smooth. In fact, it is painful. At every step of the way, there are obstacles and problems that seem huge to Melvin. But he has truly seen the separate suffering of Carol and Simon, and he can no longer live without trying to relieve their pain. In the end, Melvin is still far from perfect. But he is committed to being a better person and trying to relate to others.

At one point in the movie, Simon says, "If you look at people long enough, you discover their humanity." Seeing the suffering of others makes them "real" to us. Sharing in their sufferings makes us more human.

bigot Person who is intolerant of the different opinions and lifestyles of others. Bigots usually think their own views are the only correct ones.

> **S**uffering *is, in fact,* **guaranteed** *for anyone who takes on the task of* **loving.** *Persons who* **love** *will* **suffer,** *but they will also find a* **fullness** *of life and a personal* **experience** *of the* **Spirit's** *presence.*
>
> Eugene Kennedy,
> *The Pain of Being Human*

 Discussion
1. What kind of work most gives you a sense of purpose and accomplishment?
2. What sacrifices have you made to attain a goal?
3. Who, in real life, are three of your heroes? What have these people done to confront suffering, either their own or the suffering of others?

 Journal
If you had a choice of living a dramatic life (a story worth telling) or a boring, secure life, which would you choose? Why?

Pain and dying are not enemies to true love or human happiness. They are necessary conditions for real living.

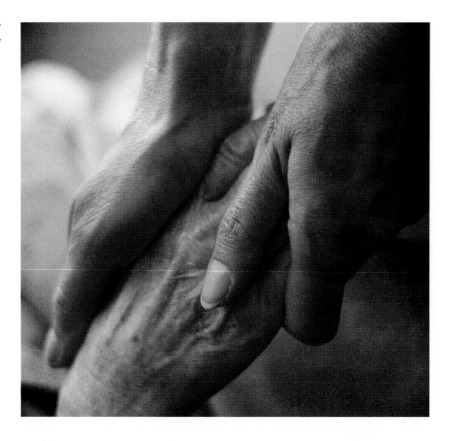

passion *From a Latin word that means "to suffer." To be passionate means to experience intense, driving, overwhelming emotion and feeling. It also means having a strong liking toward, desire for, or ardent devotion to something or someone else.*

compassion *To suffer with others; to be moved by the suffering of others in such a way that we try to alleviate that suffering.*

Suffering and Love

Ironically, we use the same word to describe suffering and to describe love. This word is *passion*. The word *passion* comes from a Latin word that means "to suffer." To be passionate means to experience intense, driving, overwhelming emotion and feeling. It also means having a strong liking toward, desire for, or ardent devotion to something or someone else. As the true story from the Vietnam War on the following page shows, people who truly love know how to suffer. They endure hardships and sacrifices for the ones they love. They are even willing to sacrifice their own lives, if necessary, for their friends.

Loving people also suffer when their loved ones suffer. They feel true **compassion** and seek to alleviate the suffering of those they love. Think of the parent who is up all night with a sick child. Or the teen who comforts a friend whose boyfriend has dumped her for someone else. Loving people especially suffer when there is nothing they can do to help relieve the suffering of loved ones.

Indeed, the mystery of love is intimately tied up with the mystery of suffering and death. Just as love makes us more alive, so suffering and death make us more "human." Pain and dying are not enemies to true love or human happiness. They are necessary conditions for real living. ▪

 Discussion

1. Some people think that "suffering for love" means putting up with physical violence or rude behavior from a loved one. Do you think this type of suffering is involved in real love? Explain.

2. Some people think that "suffering for love" means committing suicide if there is a break-up in a relationship. They literally can't live without the loved one. Do you think this type of suffering is involved in real love? Explain.

3. Some people think that "suffering for love" means pursuing a relationship even if the other person is not interested. Do you think this type of suffering is involved in real love? Explain.

No Greater Love

Whatever their planned target, the mortar rounds landed in an orphanage run by a missionary group in the small Vietnamese village. The missionaries and one or two children were killed outright, and several more children were wounded, including one young girl, about eight years old.

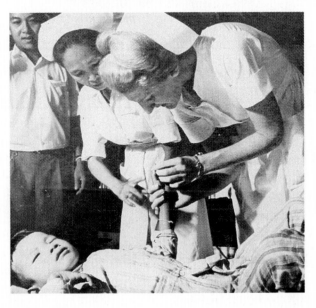

People from the village requested medical help from a neighboring town that had radio contact with the American forces. Finally, an American Navy doctor and nurse arrived in a jeep with only their medical kits. They established that the girl was the most critically injured. Without quick action, she would die of shock and loss of blood.

A transfusion was imperative, and a donor with a matching blood type was required. A quick test showed that neither American had the correct type, but several of the uninjured orphans did.

The doctor spoke some pidgin Vietnamese, and the nurse a smattering of high school French. Using that combination, together with much impromptu sign language, they tried to explain to their young, frightened audience that unless they could replace some of the girl's lost blood, she would certainly die. Then they asked if anyone would be willing to give blood to help.

Their request was met with wide-eyed silence. After several long moments, a small hand slowly and waveringly went up, dropped back down, and then went up again.

"Oh, thank you," the nurse said in French. "What is your name?"

"Heng," came the reply.

Heng was quickly laid on a pallet, his arm swabbed with alcohol, and a needle inserted in his vein. Through this ordeal Heng lay stiff and silent. After a moment, he let out a shuddering sob, quickly covering his face with his free hand.

"Is it hurting, Heng?" the doctor asked.

Heng shook his head, but after a few moments another sob escaped, and once more he tried to cover up his crying. Again the doctor asked him if the needle hurt, and again Heng shook his head. But now his occasional sobs gave way to a steady, silent crying; his eyes screwed tightly shut, his fist in his mouth to stifle his sobs.

The medical team was concerned. Something was obviously very wrong. At this point, a Vietnamese nurse arrived to help. Seeing the little one's distress, she spoke to him rapidly in Vietnamese, listened to his reply, and answered him in a soothing voice.

After a moment, the patient stopped crying and looked questioningly at the Vietnamese nurse. When she nodded, a look of great relief spread over his face.

Glancing up, the nurse said quietly to the Americans, "He thought he was dying. He misunderstood you. He thought you had asked him to give all his blood so the little girl could live."

"But why would he be willing to do that?" asked the Navy nurse.

The Vietnamese nurse repeated the question to the little boy, who answered simply, "She's my friend."

—"No Greater Love" by John W. Mansur. Reprinted with permission from the August 1987 *Reader's Digest.*

---

faith *A theological virtue that enables us to believe that God exists and loves us. Faith also enables us to have a personal relationship with God and to live by gospel values, despite situations of suffering and pain.*

Suffering and Faith

Every experience of suffering confronts us with spiritual questions. If God created everything, why did God create suffering? Where is God when innocent people suffer? Such questions can cut us to our very core. They challenge our entire belief system and sense of life's meaning and purpose.

Some people respond to suffering—their own or the suffering of others—by rejecting the gift of **faith**. They say that suffering and pain are "proofs" that God does not exist. They choose to be atheists. Other people respond to suffering by redefining who God is for them. They accept that God exists, but they believe God doesn't really care what happens to them. Still other people respond to suffering by depending even more on their religious faith. They live with suffering while still believing in a good and loving God; they choose to live with the mystery and the paradox.

This last response is the faith-stance the ancient Israelites chose to have, despite their unjust oppression as slaves in Egypt. Amidst their hardships, they continued to believe in a good God who heard their cries and cared what happened to them. Their faith was confirmed when God spoke to Moses from a burning bush.

> "I am the God of Abraham, the God of Isaac, the God of Jacob. . . . I have witnessed the affliction of my people in Egypt and have heard their cry of complaint against their slave drivers, so I know well what they are suffering. Therefore, I have come down to rescue them from the hands of the Egyptians and lead them out of that land into a good and spacious land. . . ."
>
> —Exodus 3:6–8

People's faith in God took a dramatic leap forward with the coming of Jesus. In accepting Jesus as Immanuel, a name that means "God is with us," people came to believe that God is always with us, even in times of suffering. Furthermore, God "feels" our suffering. God suffers with us. ■

Jesus Suffered

For centuries, the Church wrestled with its understanding of Jesus. Finally, its beliefs were written down in the Apostles' Creed and later in the Nicene Creed. Jesus is really divine, the second person of the Holy Trinity. But Jesus is also really human. He was born of the Virgin Mary, suffered under Pontius Pilate, was crucified, died, and was buried.

In other words, Jesus had a body exactly like the body of other human beings. He had a central nervous system and a peripheral nervous system. He really felt pain. His eyes cried real tears. Think about it—the gods of other nations could not see, hear, touch, taste, or smell. They were not moved by human suffering because they could not feel it. In Jesus, however, the God of Abraham, Isaac, and Jacob became flesh and experienced the pain of being human.

In Memory

One hundred sixty-eight men, women, and children were

killed in a bomb blast that destroyed the Alfred P. Murrah

Federal Building in Oklahoma City on April 19, 1995.

Three years later, the city constructed a shrine in their memory.

The shrine, a statue of Jesus crying, says simply,

"And Jesus wept"

(John 11:35).

Journal
How do you reconcile the reality of suffering with your ideas about God?

Jesus, in becoming human, revealed to us a side of God we could not have imagined. The Son of God actually felt physical, psychological, and spiritual pain. The Gospels record many instances of the suffering of Jesus:

- He suffered from fatigue (John 4:6).
- He knew what it meant to have his friends misunderstand him (Matthew 16:21–23).
- He grew angry at liars and cheaters, people who caused suffering to others (John 2:13–16).
- He truly pitied people who were troubled and abandoned (Matthew 9:36).
- He felt hungry (Matthew 12:1–8) and thirsty (John 4:7).
- He wept over the city of Jerusalem (Luke 13:34) and at the death of a friend (John 11:35).

- He knew the pain of being rejected by people in his own hometown (Matthew 13:54–58).
- He felt hurt by the betrayal of one of his own apostles (Matthew 26:20–25).
- He felt deep agony and distress about his impending death (Matthew 26:37–38).
- He knew what if felt like to be laughed at, scourged, cursed, and spat upon (Matthew 27:27–31).
- He felt excruciating pain caused by the thorns on his head and the nails driven into his hands and feet (Matthew 27:33–35).
- He even felt abandoned by God, his own Father (Matthew 27:46). ■

The fact that Jesus experienced the realities of suffering in his own person and was not defeated by them makes our Christian faith that much more credible. Because Jesus truly suffered the pain of being human, there are three things we can believe:

1. Suffering does not separate us from God. God cares about our suffering.
2. God does not let us face our suffering alone. God is always with us, lightening our burdens and giving us sufficient strength.
3. Suffering is not the end. It need not destroy us or defeat the possibility of eternal happiness in God's kingdom.

These three aspects of Christian faith can help us face and get through times of suffering. They can also help us stand by others when they are suffering. We are not alone. The God of passionate love is with us. ■

Of Interest

Psychologists have discovered that people with a great deal of resilience have the following seven personality traits:

1. They seize the present moment to act rather than deny the problem or procrastinate.

2. They have a strong sense of religious faith.

3. They lean on others; they ask for help rather than isolate themselves.

4. They set goals for themselves and have "contingency" plans for setbacks or problems.

5. They believe in their own worth and goodness.

6. They recognize their own strengths and put these strengths to work to solve the problem.

7. They see themselves as strategists; instead of being victimized by problems, they see each problem as a challenge and an opportunity for learning.

Activity
In a small group, look up each of the Scripture passages listed on this page that refer to the suffering of Jesus. Work together to categorize each example of suffering as physical, psychological, or spiritual. Be prepared to share your ideas with the class.

Journal
What difference has your belief in the humanity of Jesus made in the way you think about and handle suffering?

How Fast Can You Bounce Back?

Recently, psychologists have been studying the ability of people to bounce back from suffering and setbacks. People who bounce back fast and get on with their lives are said to have a great deal of **resilience**—the ability to handle whatever life deals them. Such people do not just cope with pain and suffering by merely surviving. They *thrive* despite the problems they face.

To find out how resilient you are, take the following quiz. Circle the answers that honestly reflect you. Then score yourself based on the directions your teacher will give you.

1. After completing an exhausting year on the varsity team, you get replaced for next season by a younger student. The next week, you:
   a) Map out a plan to see what other school activity you can become involved in.
   b) Decide to take the summer off and nurse your hurt feelings.
   c) Worry about how you will ever get a scholarship for college.

2. On your way to a surprise party for your best friend, you get lost on the highway. Your first response is to:
   a) Complain about not having a cellular phone so you could call and ask for directions.
   b) Stop at a gas station for help, then proceed to your destination even though you're mad about being late.
   c) Look at the map in your glove compartment, get yourself back on course, and, when you show up late, make a joke about your poor navigational skills.

3. If your parents were in a serious car accident and had to be hospitalized, what do you think you would do once you got over the shock?

   a) Pepper the doctors with questions and see that your parents were getting the best care possible.
   b) Focus mainly on practical things such as making meals, filling out medical insurance forms, and looking after the house.
   c) Feel sorry for yourself and think about finding a counselor or therapist.

4. Suppose your home has been burglarized and your most prized possessions are gone. You are most likely to:
   a) Consider how the situation could have been worse—for example, if you'd been home when the burglar broke in.
   b) Yell at your next-door neighbor for not calling 911 the second he heard suspicious noises.
   c) Help your parents install another lock and dead bolt for the door and join a neighborhood crime-prevention task force.

5. If you worked on a project with a classmate who had a totally negative mind-set, how do you think you would deal with that classmate?
   a) You'd try to understand why your classmate is always in such a bad mood.
   b) You'd keep your distance so that your classmate's attitude wouldn't rub off on you.
   c) You'd probably end up complaining about having to work with someone who complains all the time.

6. Generally speaking, how do you look at change?
   a) As scary but often worthwhile.
   b) As a chance for new opportunities.
   c) As a loss. It usually means giving something up.

7. Suppose you bought, on sale, a suede jacket or designer athletic shoes you love. But, even discounted, it cost $200, which wipes out your savings account. You would:
   a) Call up a friend for reassurance that you did the right thing.
   b) Think about it, realize there are other things you need more, and return what you bought.
   c) Ask your parents for $200.

resilience The ability to handle whatever life deals us. Resilient people do not just cope with pain and suffering by merely surviving. They thrive despite the problems they are having.

What makes a person resilient? Researchers say one of the most important skills is the ability to be and feel connected to others. Other important traits include intelligence, problem-solving skills, and a quizzical mind.

8. Suppose someone has been using your name and social security number to open a credit card account. You're being charged for hundreds of dollars you didn't spend. You:

a) Feel targeted, as if somebody is out to get you.

b) Mentally retrace your steps, trying to pinpoint when you might have given out any personal information.

c) Make phone calls and write letters to figure out how to clear your name and catch the thief.

9. Think about the most distressing thing that ever happened in your life. Did you (circle all that apply):

a) Try to handle the situation the best you could?

b) Learn something useful?

c) Discover a strength or ability you didn't know you had?

d) Develop more self-confidence?

e) End up spending more time by yourself to analyze what was going on?

10. If there seemed to be something slightly wrong with your car—for instance, you heard an unusual noise— what would you do about it?

a) Ask a friend who knows a lot about cars for an educated opinion when you see your friend next week.

b) Ask a gas-station attendant to look at it the next time you fill up.

c) Remain unconcerned about it unless the problem seems to get worse.

11. Which of the following statements comes closest to describing your philosophy of life?

a) Whatever happens, happens.

b) Life's what you make it.

c) Life's a pain and then you die.

My score: _____ ▪

—Adapted from "Can You Bounce Back?" by Stacey Colino. *Mademoiselle* (December, 1996), p. 183+.

Journal

Are you happy with your score on this quiz? If so, what can you continue to do to thrive rather than just survive when suffering occurs? If not, what are some changes you can make to help yourself bounce back faster from suffering or problems in the future?

Words to Know

acute	neurosis
bigot	nirvana
chronic	paradise
compassion	passion
faith	resilience
mortality	suffering
nerves	utopia
neurons	

Review Questions

1. What are three different causes of human suffering? Why is it possible to say that suffering does not discriminate?

2. What are the three types of pain? Give an example of each.

3. According to Maimonides, what are the three evils that cause pain? Give an example of each.

4. Give two reasons that a world with no suffering may not be the best for us.

5. How are suffering and love related?

6. What three beliefs can we have regarding suffering because of the humanity of Jesus?

7. What is resilience? Why do you think Catholics should try to be resilient despite experiences of suffering and death?

C•H•A•P•T•E•R

2

The Reality *of* Death

IN THIS CHAPTER, YOU WILL

- define what death is;

- see how people have explained the origin of death;

- learn why studying about death is important;

- understand why many people deny the fact of death;

- examine some of your own fears about death;

- explore the Church's teaching on the communion of saints;

- look at how Catholics celebrate All Saints' Day and All Souls' Day;

- consider how your present behavior can affect how long you will live.

After the Shooting

Hundreds of students walked in the rain past a fence packed with flowers Monday, down a hallway once flecked with blood, and into a cafeteria still fresh with memories of a shooting rampage that left two classmates dead.

In Memory

Ben Walker, 16, died on

May 21, 1998, after being shot

in the head by a fellow student.

Walker's organs were donated

to twelve people.

Mikael Nickolauson, 17, died on

May 21, 1998, after being shot

by the same student.

Though the blood had been scrubbed away, the bullet holes spackled and painted over, students could not hide their grief or their pain.

"It felt like sheer terror, like you were going through it again, like the shooting had started again," said 15-year-old Stacy, who was in the cafeteria when shots rang out Thursday. "It was the same way I felt when it first started."

For three hours, the high school was open so the 1,400 students could look around and talk to counselors before returning to class today.

As small groups filed in, accompanied by parents and teachers, a bagpiper played "Amazing Grace." Inside, they went back to the seats where they had been at the time of the shooting and scribbled their feelings on a long sheet of paper.

"It looked like it was haunted in there. It was dead silent," said 18-year-old Brandon.

The principal of the high school said that when he first went in, "I sat in a corner and probably cried for 45 minutes."

Memorial Day was a somber time for this city of 51,000, a day for citizens to begin taking their lives back and burying the dead.

The fifteen-year-old student in custody was on suicide watch Monday at a juvenile detention center, accused of shooting and killing his parents in their home, then driving to school and opening fire in the crowded school cafeteria with a .22-caliber semi- automatic rifle.

Just a day before the rampage, the accused juvenile had been arrested and suspended after he bought a gun from another boy on the school grounds and put it in his locker. He was booked and sent home with his parents. ▪

—Adapted from "Oregon town buries first shooting victim," © Associated Press (May 26, 1998). Article by Jeff Barnard.

Discussion

1. Is death fair? Why did the two students die?
2. How do you think the arrested 15-year-old felt after killing his parents and the two students?
3. What were some of the other students' feelings?
4. Would you have gone back to the cafeteria on Memorial Day? Why or why not?

A Fact of Life

Perhaps you are like many young people in today's society. You may think that death is something far removed from you and your friends—something that happens only after you grow old. Often it takes a tragedy such as the one at the high school in the story to make teenagers face the reality of death.

Death is a fact of life. Everyone, sooner or later, is going to die. There's no way to cheat death or to run away from it. The mortality rate for human beings is 100 percent. Here are some other sobering statistics: In 1994, more than fifty thousand people under the age of twenty-four died. Twenty thousand of these young people died in accidents; over one thousand died of AIDS.

Talking about death is morbid only if it has no other point. This course on suffering and death is not intended to be morbid. Rather, it is intended to help you deal with suffering and death as an important part of life. Hopefully, this course will give you information that can help you handle death when it happens in your own family and relationships. More importantly, it will hopefully provide you with a faith vision that can be your source of strength in times of sorrow. While this book presents the specific view of the Catholic Church about death and the afterlife, it also takes the generalized human universal, approach—universal in that sense of the word *catholic*.

Before proceeding, take some time to reflect on your present attitudes toward and experiences with death. Write your responses to the above survey in your notebook. ■

Attitude Survey	I agree	I disagree	I'm not sure
It's hard for me to accept that one day I will die.			
Modern-day society treats death realistically.			
Most people are comfortable talking about death.			
Learning about death can make life more meaningful.			
I'm afraid of ghosts, funeral homes, cemeteries, and other things related to dead bodies.			

In 1994, over one thousand people under the age of twenty-four died from AIDS.

Journal

1. Have you had any personal experience of death? If so, who died? (relative, parents, neighbor, classmate, pet)
2. When did you first learn about death? How did you react?
3. What are your present feelings about death?
4. What topics and questions about death do you want to be covered?

Of Interest

In medieval times, a pleasant smell emitting from a dead body was considered evidence of sanctity. This scent contributed to the term the *odor of sanctity*. For nine months after the death of Saint Teresa of Avila, a fragrant perfume arose from her grave.

---

sepulchre A place of burial; tomb.

death The permanent cessation of all vital bodily functions: (1) total brain function, (2) spontaneous function of the respiratory system, and (3) spontaneous function of the circulatory system.

coroner Public official given the responsibility of determining the cause of death in cases where death is not from a natural or apparent reason. The coroner is also responsible for the disposition of unclaimed bodies.

Some Basic Questions

People of every century have asked questions about death. Among the more basic questions are these: "What is death? How do we know when someone is truly dead?" "Why do people die?" and "What does death teach us?" To begin to understand the mystery of death, it is important to take a closer look at each of these questions.

"What is death? How do we know when someone is truly dead?"

Until recently, it was difficult to tell if a person was dead or in a coma or in shock. The techniques used to determine whether or not a person was dead were primitive. In ancient Rome, for example, the family called the person's name three times to "make sure" he or she was really dead. The Jews at the time of Jesus laid the "dead" person in an open **sepulchre** for three days. If there were no signs of life by then, the body was buried. In the early twentieth century, people held a mirror to the "dead" person's lips. If no beads of moisture formed, the person was pronounced dead.

Only recently, with the advances of medical science, do we have a more accurate understanding of what **death** is. Today we do not consider someone dead until total brain function, spontaneous function of the respiratory system, and spontaneous function of the circulatory system cease permanently.

After a person dies, the body undergoes certain changes. These changes, used by doctors and **coroners** to determine the time of death, include the following:

- Cooling (*algor mortis*). The temperature of the body drops. The amount of cooling depends upon environmental temperature, type of clothing, and amount of body fat.

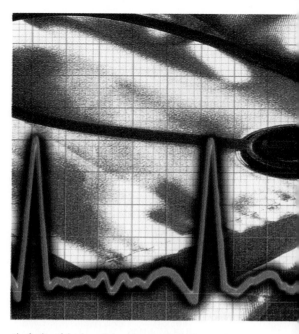

The finality of death can help us keep in perspective experiences of loss, failure, and rejection, which we all experience. We can survive these losses with hope and courage.

- Rigidity (*rigor mortis*). Five to ten hours after death, the muscles usually stiffen. Jaw muscles often stiffen first. The muscles again relax after three or four days.
- Blood clotting. The blood clots shortly after death; sometimes clotting occurs before the heart stops.
- Staining (*livor mortis*). Gravity draws unclotted blood downward, resulting in reddish-blue discoloration on portions of the body.
- Cell breakdown. This breakdown occurs due to a lack of blood supply.
- Putrefaction. After death, decomposing bacteria and fungi start to work, producing gases, greenish discoloration of the tissues, and a foul smell.

These signs, along with machines that measure brain waves and heartbeat, virtually rule out the possibility of mistaken death pronouncements today. ■

Activity

Find out how the term **odor of death** is used in the Bible. Read the following passages, and explain what you think they mean.
- John 11:1–44
- 2 Corinthians 2:14–17

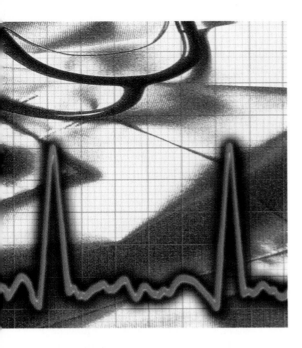

Why do people die?

In ancient times, people in many different cultures told stories to explain why people die. In many of these myths, the origin of death was connected with snakes, which were thought to live forever since they could shed their skins. Here are two tales, one from Melanesia and the other from Vietnam, that "explain" why people die:

In the beginning, people lived forever. They were like snakes; when they got older, they shed their skins and became young again. One day, an old woman went down to the stream to peel off her wrinkled skin. When she returned, looking young and beautiful, her two-year-old daughter no longer recognized her and began to cry. No matter what the woman did, the child would not let her come near. So the woman went back to the stream and put on her old skin. The daughter recognized her mother immediately and went to her. Ever since then, people lost the ability to shed their skins and live forever. (*Melanesian tale*)

God hated snakes and loved people. God wanted snakes to die and people to live forever. So God sent a messenger to earth to explain these wishes. When the snakes heard the message, they threatened to bite the messenger and kill him if he did not change the message. Fearing for his own life, the messenger said, "When snakes are old, they will shed their skins and live; when humans grow old, they will die." And that is how death entered the world. (*Vietnamese tale*) ■ ■

What does death teach us?

Because death is a fact of life, it can teach us some important lessons about life and what it means to be truly alive. ■

First, death can motivate us to make sense out of life and being human. We are not immortal; we are not gods. And yet we are the highest form of life on this planet. As the psalmist writes: "Yet you have made [us] a little lower than God, and crowned [us] with glory and honor" (Psalm 8:5). Death forces us to reflect on our identity and destiny. Death challenges us to approach life with faith and trust that God's wisdom is greater than our own. Because death surrounds us, the prophet Jeremiah states:

Do not let the wise boast in their wisdom, do not let the mighty boast in their might, do not let the wealthy boast in their wealth; but let those who boast boast in this, that they understand and know me, that I am the LORD . . .

—Jeremiah 9:23–24

 Activity

Read Genesis 3 for the Jewish story about the origin of death.
- Retell the story in your own words.
- Compare the Genesis story to the Melanesian and Vietnamese tales. How are they similar? How do they differ?

 Journal

Why do you think people die? Write your own story to explain the origin of death

 Discussion

1. Have you ever had a close brush with death? What happened? How did you feel about life after that experience?
2. Would you like to know the exact time you are going to die? Why or why not?
3. Would you like to know how you are going to die? Why or why not?
4. What would you do if you knew you only had three months left to live?

God alone can make sense out of death; God can give true and lasting meaning to our lives. ▪

Second, the inevitability of death can lead us to prepare wisely for death. People naturally prepare for important events in their lives—a vacation, the birth of a child, a wedding, a college entrance test. And yet many people do not prepare for death. In many instances, we are stunned and unprepared when death strikes. We react with disbelief and shock.

Maybe we are afraid that if we prepare for death, death will actually come. We think that by not preparing, we can somehow fend off death or keep it at arm's length. As Jesus himself tells us, such thinking is not logical.

> "But know this: if the owner of the house had known at what hour the thief was coming, he would not have let his house be broken into. You also must be ready, for the Son of Man is coming at an unexpected hour."
>
> —Luke 12:39–40

Once we are dead, it is too late to prepare for death. ▪

Third, death can provide us with insights about dealing with the little deaths that happen all through life—experiences of loss, failure, and rejection. These types of death are familiar to everyone. No one in our society could live to be a teenager without some experience of loss: moving to a new town, changing schools, illness, rejection, divorce of parents, broken relationships, having something stolen or broken, separation from friends, low self-esteem, disappointment, the death of a pet, and so forth.

Just as death is a part of life, so life is bound up with various forms of death—sorrow, betrayal, disappointments, and tragedies. The finality of death, however, can help us keep these smaller deaths in perspective. The reality of death can help us survive these losses with hope and courage.

Lastly, death can teach us the importance of living fully. Talk with anyone who has had a close brush with death, and that person will tell you that life is short, that we should cherish each moment. In other words, there is no better time than the present to explore, to search for knowledge, and to love others. Indeed, we may not have a tomorrow in which to do these things.

Coming to grips with death can itself be a source of spiritual insight and creativity. As the poet Kahlil Gibran wrote in *The Prophet:*

> If you would indeed behold the spirit of death, open your heart wide unto the body of life.
>
> For life and death are one, even as the river and the sea are one. . . .
>
> Only when you drink from the river of silence shall you indeed sing,
>
> And when you have reached the mountaintop, then shall you begin to climb.
>
> And when the earth shall claim your limbs, then shall you truly dance.

Many poems, plays, novels, paintings, statues, and musical compositions deal with the theme of death. Just as death has inspired their creation, so they continue to inspire us to "have life, and have it abundantly" (John 10:10). ▪

Activity
Read Matthew 6:25–33. Explain how the passage relates to death and making sense out of life.

Activity
Discuss one of the following Bible passages in connection to preparing for death:
- Matthew 24:45–50
- Matthew 25:1–13
- Matthew 25:14–30

Activity
Research a poem, play, novel, painting, statue, or piece of music that deals with death. Discuss the message it conveys about death and/or the meaning of life.

Why Some People Deny Death

Though many people have questions about death, some shy away from talking about it. In fact, most people talk around death rather than talk about it straight on. They speak gingerly about the "**deceased**," the "**decedent**," or the "dearly departed" rather than the dead person. They use phrases such as "passed away" or "expired" instead of saying that someone died. These expressions are meant to soften the blow of death. In reality, they may contribute to an elaborate conspiracy of silence. Death makes us uncomfortable because we have no control over it. Thus it is something we must continually strive to deny.

Possibly the greatest example of the denial of death in our modern society is the **cryonics** movement. Some people actually believe if their bodies (or heads, in some cases) are frozen immediately after death, they will be kept in a state of suspended animation indefinitely. These people hope that sometime in the future, when science has discovered a cure for whatever disease they died of, their bodies will be revived and the disease cured. Theoretically, a person kept alive by these means could live forever. ■

There are many reasons a lot of North Americans deny death. Here are just a few of them:

1. Since the Civil War (1861–1864), North Americans have not had firsthand experience of wide-scale death. No war has been fought on American, Canadian, or Mexican soil since the Civil War. The news media may run stories of war casualties and of the "human cost" of war, but these statistics are quickly hushed up after victory. Politicians, generally, do not want to mention death because it is a sign of failure.

2. In former times, executions of criminals were public events. The crucifixion of Jesus, for example, was witnessed by Romans and Jews alike. Throughout medieval Europe, guillotines and firing squads executed criminals as people watched. In the Wild West, trees or constructed gallows were used to hang outlaws as many people looked on. Today public executions have been banned. Capital punishment is a theoretical subject to debate, not something for general audiences.

deceased *A person who has died.*

decedent *A dead person, including a stillborn infant or fetus.*

cryonics *The practice of freezing a person who has died of a disease, with the hope of bringing him or her back to life in the future when a cure for the disease has been found.*

Of Interest

Two hundred and twelve United States men and women lost their lives in the Persian Gulf War against Iraq. If the same number of people had died in an airplane crash or a natural disaster, the event would have been treated as a major tragedy. Instead, the news media reported the number of deaths as "relatively few."

Discussion

1. When you were a child, did your family ever talk about death? If so, what was said? If not, why wasn't it discussed?

2. Would you want to live forever? What would the world be like if no one ever died?

3. Would you like to have your body frozen after death with the hope of being restored to life in the future? Why or why not?

Of Interest

In 1984, a person born in the African nation of Upper Volta had only a 50 percent chance of living to age 5.

---

gerontology *The study of aging.*

thanatology *The study of death.*

3. Medicine and better nutrition have prolonged life. Fewer women die in childbirth; fewer children die in infancy. In 1995, the average life span of whites in the United States was 76.5 years; the average life span of African Americans was 69.7 years.

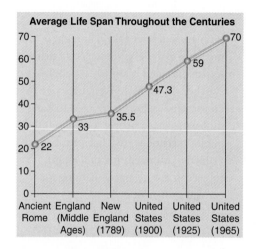

Average Life Span Throughout the Centuries

Ancient Rome: 22
England (Middle Ages): 33
New England (1789): 35.5
United States (1900): 47.3
United States (1925): 59
United States (1965): 70

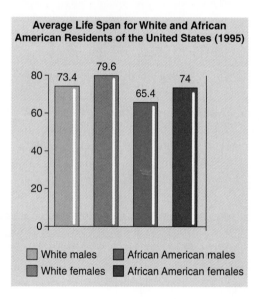

Average Life Span for White and African American Residents of the United States (1995)

73.4 — White males
79.6 — White females
65.4 — African American males
74 — African American females

■ White males ■ African American males
■ White females ■ African American females

4. Death has been removed from mainstream living. New church buildings usually do not have their own adjacent cemeteries. People are not buried in the floor of the church, as in traditional European churches. In the past, people died at home. Now they die in hospitals or care centers. Death is treated as a sickness rather than as a normal part of life.

The removal of death also affects the way our society treats the elderly. Instead of living with their children and grand-children, many elderly people live in leisure villages, retirement homes, care centers, and convalescent homes. Entire communities in Florida and Arizona have been developed solely for those who are elderly and retired. Only recently have **gerontology** and **thanatology** become recognized fields of science.

5. Society glorifies youth. Youth is big business. Just think of the millions of dollars people spend each year on cosmetics, hair dye, anti-wrinkle creams, health food, plastic surgery, and exercise equipment. Despite laws to the contrary, businesses still discriminate against people who are "too old." Such discrimination was seen in the 1980s when some news broadcasters were fired for being "over the hill." Age discrimination also surfaced when Ronald Reagan first ran for president in 1980 at age 69. His opponents argued that he was "too old" for the job. Despite his age, Reagan went on to become one of the most popular presidents of recent times. ■ ■

Discussion

1. If you were old and could not take care of yourself, where would you want to live? Why?
2. What are your present attitudes toward the elderly?
3. What would you like to accomplish with your life before you are "too old"?

Activity

1. Develop a list of familiar euphemisms for death, dying, a dead person, and cemeteries.
2. Find out what the major causes of death were in 1600, 1700, 1800, 1900, and what they are today.
3. Make a collage of newspaper and magazine ads that glorify youth and fight against the aging process.

The Fear of Death

One of the reasons many people deny death is because they fear it. There are many fears associated with death.

Fear of death cuts across every age and culture. Primitive peoples believed that dead spirits envied the living and would thus bring sickness, sterility, weakness, and bodily harm. Most feared were the ghosts of powerful men who died in their prime, women who died in childbirth, and those who committed suicide or died because of violence. ▪

The ancient Mesopotamians believed that the souls of those who had drowned, those whose bodies remained unburied, and those who had no one to carry out the prescribed funeral duties never found rest in the abode of the dead. These restless souls roamed the earth, bringing sickness, misfortune, and other ills. Because people feared these souls, they tried to placate the spirits through magic and **necromancy**. In Babylon, a special class of priests was in charge of **spiritualism**.

Anglo-Saxons used to remove a tile or cut a hole in the roof to "let out" the spirit of someone who was dying. They so feared the dead that they cut off the feet of corpses to prevent them from walking back home. They also drove stakes through the bodies of people who had committed suicide in order to "keep them down." Until recently in Europe, people turned the mirrors inside their homes toward the wall so the mirrors wouldn't "catch" the dead soul and keep it present.

Other cultures also worried about getting the spirit of the dead person out of the house for good. In Russia, people were afraid to take a corpse out through the regular door. Instead, they took the dead out through a window and then hurriedly shut the window. In old Italy and Denmark, people built special doors for the dead. In Thailand, pallbearers rushed the dead person around the house three times to

A fear of . . .	Explanation
Losing life itself	We don't want to be separated from loved ones; we have so much more we want to accomplish.
The process of dying	We are afraid of losing control over our lives and bodily functions. We shy away from pain and indignity; we don't want to be a burden to others.
Death itself	We are afraid of the unknown or of personal annihilation; maybe we are afraid of eternal punishment.
Those who are dead	We are afraid of ghosts, goblins, zombies, and evil spirits. (Just think of the scary movies you've seen or the books you've read!)

make the spirit dizzy and thus disorient it. Koreans put blinders on corpses so they couldn't find the way back from the cemetery.

Cemeteries themselves were sometimes built to keep in the spirits of the dead. The ancient Minoans of Crete built tombs shaped as a maze or labyrinth so the ghosts couldn't find their way out. After burial, mourners covered their footsteps as they walked home so the ghosts could not follow them. Because they believed that ghosts could not cross water, the Etruscans in Italy always built their cemeteries on the other side of a river. They also made sure the tombs had plenty of food in them so the ghosts wouldn't get hungry and come home looking for food.

Some modern-day customs concerning death also reflect ancient fears. Closing the eyes of a person soon after death was originally done so that the ghost couldn't "see" the living and then haunt them. Covering the face of a dead person with a cloth or sheet was done for the same reason. The customs of loud wailing, funeral bells, and gunshots were based on the belief that ghosts can't stand loud noises. Tombstones, in addition to marking who was in the grave, were meant to weigh down the dead and keep them in the ground.

necromancy Supposed communication with the dead.

spiritualism Attempts to communicate with spirits and departed souls by seances, table tapping, Ouija boards, and other methods. Spiritualistic practices, which often involve fraud, are considered a violation of the virtue of religion because they attribute to spirits' certain godlike powers over the present and the future.

Journal
What is your biggest fear about death? Why?

Of Interest

Necromancy was forbidden by ancient Jewish law (cf. Leviticus 19:31; Deuteronomy 18:11). Nevertheless, some Israelites seem to have practiced it (cf. Leviticus 20:6, 27; 1 Samuel 28:3, 7, 9; 2 Kings 21:6; 23:24; Isaiah 8:19; 29:4). Other Old Testament practices evidenced fear of the dead. Rending garments, wearing sackcloth, imposing ashes, pulling out one's hair, self-mutilation, or covering one's face with a veil were supposedly ways to make oneself unrecognizable to the spirits. Other customs based on fear of the dead included burial of executed criminals before evening (cf. Deuteronomy 21:22–23) and heaping stones on the tomb (cf. Joshua 7:26; 8:29; 2 Samuel 18:17).

Our present-day custom of trick-or-treating on Halloween has its roots in an old European festival of the dead, when the spirits were invited inside to eat with the living. Bonfires and candles were lit to show the way for the spirits (perhaps the origin of our lighted jack-o'-lanterns). After the "meal," people put on gruesome masks and costumes to frighten the spirits back into their graves. ▪

The Communion of Saints

The early Christians did not deny the fact of death, nor did they fear those who were dead. On the contrary, they saw death as a passage through which those who had been faithful to the teaching of Jesus would be united with him in **heaven**. The faithful dead were regarded as good spirits who cared about the Christians still on earth. When the Christians gathered for Eucharist, they celebrated it as a time to be united, not only with Christ and with one another, but also with all the faithful who had died, both those in heaven and in **purgatory**. For this reason, the earliest prayers, hymns, and canon of the Mass contained references to the saints and to the dead.

By the fifth century, this belief in the solidarity of all the faithful—living and dead—found its way into the Apostles' Creed with the expression "I believe in . . . the **communion of saints**." Because the early Christians believed that all the faithful formed the one Body of Christ, each part of that Body had a responsibility to help the other parts. People living on earth could affect the well-being of those in purgatory by praying for them. Likewise, the saints in heaven could intercede with God for the needs of the living.

Quite early in the Church's history, martyrs were remembered and honored at

The belief in the solidarity of all the faithful—in the communion of saints—is depicted in Andrea di Bonaiuto's painting The Triumph of Saint Thomas Aquinas.

Eucharistic gatherings, especially on the anniversaries of their deaths. Gradually these death anniversaries were recognized as the saints' feast days. These days eventually formed the **sanctoral cycle** of the Church's liturgical year. In the sanctoral cycle, the feast day of a saint (as a general rule) is observed on the day of death. (Some exceptions include the feast of Saint John the Baptist, who is honored on June 24, believed to be the day of his birth, and joint feasts, such as Saints Basil the Great and Gregory Nazianzus and Saints Cyril and Methodius.)

At first the Church celebrated each saint's day separately. As more and more Christians died and were revered as saints, the need arose for a common celebration of all known and

---

heaven *The fullness of human existence in which people, after passing through earthly death, experience God's life and love forever.*

purgatory *State of purification through which some people pass after death and before they experience heaven.*

communion of saints *The union of all faithful people, living and dead, who belong to the family of God.*

sanctoral cycle *A Church calendar of saints' feast days. Commemorations on these days are intended to illustrate how each saint followed Christ, to honor the saint as a hero of holiness, and to appeal for the saint's help.*

Activity

1. Investigate numerous folk legends regarding zombies, vampires, dybbuks, and so forth. Discuss how these legends may have started.
2. Review a book, movie, play, television show, or pop song that expresses fear of the dead.
3. Find out why the Church frowns upon seances and spiritualism.

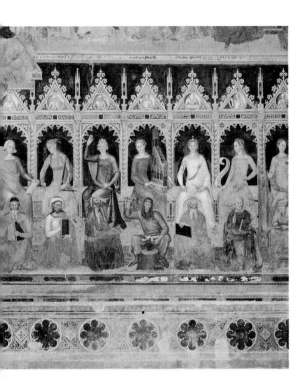

unknown saints. This celebration is called *All Saints' Day*, a holy day of obligation for Catholics in the United States and in many other countries.

It seems that All Saints' Day was originally celebrated on May 13, possibly to offset *Lemuria*, a festival of the dead observed by non-Christians on May 9, 11, and 13. According to one historian, Pope Gregory IV (827–844) moved the feast to November 1 one year because provisions were inadequate in May for the many pilgrims coming to Rome for the feast. Another historian states that the Irish originated the feast on November 1 because that day was the beginning of the Celtic winter and because they had a custom of assigning the first day of the month to important feasts.

In A.D. 988, Saint Odilo of Cluny established a second feast to pray for all the faithful departed. This day, known as All Souls' Day, quickly became an established custom in many churches. It was added to the Roman calendar of feast days in the thirteenth century. Today, the Catholic Church celebrates All Souls' Day on November 2, unless that day falls on a Sunday. Then the feast is celebrated on November 3.

In some parts of Europe, All Souls' Day is a day of the dead. People visit cemeteries and put flowers and candles on family graves, much as the ancient Romans did. On the eve of All Souls' Day, children used to beg from house to house for doughnuts called *soul cakes*. (The circle made by the hole in the center of the doughnut represented eternity, with no beginning and no end.) The soul cakes were eaten in remembrance of the dead or were put on relatives' graves. In return, the children were obligated to pray for the dead and for a good harvest.

Today, in addition to celebrating All Saints' Day and All Souls' Day, the Catholic Church sets aside the entire month of November as a time to remember the dead. Often, parishes are encouraged to make available a book near the entrance of the church, the baptistery, or some other convenient location, in which people can write the names of their deceased loved ones. These dead are then remembered in prayers throughout the month. ▪

Of Interest

Eastern Rite Catholics traditionally celebrate All Saints' Day and All Souls' Day on different dates than the Latin Rite. For example, Maronite Catholics set aside three Sundays during the Season of Epiphany for remembering the dead. These Sundays are known as the Sunday of Deceased Priests, the Sunday of the Righteous and the Just (All Saints), and the Sunday of the Faithful Departed (All Souls).

Of Interest

In the Latin Rite, each priest is allowed to celebrate three Masses on All Souls' Day: (1) for particular people who have died, (2) for all the faithful departed, and (3) for the intentions of the pope.

Catholics Believe

"We believe in the communion of all the faithful of Christ, those who are pilgrims on earth, the dead who are being purified, and the blessed in heaven, all together forming one Church; and we believe that in this communion, the merciful love of God and his saints is always [attentive] to our prayers" (Paul VI, CPG § 30). (Catechism, #962)

 Activity

1. Research the life and death of your patron saint, including his or her feast day. Present your findings to the class in the form of a play or song.
2. Study and compare the four Eucharistic Prayers for Mass. How are the saints and the faithful departed mentioned in each prayer?
3. Read the following Bible passages from the Mass for All Saints' Day, and then explain what they tell you about the communion of saints.
   - Matthew 5:1–12
   - 1 John 3:1–3
   - Revelation 7:2–4, 9–14
4. Read the following Bible passages suggested for the Mass for All Souls' Day and then explain what they tell you about those who have died.
   - Wisdom 3:1–9
   - Romans 14:7–12
   - John 6:37–40

How Long Will You Live?

Many factors work together to determine how long you will live. You have no control over the genetic factors you have inherited or your family's medical history. But you do have choices about the kind of life you lead and the risks you take. Environment, stress, and general behavior can add or subtract years from your life.

The following quiz will give you a rough idea of how long you can expect to live, based on your present lifestyle. If you don't like the results, now is the time to make some changes in your behavior and habits. The earlier you start to take care of yourself, the more you can expect to make a difference in the length and quality of your life.

Directions:

Start with the number 72. Then add or subtract, based on your answers to the following facts.

Genetic Factors and Medical History

- If you are male, subtract 3. If you are female, add 4.
- If you are Caucasian or Asian American, add 3. If you are African American, Latino, or Native American, subtract 4.
- If any grandparent lived to 85, add 2.
- If all four grandparents lived to 80, add 6.
- If either parent died of a stroke or heart attack before the age of 50, subtract 4.
- If any parent, brother, or sister committed suicide, subtract 4.
- If any parent, brother, or sister under 50 has (or has had) cancer or a heart condition or has had diabetes since childhood, subtract 3.
- If your blood pressure or cholesterol level is high, subtract 3.
- If you have asthma, subtract 2.
- If you are female and your grandmother, mother, or sister has (or has had) breast cancer, subtract 4.

Lifestyle History

- If you live in an urban area with a population of more than two million, subtract 2. If you live in a town under 10,000 or on a farm, add 2.
- If you are actively homosexual or if you use intravenous drugs, subtract 5.
- If you work behind a desk or watch more than fifteen hours of television per week, subtract 3.
- If you exercise strenuously (tennis, running, swimming) five times a week for at least a half hour, add 4. If you exercise two or three times a week, add 2.
- If you sleep more than ten hours each night, subtract 4.
- If you are a member of a gang, subtract 4.
- If you tend to be intense, aggressive, and easily angered, subtract 3. If you tend to be easygoing and relaxed, add 3.
- If you are happy at home and at school, add 1. If you are unhappy either at home or at school, subtract 1.

Of Interest

Where you live in the United States seems to make a difference in how long you will live. People who live in Hawaii have the longest average life span. Those living in Louisiana tend to have the shortest life span. Those living in Montana, Missouri, Indiana, and Wyoming can expect to live to the national average.

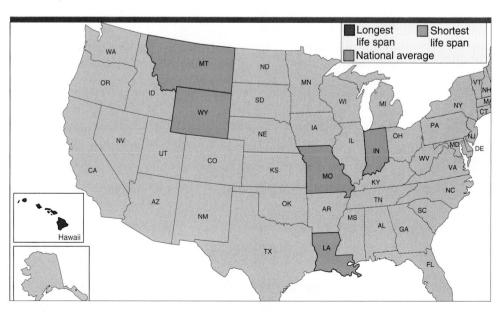

- If you have good friends, add 1. If you have no close friends, subtract 1.
- If you have a pet, add 1.
- If you have had a speeding ticket in the past year, subtract 1.
- If you smoke more than two packs of cigarettes per day, subtract 8. If you smoke one or two packs a day, subtract 6. If you smoke one-half to one pack a day, subtract 3.
- If you tend to get drunk each weekend and then drive, subtract 6. If you drink the equivalent of 1 1/2 oz. of liquor a day, subtract 1.
- If you are overweight by 50 pounds, subtract 8. If you are thirty to fifty pounds overweight, subtract 4. If you are ten to thirty pounds overweight, subtract 2.
- If you have regular medical checkups each year, add 2.
- If you have regular dental checkups each year, add 1.

Now add up your score to get your life expectancy. _____

Are you satisfied with this result? If not, what are some changes you can begin to make in your lifestyle? ■

Adapted from "How Long Will You Live?" *Time* (November 2, 1981), p. 106, which in turned was quoted from *Lifegain* by Robert Allen with Shirley Linde (Appleton Books/a division of Prentice Hall Inc.).

Of Interest

According to the 1997 *Guinness Book of World Records*, the oldest living person in the world whose date of birth could be authenticated was Jeanne Louise Calment, who was born in France on February 21, 1875. She died August 4, 1997, in a nursing home in Arles, France, at the age of 122.

Discussion

1. Why do you think women usually live longer than men?
2. What are possible reasons that African Americans have a shorter life expectancy than whites?
3. What might be done to increase the life expectancy of African Americans?

Words to Know

communion of saints	heaven
coroner	necromancy
cryonics	purgatory
death	sanctoral cycle
deceased	sepulchre
decedent	spiritualism
gerontology	thanatology

Review Questions

1. How do we know when someone is dead? What are the signs of death?
2. What does the Bible tell us about the origin of death?
3. What four things can death teach us?
4. What are five reasons our society tends to deny death?
5. Give one example of an ancient custom that shows fear of death. Give one example of a modern-day custom that originally expressed fear of death.
6. What does it mean to belong to the communion of saints?
7. What is the purpose of All Saints' Day? All Souls' Day?

C•H•A•P•T•E•R

3

Why Did This Happen

IN THIS CHAPTER, YOU WILL

- explore some of the questions people ask when suffering and death strike suddenly, without warning;

- understand why people are sometimes more upset by the unjust distribution of suffering than the actual fact of suffering;

- consider how original sin may be the cause of suffering and death;

- uphold our Christian belief in a good God and human goodness;

- reflect on whether or not God sends suffering to test our faith;

- discuss whether or not suffering is God's way of strengthening our character;

- see how the Church connects suffering and freedom;

- discover traits and actions that can help you imitate Jesus' approach to suffering.

Without Warning

Penny Hall and Kevin Taylor planned to be together in marriage. Instead, they were united in death, buried side by side Saturday, nearly a week after they perished in a fierce night of tornadoes.

More than 300 mourners came to the funeral for the couple and for Hall's parents, Ed and Debra, who also were killed when a twister demolished the family's mobile home early Monday morning.

Hall's five-year-old daughter, Ashley, the only survivor in the house, is hospitalized in stable condition with a ruptured spleen and bruised lung. She had been found wandering dazed in the woods after the tornadoes struck.

Another funeral service was held Saturday in nearby St. Cloud for nine-month-old Niles David Bourke, who was sucked from his father's arms and dumped 300 feet from his mobile home. He lay in a white casket trimmed with blue lace. The white *Sesame Street* socks he wore had the words "Why? Why? Why?" printed on them. A new brown teddy bear sat beside him to replace the one he lost in the storm.

In Memory

Penny Hall, Kevin Taylor, Ed Hall, and Debra Hall—all from Apopka, Florida—and 9-month-old Niles David Bourke of St. Cloud, Florida, were killed by fierce tornadoes in late April 1998.

Niles' parents, Karen and Guy, wept quietly for their son. "As I tried to close the closet door, the floor lifted up and threw me against the wall and slapped me against the ceiling. When I woke up a half-hour later, Niles was gone and my jaw was just hanging there covered with blood," Guy said. Karen Bourke's brother found Niles' body under a pile of debris fourteen hours later.

Heavy sobs punctuated the hour-long service for the Hall family. The Rev. Robert Welch read from Scripture, talked of mortality, resurrection, and eternal life. "Death at any hour is sad. It's difficult to deal with and especially so when it comes without warning."

A carpet of white carnations draped Penny Hall's pink casket, which sat at the front of the chapel between the caskets of her parents, each also adorned with carnations. Floral crosses stood among the dozens of flower baskets.

State officials said forty people died when the tornadoes swept through central Florida late last Sunday and early Monday. Several families buried their dead in services Friday and Saturday. Others spent the day trying to secure belongings as heavy rain moved into the area for the first time since the tornadoes. ▪

—Adapted from "'Why? Why? Why?' Victims of tornadoes buried in Florida," © Associated Press (March 1, 1998). Article by Pat Leisner.

Discussion

Has sudden and unexpected suffering or death ever happened in your life? If so, what were some questions you had about suffering and death?

Unanswered Questions

Suffering at any time in life is difficult to handle. When suffering and death strike without warning, however, the suffering intensifies. Survivors are left not only with grief but also with many unanswered questions. Above all, there is the question "Why?"

This question takes many forms. When tragedy strikes, especially without warning, we ask "Why did this happen?" "Why did it happen to me (my family, my friend)?" "Why did this happen now?" "Why isn't life more fair?"

Throughout the centuries, people have sought satisfactory answers to these questions. Some people have found their answers in **superstition**. Superstition involves the belief that bad luck has irrational causes—magic or certain actions, such as walking under a ladder, crossing the path of a black cat, stepping on a crack in the sidewalk, breaking a mirror, or traveling on Friday the thirteenth. While Christians reject such superstitions as meaningless, some religious people ascribe tragedy to other superstitions—their failure to say certain prayers, wear blessed scapulars, honor certain relics, or maintain specific devotional practices. Such good religious practices become superstitious when people attribute magical or miraculous effects solely to external performance, apart from interior dispositions. ■

In this chapter, you will explore how the Catholic Church answers the questions evoked by sudden tragedy. Before proceeding, take some time to think about your own answers to the question "Why did this happen?" Write in your notebook your responses to the above Attitude Survey.

Attitude Survey	I agree	I disagree	I'm not sure
People get what they deserve; the good prosper and the wicked are punished.			
Suffering and death are forms of punishment for our sins.			
God sends us suffering and death to test our faith.			
Suffering is ennobling; it strengthens our character and brings us closer to God.			
God wants us to learn a lesson from suffering and death.			

Our Quest for Justice

It's true: Life isn't fair. Perhaps that is why most people yearn for a God who is just. We long for a God who will reward good people and punish those who are cruel, selfish, hardhearted, and evil. We long for another world where the injustices of life will finally be rectified.

The type of justice we seek is called **retributive justice**. If we do something good, we expect to be rewarded. If we do something bad, we expect to be punished. The Old Testament is filled with this idea of retribution. "The fear of the LORD prolongs life, but the years of the wicked will be short" (Proverbs 10:27). "Tell the innocent how fortunate they are, for they shall eat the fruit of their labors. Woe to the guilty! How unfortunate they are, for what their hands have done shall be done to them" (Isaiah 3:10–11). "No harm happens to the righteous, but the wicked are filled with trouble" (Proverbs 12:21).

superstition *The non-Christian belief that bad luck has irrational causes—magic or certain actions, such as walking under a ladder, crossing the path of a black cat, stepping on a crack in the sidewalk, breaking a mirror, or traveling on Friday the thirteenth.*

retributive justice *The type of justice in which good people are rewarded and evil people are punished.*

Discussion

1. Some athletes in our society wear certain charms or articles of clothing for good luck. Do you think this action really affects their performance? Why or why not?
2. If you wear a medal or scapular, does it automatically mean you are superstitious? Explain.
3. What do you think are the causes of suffering and death? Why do tragedies happen?

The Old Testament also has many examples of God rescuing people from unjust suffering. God delivers Noah and his family from a terrible flood (cf. Genesis 6:5–9:17). God saves the Israelites from their oppression in Egypt (cf. Exodus 12–15). God frees Daniel from harm in the lion's den (cf. Daniel 6:2–29). God protects Shadrach, Meshach, and Abednego in the midst of the fiery furnace (cf. Daniel 3:13–97). And God brings Jonah to safety from the belly of a whale (cf. Jonah 1–4).

The problem in Scripture is not the question of why suffering exists. Rather, it is the question of why suffering afflicts some people and not others. The problem is not the *fact* of suffering but its *distribution*. Reality doesn't always affirm our perceptions of God's justice. Sometimes sinful people prosper in this world, and those who try to keep faith with God suffer. In the Old Testament, the prophet Jeremiah was upset by this unfair reality, so he confronted God: "You will be in the right, O LORD, when I lay charges against you; but let me put my case to you. Why does the way of the guilty prosper? Why do all who are treacherous thrive?" (Jeremiah 12:1). "For I was envious of the arrogant; I saw the prosperity of the wicked. For they have no pain; their bodies are sound and sleek. They are not in trouble as others are; they are not plagued like other people" (Psalm 73:3–5).

Unjust suffering challenges our very faith in God. How can we uphold the justice and righteousness of God when daily we see examples of unjust suffering? This age-old problem of reconciling God's justice with the fact of evil and suffering is called **theodicy**. This word comes from two smaller Greek words—*theos*, which means "God," and *dike*, which means "justice." Another way of expressing the problem of theodicy is this: Why do bad things sometimes happen to good people? How could a good and just God let tragedies such as the tornadoes in Florida happen? ▪

 Journal

Have you ever had a problem reconciling a God who is just with the fact of unjust evil and suffering in the world? If so, explain what happened. If not, tell why you think this has never been a problem for you.

Punishment for Sin

A common response in the face of suffering is to think that suffering must be God's way of punishing us for our sins and wrongdoings. Interestingly, the word *pain* comes from the Latin root *poena,* which means "punishment" or "penalty." In this way of thinking, *God* doesn't cause suffering; *we* cause it by choosing to sin. The suffering we endure is simply God's way of maintaining justice. ■

The idea that human sin is to blame for suffering and death is found in the Book of Genesis. Adam and Eve sin by choosing to disobey God. As a result, God punishes them by sending suffering and death into their lives (cf. Genesis 3). Furthermore, God punishes all humans for the sin of Adam and Eve. All humans inherit **original sin**, the tendency to choose evil over good. ". . . I the LORD your God am a jealous God, punishing children for the iniquity of parents, to the third and the fourth generation of those who reject me . . ." (Exodus 20:5).

Indeed, the human propensity to sin is repeated in story after story in the Bible.

- Cain kills his brother Abel out of jealousy; God condemns Cain to a life of aimless wandering (cf. Genesis 3:1–16).
- The peoples of the world think they can be God's equal by building a great tower; God punishes their false pride by dividing them into different language groups (cf. Genesis 11:1–9).
- Lot's wife sins by looking back at the cities of Sodom and Gomorrah; God reacts by changing her into a pillar of salt (cf. Genesis 19:15–29).
- In disobedience to God, Moses strikes a rock more than once to get water; God punishes him by not letting him enter the promised land (cf. Numbers 20:1–12).

- David kills Uriah so he can marry Uriah's wife, Bathsheba; God punishes him by killing the baby David and Bathsheba conceive (cf. 2 Samuel 12:13–23).
- The Israelites are not faithful to God's covenant; God punishes them by having them lose in battle to the Babylonians and endure exile from their country (cf. Jeremiah 12:7–9; Amos 3:2).

The idea that suffering is a deserved punishment is actually consoling—not for the person who suffers but for those who don't. It is a way of reassuring ourselves that life is not so unfair after all. We tell ourselves there are good reasons for people's suffering, even if we don't know what the reasons are. Most likely, the people themselves are to blame for their own misfortunes. We, on the other hand, "deserve" our good fortune; God must be pleased by our choices and actions.

Why This Idea Is Inadequate

There are two main problems with the belief that suffering is a punishment for one's sins. First of all, the explanation doesn't present God in a very attractive light. And second, it doesn't account for the suffering of innocent people, especially children and babies. Let's examine these problems more closely.

The Goodness of God

To say that God sends us suffering as a form of punishment is to describe God as an exacting judge. This type of God upholds the law, down to its most minute letter. But is this really the type of God we have? Is our God a strict enactor of justice? Certainly that is not the type of God Jesus speaks about. For Jesus, God is Abba, a loving father.

Of Interest

The idea that guilt for sin can be inherited by one's children influenced the Church's punishment of heretics. In the eleventh century, Pope Gregory VII excommunicated descendants of heretics down to the seventh generation.

---

original sin The sin of Adam and Eve; the lack in humans of the original holiness and justice that the first humans had, resulting in concupiscence, which is the inherited tendency within all humans to be attracted to evil and to choose sin over virtuous living, even after Baptism.

Activity

In a small group, read one of the Scripture passages listed below. Then discuss the questions that follow.

- Genesis 3:1–16
- Genesis 19:15–29
- 2 Samuel 12:13–23
- Genesis 11:1–9
- Numbers 20:1–12
- Jeremiah 12:7–9; Amos 3:2

1. How does the passage describe God?
2. Do you believe in this type of God? Why or why not?

"Is there anyone among you who, if your child asks for bread, will give a stone? Or if the child asks for a fish, will give a snake? If you then, who are evil, know how to give good gifts to your children, how much more will your Father in heaven give good things to those who ask him!"

—Matthew 7:9–11

We can get an idea of the difference between the God who is a strict judge and the God who is a loving father by studying the story of *Les Miserables*. In this epic story by Victor Hugo, the Frenchman Jean Valjean steals a loaf of bread because he and his family are hungry. He is arrested and sentenced to years of hard labor in prison. After serving his time, he is released. Circumstances, however, prevent him from making a required appointment with his parole officer. So once again, the authorities begin looking for him. If they catch him, the punishment will be additional time served in prison.

Jean Valjean changes his name and becomes a model citizen. He lives in a small town as a kind employer and a beloved mayor. At the deathbed of Fantine, one of his employees, Valjean promises to take care of her daughter and raise her as his own. He is true to his word; young Cosette grows up believing he really is her father.

Inspector Javert, however, continues to look for Valjean. For him, Valjean is a recalcitrant criminal who must be punished. Javert is obsessed with the idea of catching Valjean and exacting justice. He finds Valjean and sees how the "criminal" has turned his life around, but even then Javert cannot bend. He insists on enforcing the law. In the end, Javert sees that his strict adherence to justice has made Javert himself the prisoner. No one loves him; he despises even himself.

Javert represents the God of strict justice; he is a type of God we can only fear. Valjean, however, represents the God who is a loving father. He is the type of God we find attractive and approachable. He is not only capable of true and selfless love; he is also someone we want to love. In this God, love and mercy are stronger than justice. Instead of punishing us as our sins deserve, God forgives us and welcomes us back home as the merciful father welcomed home his prodigal son (cf. Luke 15:11–32). ■

Human Goodness

It is true that all people are sinners. But it is not always true that we "deserve" the torments we suffer. There are real situations in which innocent people suffer. For them, suffering is most certainly not a punishment for sin. ■

In the Bible, the Book of Job explores the possibility that some people who suffer might be innocent. Job is a rich man who, without any fault of his own, experiences sudden tragedy and innumerable sufferings. He loses his possessions and his children, and finally, he himself is afflicted with a grave illness. In this horrible situation, three "friends" visit Job and try to convince him that he must have done something wrong to "deserve" such suffering. One friend, named Eliphaz, urges Job to repent for his sins and beg God for mercy. Job, however, cannot accept this type of thinking. "Far be it from me to say that you are right; until I die I will not put away my integrity from me. I hold fast my righteousness, and will not let it go; my heart does not reproach me for any of my days" (Job 27:5–6).

Activity

View the movie *Les Miserables*. Discuss how the story compares the virtue of justice with the virtues of love and mercy. Then read the parable of the prodigal son (Luke 15:11–32). How do you think the parable would have ended if the father had responded as Inspector Javert did? Why do you think the father responds as Jean Valjean instead?

Discussion

Find out what Jesus said about the idea that suffering is punishment for sin. Read John 9:1–3. Then, in a small group, discuss these questions:

- Why do you think God allows some babies to be born with birth defects, with the HIV virus, or addicted to crack cocaine?

- How do you think "the works of God" (evidence of God's love and mercy) can be found in situations involving babies with birth defects, with the HIV virus, or addicted to crack cocaine?

As the friends continue to talk, they come up with another idea. If Job truly has not committed any sin, perhaps he has *omitted* to do something good. Perhaps Job has forgotten to perform one of the **works of mercy**—to help the poor or to deal justly with others.

Again, Job protests his innocence.

> If I have withheld anything that the
>   poor desired,
> or have caused the eyes of the widow
>   to fail,
> or have eaten my morsel alone,
> and the orphan has not eaten from it; . . .
> if I have seen anyone perish for lack of
>   clothing,
> or a poor person without covering,
> whose loins have not blessed me,
> and who was not warmed with the
>   fleece of my sheep;
> if I have raised my hand against the
>   orphan,
> because I saw I had supporters
>   at the gate;
> then let my shoulder blade fall
>   from my shoulder,
> and let my arm be broken
>   from its socket.
> For I was in terror of calamity
>   from God,
> and I could not have faced his majesty.
>
> —Job 31:16–17, 19–23

Job is truly an innocent man, yet he suffers grievously. His story foreshadows the sufferings and death of another innocent man—Jesus.

A Test of Faith

If suffering is not a punishment for sin, perhaps it is a test. Maybe God is testing us to find out the quality of our faith. Many people have espoused this type of thinking.

Consider the Old Testament story of Abraham and his son Isaac. God promised to make Abraham and Sarah the parents of a son. And yet they were very old and had no children. Finally, when they miraculously did have a son, God asked Abraham to conform to the traditional custom—sacrificing his firstborn.

> After these things God tested Abraham. He said to him, "Abraham!" And [Abraham] said, "Here I am." [God] said,

Works of Mercy	
Corporal	**Spiritual**
Feed the hungry.	Admonish the sinner.
Give drink to the thirsty.	Instruct the ignorant.
Clothe the naked.	Counsel the doubtful.
Visit the imprisoned.	Comfort the sorrowful.
Shelter the homeless.	Bear wrongs patiently.
Visit the sick.	Forgive all injuries.
Bury the dead.	Pray for the living and the dead.

> "Take your son, your only son Isaac, whom you love, and go to the land of Moriah, and offer him there as a burnt offering on one of the mountains that I shall show you." So Abraham rose early in the morning, saddled his donkey, and took two of his young men with him, and his son Isaac; he cut the wood for the burnt offering, and set out and went to the place in the distance that God had shown him. On the third day Abraham looked up and saw the place far away. Then Abraham said to his young men, "Stay here with the donkey; the boy and I will go over there; we will worship, and then we will come back to you."

works of mercy *Charitable actions directed toward meeting the physical (corporal) and spiritual needs of others.*

Of Interest

The sacrifice of Isaac has been the subject of numerous paintings throughout the centuries. One of the most beautiful and emotion-wracked depictions of this Bible story was created by Rembrandt, a seventeenth-century Dutch artist. The painting, which shows the angel stopping the hand of Abraham as he is about to slay Isaac, is entitled *Abraham and Isaac*. Painted in 1634, it may now be seen in the Hermitage Museum in Russia.

Of Interest

Abraham took the wood of the burnt offering and laid it on his son Isaac, and he himself carried the fire and the knife. So the two of them walked on together. Isaac said to his father Abraham, "Father!" And [Abraham] said, "Here I am, my son." [Isaac] said, "The fire and the wood are here, but where is the lamb for a burnt offering?" Abraham said, "God himself will provide the lamb for a burnt offering, my son." So the two of them walked on together.

When they came to the place that God had shown him, Abraham built an altar there and laid the wood in order. He bound his son Isaac, and laid him on the altar, on top of the wood. Then Abraham reached out his hand and took the knife to kill his son. But the angel of the LORD called to him from heaven, and said, "Abraham, Abraham!" And [Abraham] said, "Here I am." [The angel of the Lord] said, "Do not lay your hand on the boy or do anything to him; for now I know that you fear God, since you have not withheld your son, your only son, from me." And Abraham looked up and saw a ram, caught in a thicket by its horns. Abraham went and took the ram and offered it up as a burnt offering instead of his son. So Abraham called that place "The LORD will provide"; as it is said to this day, "On the mount of the LORD it shall be provided."

—Genesis 22:1–14

A second story in the Old Testament reflects the same type of thinking, that suffering seems to be a way God tests us.

One day the heavenly beings came to present themselves before the LORD, and Satan also came among them. The LORD said to Satan, "Where have you come from?" Satan answered the LORD, "From going to and fro on the earth, and from walking up and down on it." The LORD said to Satan, "Have you considered my servant Job? There is no one like him on the earth, a blameless and upright man who fears God and turns

away from evil." Then Satan answered the LORD, "Does Job fear God for nothing? Have you not put a fence around him and his house and all that he has, on every side? You have blessed the work of his hands, and his possessions have increased in the land. But stretch out your hand now, and touch all that he has, and he will curse you to your face." The LORD said to Satan, "Very well, all that he has is in your power; only do not stretch out your hand against him!" So Satan went out from the presence of the LORD.

—Job 1:6–12

All of Job's sufferings—the death of his sons and daughters, the loss of his livestock and possessions, and eventually the loss of his own health—were a means of testing his faith in and loyalty to God.

This same type of thinking is found in the letter of James in the New Testament.

My brothers and sisters, whenever you face trials of any kind, consider it nothing but joy, because you know that the testing of your faith produces endurance; and let endurance have its full effect, so that you may be mature and complete, lacking in nothing.

—James 1:2–4

Blessed is anyone who endures temptation. Such a one has stood the test and will receive the crown of life that the Lord has promised to those who love him.

—James 1:12

To say that God sends us suffering to test us could imply that God is sadistic and cruel; we are simply pawns in a game God is playing with Satan. Furthermore, such thinking says that God is not **omniscient**, all-knowing, that God only knows the extent of our faith by our external actions, that God does not read our thoughts or know what is in our hearts. Jesus, however, preaches a different type of God. God is not just outside us, but inside us, too. God is a Father who "sees in secret" (Matthew 6:6), who knows what we need before we ask him (cf. Matthew 6:8).

---

omniscient *The ability of God to know everything— past, present, and future. God can read human hearts and know what we need before we say the words.*

A Form of Discipline

If suffering is not a punishment or a test, then perhaps it is a form of discipline. Maybe God sends us suffering to teach us a lesson, to help us grow. Perhaps the suffering purifies and strengthens us; it "ennobles" us and brings us closer to God. This type of thinking is found in many of the Old Testament prophets. According to some of their teachings, God inflicts suffering upon his chosen people, not to destroy them, but to discipline them and make them stronger. The suffering is creative and formative. It makes them better people. ▪

Suffering is like graceful pottery that emerges from the fire. God is the potter, and we are the clay (cf. Jeremiah 18:1–6). That is why the authors of Scripture tell us not to turn away from suffering: ". . . for the LORD reproves the one he loves, as a father the son in whom he delights" (Proverbs 3:12).

> Endure trials for the sake of discipline. God is treating you as children; for what child is there whom a parent does not discipline? If you do not have that discipline in which all children share, then you are illegitimate and not his children. Moreover, we had human parents to discipline us, and we respected them. Should we not be even more willing to be subject to the Father of spirits and live? For they disciplined us for a short time as seemed best to them, but he disciplines us for our good, in order that we may share his holiness. Now, discipline always seems painful rather than pleasant at the time, but later it yields the peaceful fruit of righteousness to those who have been trained by it.

Therefore lift your drooping hands and strengthen your weak knees, and make straight paths for your feet, so that what is lame may not be put out of joint, but rather be healed.

> —Hebrews 12:7–13

The argument is somewhat persuasive. But we must ask: Is this explanation truly adequate to explain suffering?

The answer is "No," for three reasons. First, while it is true that suffering can be a form of discipline and can strengthen our character, suffering in itself is no guarantee that we will become better persons. Some people respond to suffering by becoming crabby, angry, vindictive, selfish, and bitter. Again, consider the differences between Inspector Javert and Jean Valjean in *Les Miserables*. Javert thinks nothing of making life miserable for everyone around him. It doesn't bother him that his treatment of the poor is unjust, because he himself is suffering. Valjean, on the other hand, uses his experience of suffering to help him be more sensitive to the pain of others. He sacrifices himself to relieve the suffering of others.

> *W*e have more **resources** than we usually think; we may never **discover** them, and therefore never discover **ourselves** fully, if we do not enter the pain and suffering that test our **depths** and test them **true**. There is a **place** in life for the experience of **pain**, not for its own sake, but because it **burns** the dross off us in a way that nothing else can.
>
> Eugene Kennedy, *The Pain of Being Human*

Journal

1. Write about a time when enforced discipline helped you become a better person.
2. Write about a time when enforced discipline did not help you become a better person.
3. In the future, how do you think you will discipline your children? How much discipline will you use? What kinds of discipline will you use? Why?

masochism *An unhealthy desire to inflict pain, humiliation, abuse, or suffering on oneself.*

sadism *An unhealthy desire to inflict pain, humiliation, abuse, or suffering on someone else.*

capital sins *Evil tendencies within us that predispose us to sin. The seven capital sins— pride, covetous, lust, anger, gluttony, envy, and sloth—are the root causes of most sins. They also cause a great deal of suffering in this world.*

Second, if suffering is always a form of discipline, then being "virtuous" would entail the seeking of suffering for its own sake. At every possible opportunity, we would strive to inflict pain on ourselves and pain on others. Such a stance is hardly healthy and far from being "religious." Deliberately inflicting pain on ourselves is **masochistic**; deliberately inflicting pain on others is **sadistic**. Such actions deny respect for the human body— both our own and that of others. These acts violate the fifth commandment. Such actions also reject God's gift of health as something good.

It may be that there is no answer to the question "Why?" In fact, "Why?" may be the wrong question to ask altogether. Maybe suffering just is. Perhaps we can't have happiness without sorrow—like two sides of the same coin. Perhaps suffering is not a punishment, test, or form of discipline; perhaps happiness is not a reward. Maybe, as Father William O' Malley suggests in his book *Redemptive Suffering*, "each is essential, even to understand the other exists." ▪

Suffering and Freedom

The Church has long taught that some suffering is the consequence of human sin. Indeed, the seven **capital sins**—pride, covetousness, lust, anger, gluttony, envy, and sloth—are the root causes of a great deal of suffering in this world. But not all suffering is caused by these sins. As Saint Augustine taught, evil and suffering are the consequences not of sin, but of human freedom. God created humans free to choose between good and evil, between rejecting him and loving him. A world without suffering would definitely limit our decisions and impair our freedom. For God, human freedom is more important than creating a world without suffering. Suffering exists so that we might be truly free. ▪

In a way, human evil and suffering also underline God's freedom. Instead of responding to humans with strict justice, God is free to respond with mercy, love, forgiveness, and compassion. Nothing we do—good or bad—controls what God will do. For example, if we sin, God responds accordingly. God's response to us and to suffering is always free. This idea is part of the theme of Jesus' parable about the weeds and the wheat.

"The kingdom of heaven may be compared to someone who sowed good seed in his field; but while everybody was asleep, an enemy came and sowed weeds among the wheat, and then went away. So when the plants came up and bore grain, then the weeds appeared as well. And the slaves of the householder came and said to him, 'Master, did you not sow good seed in your field? Where, then, did these weeds come from?' He answered, 'An enemy has done

Discussion
Do you agree or disagree with Father O'Malley? Do we "need" suffering to know what happiness is? Explain your position.

Activity
In a small group, find out more about one of the seven capital sins. Discuss ways this evil tendency might lead teens to sin—in their thoughts, words, and actions.

this.' The slaves said to him, 'Then do you want us to go and gather them?' But he replied, 'No; for in gathering the weeds you would uproot the wheat along with them. Let both of them grow together until the harvest; and at harvest time I will tell the reapers, Collect the weeds first and bind them in bundles to be burned, but gather the wheat into my barn.' "

—Matthew 13:24–30

The Church teaches that there is another link between suffering and freedom as well. We are always free to choose how we will react to evil and unmerited suffering. The experience of suffering does not determine who we are or how we must act. We can either be victimized by our suffering, or we can be victors—people who transform our suffering into something that benefits both ourselves and others, something that is redemptive.

The Suffering Servant

You have already seen how Jesus, during his life on earth, suffered the pain of being human. It is important to remember that God did not cruelly send Jesus to earth to suffer and die. Instead, God sent Jesus to save humans from suffering and death. It is also important to remember that Jesus himself was not a masochist. He did not seek suffering and pain, nor did he enjoy it when it came. What he sought was to love—freely and forgiving.

Because of his great love for us, Jesus chose to give up his life as a sacrifice for our sins. When faced with unmerited suffering and death, he accepted his reality and made it redemptive. He became the perfect sacrifice. He endured suffering—not just as a victim, but as a priest and victor. In every way, Jesus became the Suffering Servant described centuries earlier by Deutero-Isaiah.

The concept of a Messiah who was God's Suffering Servant was formulated during the Babylonian exile. After the fall of Jerusalem, the people remaining in Israel had to live among the ruins of national defeat. They suffered in their own land. The Israelites who were taken as hostages to Babylon also experienced desolation and misery. Their very faith in God was shaken. They questioned why this fate had befallen them; they wondered if God was not strong enough to relieve their suffering.

In the midst of such pain, Deutero-Isaiah offered the Israelites a role model—God's Suffering Servant. This servant would endure unmerited suffering and death for the sake of others. Like a scapegoat, he would take on the punishment of sins he had not committed. Here is how Deutero-Isaiah describes him:

He was . . . a man of suffering and acquainted with infirmity; . . .

Surely he has borne our infirmities and carried our diseases;

yet we accounted him stricken, struck down by God, and afflicted.

But he was wounded for our transgressions, crushed for our iniquities;

upon him was the punishment that made us whole, and by his bruises we are healed.

He was oppressed, and he was afflicted, yet he did not open his mouth;

like a lamb that is led to the slaughter, and like a sheep that before its shearers is silent, so he did not open his mouth.

By a perversion of justice he was taken away. Who could have imagined his future?

—Isaiah 53:3–8

Catholics Believe

. . . Jesus is . . . the suffering Servant who silently allows himself to be led to the slaughter and who bears the sin of the multitudes. . . . Christ's whole life expresses his mission: "to serve and to give his life as a ransom for many" (Mk 10:45). (Catechism, #608)

Despite his unspeakable torments, Jesus, the Suffering Servant, would still keep faith in his Father as a good and loving God. He accepted it as his own and offered it to God his Father as an expression of love. Suffering and death did not conquer him; he conquered them and made them the gateway to a better and eternal life. ▪

Following Jesus

Jesus once said, "If any want to become my followers, let them deny themselves and take up their cross daily and follow me" (Luke 9:23–24). These words have a lot to tell us about discipleship, or following Jesus. We are to approach suffering and death as he did.

Characteristics of Discipleship

What was it about Jesus' personality that enabled him to accept unmerited suffering and turn it into a redemptive force? Here are some characteristics that most likely helped. For each trait listed in the following table, rate yourself on a scale of 0 to 10 on how much you find this same trait in yourself.

	0	1	2	3	4	5	6	7	8	9	10
1. Optimism	❑	❑	❑	❑	❑	❑	❑	❑	❑	❑	❑
2. Courage	❑	❑	❑	❑	❑	❑	❑	❑	❑	❑	❑
3. Self-understanding	❑	❑	❑	❑	❑	❑	❑	❑	❑	❑	❑
4. Faith in God's goodness	❑	❑	❑	❑	❑	❑	❑	❑	❑	❑	❑
5. Personal relationship with God as Father	❑	❑	❑	❑	❑	❑	❑	❑	❑	❑	❑
6. Perspective	❑	❑	❑	❑	❑	❑	❑	❑	❑	❑	❑
7. Perseverance	❑	❑	❑	❑	❑	❑	❑	❑	❑	❑	❑
8. Flexibility	❑	❑	❑	❑	❑	❑	❑	❑	❑	❑	❑
9. Insight and intuition	❑	❑	❑	❑	❑	❑	❑	❑	❑	❑	❑
10. Humor	❑	❑	❑	❑	❑	❑	❑	❑	❑	❑	❑
11. Belief in one's own strengths and abilities	❑	❑	❑	❑	❑	❑	❑	❑	❑	❑	❑
12. Sense of morality	❑	❑	❑	❑	❑	❑	❑	❑	❑	❑	❑

If your rating to most or all of the traits is near "10," you are probably a person who looks at suffering and death as Jesus did. If your rating to most or all of the traits is near "0," you may need to take a closer look at your personal stance toward suffering and death. In your notebook, list ideas that may help you grow in the traits that need strengthening.

Activity

In a small group, read one of the following prophecies about God's Suffering Servant. Then discuss how Jesus fulfilled this prophecy.

- Isaiah 42:1–4
- Isaiah 49:1–6
- Isaiah 50:4–11
- Isaiah 52:13–53:12

From Victim to Victor

The ability to give suffering a positive, redemptive meaning is based on the ability to see yourself as a victor rather than a victim. But how do you get from a victim mentality to a victor mentality? Psychologists offer the following suggestions.

1. **Face problems rather than dodge them.** Remember, suffering is not necessarily evil or opposed to God. Suffering can be an opportunity to grow and learn something new about yourself and the world around you.

2. **Keep close to the people you love.** Continue to have a social life. Ask for advice of trusted others. Lean on them when you need help. Don't isolate yourself or think you have to suffer stoically alone in silence.

3. **Discover what you are really feeling.** Let yourself feel the pain. Then express these feelings in healthy and creative ways. (Yell at a stuffed animal or magazine picture; hit a pillow; run around the block.)

4. **Balance the ongoing problem with other parts of your life.** Have some perspective. Just because one thing in your life is going wrong doesn't mean that everything is; it just seems that way.

5. **Be responsible for your own decisions.** Don't wait for a knight in shining armor or a warrior princess to come rescue you.

6. **Be true to your moral, religious, and spiritual beliefs.** Remember, bad times are usually temporary. God is with you in your suffering. Jesus knows exactly how you feel because he has been there.

7. **Be proactive, not reactive, to your situation.** Proactive people strategize. They plan ahead for possible problems so that they aren't blindsided or paralyzed when problems or setbacks occur. Take initiative rather than let the situation victimize you. Act NOW rather than wait for some future time when conditions are "right."

8. **Maintain your sense of humor.** If you can learn to laugh at yourself and your situation in life—both good and bad, you will be better able to ride out the tough times and appreciate the good times. ▪

Journal

Write about a problem or unpleasant experience you are going through right now. Then map out a plan of action, based on the eight steps found on this page, for transforming yourself from a victim to a victor.

Words to Know

capital sins	sadism
masochism	superstition
omniscient	theodicy
original sin	works of mercy
retributive justice	

Review Questions

1. What is the difference between superstition and healthy religious devotional practices?
2. Explain how our sense of retributive justice leads to the problem of theodicy.
3. What are two problems with thinking that suffering is always a punishment for one's sins?
4. What are two problems with thinking that suffering is always God's way of testing our faith?
5. What are three problems with thinking that suffering is always God's way of disciplining us and making us stronger?
6. According to Church teaching, what is the relationship between suffering and freedom?
7. How did Jesus approach suffering and death so that it would be redemptive?
8. List three actions you can take to help transform yourself from a victim mentality to a victor mentality in the face of suffering.

C•H•A•P•T•E•R

4

Healthy *and* Unhealthy Reactions

IN THIS CHAPTER, YOU WILL

- see how some people respond to the mystery of suffering and death by taking risks with their lives;

- learn what several philosophers have to say about death;

- consider why some people attempt suicide;

- explore the warning signs of suicide and learn some ways to help prevent it;

- examine what motivates some people to give their lives for others;

- explore why Christians believe the death of Jesus conquered death once and for all;

- appreciate how religious faith can help us view death as the beginning of new life;

- assess your own values and attitudes regarding life, death, and risk-taking.

Gambling with Life

People react differently to the unexplainable mystery of suffering and death. Some people respond in healthy, productive ways. Other people respond in unhealthy, self-destructive ways. Here is the story of one teen who gambled with his life and lost.

As easy as it would be to blame William Smith's death on a movie, or on easy access to guns, or on teenage angst, none fully explains why the 13-year-old decided to load a six-shot revolver with five bullets, spin the cylinder, then put the gun to his head and fire.

"He knew what guns could do," his father, a retired reserve officer with the Department of Public Safety, said. "I taught him safety—that guns are not to be played with. They can kill you." The gun William Smith used to shoot himself was his father's old DPS service revolver.

The family theorizes that William was trying to imitate a scene from the movie *187*, which the teen had seen about two weeks ago. At the end of the film two of the characters play a variation of Russian roulette, putting two bullets in the gun and firing more than once on a turn. Both end up dead.

"Oh, that was stupid," William said after watching the scene.

William had plenty of friends and high self-esteem. The two boys he was with on Friday, one 10, the other 15, weren't part of his normal circle; but then, William was always making new buddies.

Friday was a day off at William's middle school. It was also the start of the two-week spring break at the year-round school. With both parents working, William was home alone. He had spent Thursday night at a friend's house. The next morning, he came home, grabbed his father's revolver, and went back to that friend's home. The boys played Russian roulette with a single bullet, the family learned after the shooting. They all cheated death.

That afternoon they ate lunch at William's house. Around 3 P.M. William decided to play Russian roulette with raised stakes. The gun William was playing with was loaded with five bullets. William took the first and only shot of the accelerated game. ■

—Shortened from "'A Nightmare,' Russian roulette victim's family seeks answers," © *The Arizona Republic* (March 16, 1998). Article by Richard Ruelas. Used with permission. Permission does not imply endorsement.

In Memory

William Smith, 13, was killed by a self-inflicted gunshot wound to the head during a game of Russian roulette. He died Friday, March 13, 1998, in Chandler, Arizona.

Discussion

1. How much do you think television shows and movies influence the actions of most teens? Explain your position.
2. Do you think people who take life-threatening risks are trying to kill themselves? Explain.

Staring Death in the Face

TV and modern forms of communication have brought us face-to-face with death. On the nightly news, we now see the victims of car accidents, murders, famines, wars, and natural disasters. In addition to real-life scenarios, many TV shows and movies include death-defying stunts and spectacularly faked deaths. Explicit accounts of suicides and murders are also found on the Internet. ▪

Instead of making us more responsive to death, such media overexposure numbs us. Because death, Hollywood style, is not real, it is hard not to view real-life suffering and death as fiction. Because cinematic suffering and death are so commonplace, many people look for more sensational ways to overcome their boredom both with TV and with their own lives. Thus, ordinary people turn to high-risk activities, such as bungee jumping, Russian roulette, taking drugs, and motorcycle racing. ▪

Just think of the professional death-defiers you have seen: high-wire circus acts, stunt persons, magicians, high divers. What motivates a David Copperfield to go over Niagara Falls tied to a flaming raft, or a Harry Houdini to allow himself to be put in a locked coffin submerged in water, or an Evel Knievel to attempt jumping over thirty limousines on a motorcycle? Certainly, money is one motivation. Another motivation is the "thrill" of looking death in the face and living to tell about it.

In the last chapter, you learned that questions about suffering and death that ask "Why did this happen?" have no completely satisfactory answers. In this chapter, you will learn about healthy and unhealthy reactions to the mystery of suffering and death. Before beginning the chapter, respond in your notebook to the survey statements above.

Attitude Survey	I agree	I disagree	I'm not sure
High-risk activities make life more interesting.			
We can only approach death realistically if we accept that there is nothing beyond life.			
Sacrificing your life for an ideal is stupid.			
Suicide is sometimes justified.			
Jesus conquered death; his followers will share his victory.			

Response One: Death Is Final

What people believe often determines how they respond to suffering and death. In this section, you will look at the view of some philosophers who believed that death is final, that there is no life after death. Some of these philosophers believed in God; others were atheists.

Socrates (470–399 B.C.)

Socrates was sentenced to death by the Greek government for presumably corrupting the youth of Athens with his teachings. He spent considerable time in prison before his death describing his feelings and attitudes during the final days of his life. Although he could have escaped from prison and lived out his days in peace, Socrates chose to abide by the decision of the state. In the end, he administered his own death by drinking hemlock. Because Socrates approached death with dignity and courage, many people have considered him a role model of **Ars Moriendi**, the art of dying.

Of Interest

Over the past thirty-five years, TV has brought us extensive accounts of death: the assassination of John F. Kennedy and the killing of his accused assassin by Jack Ruby; the murder of Martin Luther King Jr.; the slaying of Robert F. Kennedy; the attempted killings of Pope John Paul II and President Ronald Reagan; the murder of musician John Lennon; the Persian Gulf War; the death of Princess Diana.

Ars Moriendi *Latin for "the art of dying." This art is thought to be acquired by the practice of right living.*

Journal
What are your feelings when you hear about suffering and death on the nightly news?

Discussion
Think about the TV shows or movies you have seen recently. How was death portrayed in these shows? How many people died?

Because Socrates himself left no written records of his philosophy, it is difficult to sort out his thoughts about life and death from those of Plato, his biographer. According to Plato's report, Socrates wanted to convince his followers that death is not to be feared. Socrates himself was unclear about whether or not the soul lived on after death. In Plato's *Apology*, Socrates is presented as not believing in **immortality**. Later, in the *Phaedo*, Plato has Socrates giving many arguments for immortality. In short, Socrates did not pretend to know what, if anything, exists after death. Yet his belief in God's goodness and justice led him to overcome all fears about death. "Since there is God, no evil can happen to a good man, either in life or after death," Socrates argued. "Death is an unspeakable gain, perhaps a journey to another place. What can be greater than this? . . . It is always better to die than to do evil."

immortality Continued existence beyond death.

Martin Heidegger (1889–1976)

According to German philosopher Martin Heidegger, dying is one thing no one can do for another; we all must die our own death. Because we die alone, the reality of death gives us a sense of individuality and uniqueness. We define who we are and what our lives are to be, only in light of death.

Indeed, Heidegger saw all of life from the standpoint of death. "As soon as we are born, we are old enough to die," he wrote. For him, the important thing is to face death as final and to take possession of it. We are to "advance" resolutely toward death, taking charge of our lives and seizing each moment as an opportunity to fulfill ourselves as much as possible. Just as no one else can die for us, so no one else can live our lives for us. We are ultimately responsible for finding meaning and purpose in our lives.

Jean-Paul Sartre (pictured above) believed that death deprived people of their full potential. However, German philosopher Karl Jaspers (pictured on page 53) defined death as the fulfillment of human life.

Jean-Paul Sartre (1905–1980)

For the French philosopher Jean-Paul Sartre, death is absurd. The soul is not immortal; after death, there is only nonbeing. Death is something we can never understand or control. It prevents our completion and wholeness; it deprives us of our full potential.

Faced with his own finiteness, Sartre discovered a sense of personal freedom. "I am free to make meaning out of my life, despite my mortality," he wrote. What we make of ourselves, what we accomplish in life, is entirely our own responsibility. We must make sense out of life while we have it. We must celebrate our days while we have them; we must engage in a daily effort to find meaning in life. ▪ ▪

Journal

1. Do you believe the soul lives on after death? Why or why not?
2. If you had been Socrates, would you have chosen to drink the hemlock? Explain.
3. At this point in your life, what gives you meaning? Do you think this will change in the future?

Discussion

1. According to Heidegger, no one else can die for us or live our lives for us. What do you think this statement means for teenagers today?
2. What do you think Socrates meant when he said we should fear doing wrong more than we should fear death? Give examples.
3. In what sense does death prevent us from achieving our

Karl Jaspers (1883–1969)

This German philosopher parted from Heidegger by defining death as the fulfillment of human life. According to Jaspers, death is entirely natural and in keeping with human identity. Human life belongs to a larger cycle of birth, growth, decline, and death. We are part of a cosmic process. Just as we had no control over our own birth, so we have no control over our own death. When we remember that life itself is a gift and that we did not create ourselves, then we can approach death with a leap of faith. This faith is not based on belief in God or an afterlife but rather on an understanding of the nature of the material universe. ■ ■

Response Two: Death as a Way Out

Some people look death in the face and see it as an end to their suffering. They embrace death as a way out of their problems; they end up committing **suicide**. In the traditions of some cultures, suicide has been considered an honorable way to die. For example, in ancient Rome a soldier was expected to fall upon his sword in certain adverse circumstances. The Japanese respected those who practiced *hari-kari* (ritual self-disembowelment). In Polynesia, if a man realized he had treated others unjustly, the respectable thing for him to do was to swim out to sea until he drowned.

These examples are exceptions. Almost universally, suicide has been considered wrong. Although the Old Testament contains several examples of suicide (Saul, who fell on his own sword when his enemies surrounded him in battle; Ahithophel, who hung himself after betraying King David; and Razis, who disemboweled himself instead of being taken by enemy soldiers), the Jews considered suicide to be a violation of the fifth commandment: "You shall not kill" (Exodus 20:13). The early Christians also regarded suicide as a serious moral evil. Although the Gospel of Matthew records that Judas Iscariot hung himself after betraying Jesus, the Acts of the Apostles states that his death was accidental. During the Middle Ages, Saint Thomas Aquinas refined the Church's thinking on suicide, saying that it is wrong for three reasons: (1) it violates the instinct to love oneself and to preserve one's own life; (2) it is an offense against society since it deprives the community of one of its rightful members and contributors; and (3) it is a crime against God, who alone has power to give and take away life. ■

The social dimension of suicide may be seen in many civil laws. English law once listed attempted suicide as a crime. Even today, California state law says that aiding and abetting someone in committing suicide is a felony.

suicide The intentional killing of oneself.

Catholics Believe

Suicide . . . is gravely contrary to the just love of self. It likewise offends love of neighbor because it unjustly breaks the ties of solidarity with family, nation, and other human societies to which we continue to have obligations. Suicide is contrary to love for the living God. (Catechism, #2281)

Activity

Search through newspapers and news magazines for examples of recent Catholics who are role models for the art of dying. Three examples might include Sister Thea Bowman (d. 1990), Cardinal Joseph Bernardin (d. 1996), and Mother Teresa of Calcutta (d. 1997). Prepare a three-minute news report on the death of this person.

Discussion

1. In what sense is death a fulfillment of life?
2. How does the "faith" of Karl Jaspers differ from Christian faith?

Activity

Compare the two accounts of the death of Judas Iscariot (Matthew 27:3–10, Acts 1:15–20). Can you think of any way to explain the discrepancies between the two stories?

Of Interest

Because suicide was regarded as a mortal sin, the Church for many centuries forbade those who had committed suicide from having a Catholic funeral or from being buried in a Catholic cemetery. The 1983 revised Code of Canon Law does not mention people who have committed suicide among those who are to be forbidden Church funeral rites.

In the United States, over thirty-one thousand people committed suicide in 1995. In other words, roughly twelve out of every 100,000 people saw death as a way out of their problems. Native Americans had the highest suicide rate among any race.

Teen suicide is a growing problem in our society. Indeed, it is among the top three killers of teens today. Statistics tell us that a teenager tries to commit suicide every ninety minutes.

While more girls than boys try to commit suicide, more boys actually kill themselves. Television shows that portray suicide and lyrics (sometimes subliminal) of heavy metal music may have some influence on these statistics. A significant number of suicides among teenagers occur in clusters or are "copycat" actions of earlier suicides seen on TV or committed by friends and family members. ■

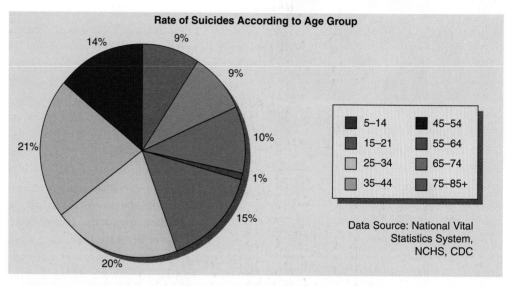

Rate of Suicides According to Age Group

14% 9% 9% 10% 1% 15% 20% 21%

Legend:
- 5–14
- 15–21
- 25–34
- 35–44
- 45–54
- 55–64
- 65–74
- 75–85+

Data Source: National Vital Statistics System, NCHS, CDC

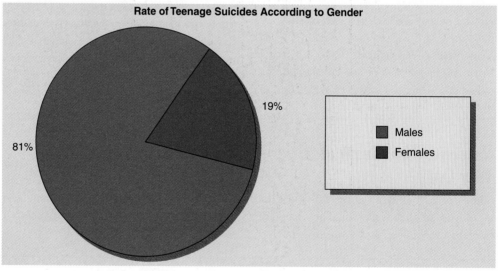

Rate of Teenage Suicides According to Gender

81% 19%

- Males
- Females

Discussion

1. It has been said that suicide is a permanent solution to a temporary problem. Do you agree or disagree with this statement? Explain.

2. Why do you think the Church changed its position forbidding those who had committed suicide from having a Catholic funeral or from being buried in a Catholic cemetery?

3. What are possible reasons Native Americans in the United States have higher suicide rates than people of other races?

4. What are possible reasons teenagers might attempt suicide? What are some alternatives for dealing with these reasons/problems?

The reasons people choose suicide vary. Marilyn Monroe, Judy Garland, Jim Morrison, and Jimi Hendrix felt they couldn't live with or without more and more drugs; they overdosed. Kurt Cobain, member of the rock group Nirvana, committed suicide in 1994 after extended heroin abuse and a troubled marriage. These people undoubtedly felt what most people who attempt suicide feel: desolate loneliness, alienation from others, despair, hopelessness, guilt, rejection, low self-esteem, and self-hatred. These negative feelings feed upon themselves and become so dominant that life no longer seems worth living. Death seems to be the only way out of pain and misery. ■

Many stereotypes about suicide are wrong. Because suicide affects so many teens, you need to be aware of these stereotypes and what really is the truth.

Stereotype 1: Only the very rich or the very poor commit suicide.

Fact: People of every economic and racial group commit suicide.

Stereotype 2: Suicide tends to run in families. The desire to commit suicide is inherited.

Fact: While there is no known gene for suicide, people who have had a family member commit suicide are more likely to commit suicide themselves. The reasons may include the survivor's feelings of guilt ("What did I do wrong?" "If only I had done this . . ."), similar problems facing members of the same family, and inherited chemical imbalances that lead to depression.

Stereotype 3: People who commit suicide are mentally ill.

Fact: In most cases, a person who commits suicide is not mentally ill but is extremely unhappy due to prolonged depression or emotional upset.

Stereotype 4: Most suicides occur around Christmas.

Fact: While most suicides occur in February, there also seems to be a correlation to the person's birthday. One study has found that half the people who commit suicide do so within ninety days of their last birthday and that nearly eight in ten suicides occur within the first six months after a person's birthday. Few people kill themselves in the three months before their birthdays.

Stereotype 5: Suicidal people want to die and there is little that can be done about it.

Fact: Most people who threaten suicide are undecided about living or dying. They gamble with death in the hope that others will save them.

Stereotype 6: People who talk about suicide will not commit it.

Fact: Eight out of ten people who give definite warnings about killing themselves will do so. Their threats should be taken seriously.

In times of severe depression, a person's outer strengths (connections to others) and inner strengths (religious convictions) can be real life-savers. ■

Of Interest

In 1997, the National Center for Chronic Disease Prevention reported that one out of four high school students seriously considered suicide.

The negative feelings people who choose suicide experience become so dominate that life no longer seems worth living. Death seems to be the only way out of pain and misery.

Activity
1. Many of the lyrics found in popular music are depressing. Some teenagers who commit suicide are discovered with copies of such song lyrics on their persons. Do you think it is possible for song lyrics somehow to encourage an individual to commit suicide? Bring to class some lyrics that illustrate your point.
2. Rent the movie *It's a Wonderful Life.* Why does George Bailey choose not to commit suicide? How would the world be different if you had never been born?

Journal
Suppose a friend tells you that he or she is thinking about suicide. How would you respond?

Some Warning Signs of Suicide

mood swings, emotional outbursts, aggressive behavior

ongoing depression, loss of interest or involvement in social activities, withdrawal from family and friends

drop in grades or work performance

change in eating habits and weight (either up or down)

change in sleeping patterns (either insomnia or sleeping all the time)

increased use of alcohol and other drugs

less concern for personal safety

saying things such as "I wish I were dead" or "Maybe people will appreciate me once I'm gone," or giving similar hints about suicide

giving important things away or making out a will

obsession with death, heaven, hell, and death drawings

---

altruistic death A form of self-sacrifice in which an individual gives up his or her life for a noble cause, a sense of patriotic duty, or a religious ideal.

martyr A Greek word that means "witness"; one who voluntarily dies for his or her faith or some Christian principle.

Response Three: Death as Self-Sacrifice

For some people, death is the ultimate expression of love—a way to express belief in a noble cause or ideal, a way of sacrificing oneself for others. Death that is motivated by the love of God and others is known as **altruistic death**.

Every century has known such deaths involving faith, courage, and love. In the Old Testament, Samson gave up his own life in fighting his people's enemies. During the Maccabean revolt in the second century B.C., many Jews gave up their lives for their religious beliefs. In the New Testament, Jesus died on the cross rather than compromise the message of God's love that he lived and preached. Many Christians in the early days of the Church gave up their lives rather than disavow their allegiance to Christ. The Church has honored such people as **martyrs**, a word that means "witness." In dying, such people gave witness to their values and beliefs. They put their lives "on the line" for what they held important.

Modern-day society has seen many examples of people who have risked and sometimes given up their lives for others. During World War II, for example, Japanese kamikaze pilots deliberately plunged their aircraft (and themselves) into American warships for the sake of their country. In every war, soldiers have risked their lives to bring the wounded to safety. In our present society, firefighters and police officers risk their lives every day to save others.

Before his own death, Jesus told his disciples that giving up one's life for one's friends is the greatest possible expression of love (cf. John 15:12–13). Here are the stories of two modern-day people who gave up their lives as expressions of love.

Of Interest

There are more than two hundred suicide prevention centers throughout the United States, and most major cities have a suicide prevention hot line that is listed in the telephone directory. Here are some places to contact if you ever need help:

- Suicide Hot Line, 1-800-827-7571
- Youth Line, 1-800-246-4646
- On-line Support, www.alt.support.depression

CRISIS LINES
-24-Hour Service-
MENTAL HEALTH COMPLEX 257-7222
• TTY/TDD (for hearing-impaired) 257-6300
-Weekdays 8AM-4:30PM-
SOCIAL SERVICES
• Adult 289-6660
• Children 289-6444
• TTY/TDD (for hearing-impaired) 289-6665
After 4:30PM & Weekends
Please Call Your Police Department Or
————————————————————— 289-6444

Maximilian Kolbe (1894–1941)

"Welcome back to Poland, Father!" the young priest said enthusiastically. "Or should I call you Doctor? Or perhaps General?"

Maximilian laughed and embraced his brother Franciscan. After a long trip in Japan, he was at last returning home to his own country and to *Militia Immaculatae*, the Army of Mary Immaculate, a religious community he had founded. "How about calling me Editor?" Maximilian quipped. "It's time I got back to work doing what I like best."

The young priest frowned. "Since the Germans took over Poland, we have been forbidden to publish the newspaper," he said. "They consider it subversive of their political viewpoint."

"And rightly so," Maximilian remarked.

That very afternoon, he began work on the next edition of the paper. Soon after the newspaper was released, the Nazis came and arrested him. He was taken to the concentration camp at Auschwitz.

The place was a death camp. Those who could not work were exterminated immediately. Those who could work were worked to death. In any event, the Nazis intended for there to be no survivors.

One day a desperate prisoner successfully escaped from Father Kolbe's barracks. The Nazi commander lined up all the men in the barracks and told them that, in retaliation for the escape, he would choose ten of them to die.

Maximilian waited in fear as the Nazi commander made his selections. He felt sad and helpless for those chosen, but he also felt relieved at not being among them.

Suddenly Francis Gajowniczek, one of the condemned men, broke down and cried. "I have a wife and small baby," he pleaded. "I can't die. They need me."

Maximilian's heart went out to the prisoner. In an act of supreme courage and selflessness, he found himself stepping forward. "Take me instead," he told the Nazi guide. "I'll die for Mr. Gajowniczek."

And so it was done. Maximilian and the other nine men were taken to Cell Block 11 to be starved to death. As the horrible days passed and death began to claim them, Father Kolbe continued to lead the other prisoners in prayers and hymns. Finally, when there were only four of the original ten remaining, the soldiers killed Maximilian with a lethal injection of carbolic acid. News of his death spread quickly throughout the camp. And everywhere the prisoners began to speak of him as "the saint" who gave his life for others. ▪

Of Interest
Maximilian Kolbe was declared a saint by Pope John Paul II in 1982. His feast day is August 14.

Activity

1. Research the life of one other Catholic Church martyr (such as Saint Felicity, Saint Perpetua, Saint Isaac Jogues, or Saint Charles Lwanga). In what way did the saint sacrifice his or her life for the faith?

2. Search through newspapers and news magazines for examples of modern-day martyrs. For what or whom did these people die?

3. Read Robert Bolt's play *A Man for All Seasons*. Write a report that explains why Saint Thomas More chose to die.

Jean Donovan (1953–1980)

"Surprise!" the voices called out in unison in the Connecticut parish hall.

Jean smiled with happiness to see all her old friends. She had just returned from a year as a lay missionary in El Salvador, and she had really missed everyone. Jean went around the room, laughing, hugging, and exchanging stories with her friends.

After a festive meal and boisterous singing, the crowd began to thin. Eventually only Jean and her closest friends remained.

"You're not thinking about going back to El Salvador again, are you?" one of them asked.

Jean looked around the room. "As a matter of fact, I am."

"But you can't," another friend warned. "It's too dangerous. If they could kill Archbishop Romero, they'd easily kill you."

Jean laughed to ease the tension in the group. "Believe me, blue-eyed blondes are safe there. We're easily identified as Americans, and no matter what, the Salvadoran army doesn't shoot Americans."

"Father Crowley told us about the death threats you'd gotten before you left," a third friend spoke. "Be smart, and don't go back."

Jean sighed. "Sometimes you can't make choices with your head," she explained. "You have to follow your heart. My heart is with the poor in El Salvador. They're hungry and homeless, and I promised them that I would come back."

Despite the warnings, Jean returned to El Salvador in the fall. On December 2, 1980, she, Ursuline Sister Dorothy Kazel, and Maryknoll Sisters Maura Clarke and Ita Ford were kidnapped a few miles from the San Salvador airport. The next day their fire-gutted van was found on a deserted road. The following day their bodies were found in a shallow grave in a cow pasture. Each had been shot in the head; at least two of them had been raped.

Almost two decades later, Jean's murderers still have not been conclusively identified or punished. ■ ■

Discussion

1. The writer Tertullian once said, "The blood of the martyrs is the seed of the Church." What do you think this statement means? Do you think the same is true of the blood of today's martyrs? Explain.

2. What do you see as the difference between a death-defier and an altruist?

3. Is an altruist really a hero, or is altruistic death just another form of suicide? Explain your position.

Journal

For what (or whom) would you be willing to give up your life?

Of Interest

Archbishop Oscar Romero (1917–1980) was shot and killed while he celebrated Mass in the oratory of the *Divina Providencia* cancer hospital on March 24, 1980. You can learn more about his life by renting the video *Romero*.

Response Four: Death as the Beginning of New Life

Seeing death as the beginning of new life marks one of the radical differences between Christianity and traditional Judaism. Usually, Old Testament authors viewed death as final. When people died, their spirit left. The deceased continued to exist in Sheol, but they were incapable of any vital activity, even the worship of God. Thus death was a terrible evil, something to avoid at all costs.

As the Israelites grew in their understanding of God as good and all-powerful, they also grew in the realization that God must have power over the forces of evil. The Messiah whom God promised to send would therefore have power over the evil of sin and the evil of death. The Messiah would not only free people from their sins; he would free them, once and for all, from death. The Messiah himself would not die; his kingdom would last forever. ■

The apostles approached Jesus with this mind-set. As they grew in their belief that he was the Messiah, they also grew in the expectation that he would live forever and that he would include them in his eternal kingdom on earth. Many actions of Jesus supported their viewpoint. He cured the sick, restored sight to the blind, made those unable to speak talk again, calmed the wind and the sea, and even revived people who had died.

It is no wonder that Peter protested ferociously when Jesus predicted his own death. Nor is it surprising that James and John would fight over the best positions in Jesus' kingdom. In some ways, it is even understandable how Judas could have told the Jewish officials where Jesus was, in exchange for silver. None of the apostles ever expected Jesus to die.

If you can put yourself in the apostles' frame of mind, then you can see why the crucifixion of Jesus was so horrible. It wasn't just that it was a painful, humiliating way to die; everything the apostles had hoped for also died with Jesus. They thought they had believed in him in vain. How disappointed and disillusioned they must have felt.

These feelings were precisely what the Gospel of Luke says two disciples were discussing on their way to Emmaus three days after the death of Jesus. On the road, they met up with a stranger who explained to them why it was necessary for the Messiah to suffer and die in order to conquer death. Only when that same stranger later broke bread with them did they recognize him. Then the truth hit them: Jesus had been raised from the dead! ■

> *T*orture us, rack us, **condemn** us, crush us; your cruelty only **proves** our **innocence**. *That is why God* **suffers** *us to suffer* **all** *this.*
>
> Quintus Tertullian

Activity

Find out more about the Old Testament concept of death by reading the following passages. Then summarize your findings in a report.
- Psalm 6:5–6
- Psalm 30:9–11
- Psalm 88:10–13
- Isaiah 38:10–11, 18

Activity

1. Act out one of the following Scripture passages that tell about the apostles' expectations of Jesus.
   - Matthew 16:21–26
   - Matthew 20:20–28
2. Read Luke 24:13–35. Tell in your own words
   - what you think the disciples were talking about;
   - why they didn't recognize Jesus at first;
   - why they finally recognized him.

resurrection *Jesus' Passover from death to life in and through the power of God. People who die believing in Jesus will rise, as he did, to new life.*

The **resurrection** of Jesus is the cornerstone of our Catholic faith. Jesus overcame death by his own dying and rising. Because he deprived death of its power, we, too, shall pass through death to new life. We no longer need to be afraid of death; death is not final. Seen with the eyes of faith, death takes on new meaning: ". . . unless a grain of wheat falls into the earth and dies, it remains just a single grain; but if it dies, it bears much fruit" (John 12:24). "I am the living bread that came down from heaven. Whoever eats of this bread will live forever" (John 6:51). ▪

Through Baptism, we enter fully into the Paschal mystery. We are baptized into the death of Jesus so we can rise with him to a new life. As Saint Paul wrote to the Romans:

> Do you not know that all of us who have been baptized into Christ Jesus were baptized into his death? Therefore we have been buried with him by baptism into death, so that, just as Christ was raised from the dead by the glory of the Father, so we too might walk in newness of life.
>
> We know that Christ, being raised from the dead, will never die again; death no longer has dominion over him. The death he died, he died to sin, once for all; but the life he lives, he lives to God. So you also must consider yourselves dead to sin and alive to God in Christ Jesus.
>
> —Romans 6:3–4, 9–11

Because of the resurrection, death has no power over us. For those who have faith in Jesus, death is merely a passage to everlasting life and the fullness of the new life they have already begun to experience here. ▪ ▪ ▪

Where You Stand

Where do you stand in response to death? How much do you really value life? Do you unnecessarily put your life in danger? Are you at risk regarding suicide?

To answer these questions, reflect on the items in the questionnaire that follows. Quietly think about and pray over each item. After you have finished, write a short paragraph in your notebook about your philosophy of life. Do you value life highly, or are there areas at which you may need to take a closer look?

Have you ever . . .

1. Used illegal drugs?
2. Driven a car above the speed limit?
3. Raced a car, boat, motorcycle, jet ski, or all-terrain vehicle?
4. Driven a car while drunk?
5. Ridden in a car with a drunk driver?
6. Played Russian roulette?
7. Carried a gun or knife?
8. Gone scuba diving?
9. Parachuted from a plane?
10. Flown a plane?
11. Surfed in an area known for dangerous undertow?
12. Gone bungee jumping?
13. Dived off a high dive or cliff?
14. Smoked cigarettes?
15. Gotten drunk?
16. Had unprotected sex?
17. Gone white-water rafting?

Activity

Choose one of the following passages in which Jesus raises the dead. Then rewrite it from the perspective of one of the apostles.
- Matthew 9:18–19, 23–26
- Luke 7:11–17
- John 11:1–44

Journal

What difference has the resurrection of Jesus made in your own life? In your own response to death?

Activity

Discuss 1 Corinthians 15:12–58. What does Paul say about
- the resurrection of Jesus;
- our own dying and rising;
- the meaning of baptism;
- why he dares to face death;
- the resurrection of the body;
- the relationship between faith and moral living?

18. Been on high-thrill amusement rides?
19. Lived on or near an earthquake fault?
20. Gone rock climbing?
21. Tried to copy stunts done on TV or in movies?
22. Thought about killing yourself?
23. Deliberately disobeyed traffic laws?
24. Been depressed for an extended period of time?

If your answer is "No" to most or all of the questions, you are probably a person who values life highly. If your answer is "Yes" to most or all of the questions, you may need to take a closer look at your personal stance toward life and death.

If you are at high-risk regarding suicide, or if you're just depressed by the way your life is going, take time NOW to make some changes. No one needs to go through life unhappy, and no one needs to commit suicide. Here are some tips that can help you build a happier and more meaningful life.

1. **Take charge of your own emotions.** You may not be able to control everything that happens to you, but you can control how you will respond to what happens. No one can make you feel a certain way. Only you can choose how you will feel.
2. **Commit yourself to projects that help others.** Donate some time each week to give generously of yourself.

3. **Take initiative in developing friendships.** If one person isn't interested in being your friend, move on to someone else.
4. **Don't count on only one activity or friendship.** In other words, find meaning in all sorts of relationships and activities. Don't put all your meaning into one person, job, team, or even grades in school. It's smart to have many things that give you meaning. Then if something bad happens in one area, you will still find positive support in the other areas.
5. **Learn to distinguish a bad situation from feelings of self-hatred.** Just because someone breaks up with you doesn't mean you are a bad person or worthless. Learn what you can from the bad situation, reaffirm your own goodness, and then move on.
6. **Develop a friendship with yourself.** Sometimes we are our own worst critics. Learn to be gentle with yourself, affirm your positive points, and look at any mistakes you make as an opportunity for learning.
7. **Never be afraid to get help.** People are social beings, and sometimes talking things over with someone else is the best way to make a problem manageable. ■ ■

 Discussion
The Bible tells us to "Choose life, not death." How do you think these words apply to teenagers today? How do they apply to your own choices each day?

 Journal
On a scale of 1 to 10 (with 10 being the highest), how happy would you say you are right now? If you are a 10, what are some things that have contributed to your happiness? If you are lower than a 10, what are some actions you might take to increase your happiness?

 Words to Know

altruistic death	martyr
Ars Moriendi	resurrection
immortality	suicide

 Review Questions
1. How has TV and movies affected people's reactions to suffering and death?
2. Summarize each of the following philosopher's response to death: (a) Socrates; (b) Heidegger; (c) Sartre; (d) Jaspers.
3. Why do Christians consider suicide wrong?
4. What are the warning signs that a person may be considering suicide?
5. How does altruistic death differ from suicide?
6. Why was the death of Jesus so difficult for the apostles?
7. How did the resurrection of Jesus shape our Christian response to death?

Dealing with Suffering

The most beautiful Credo is the one we pronounce in our hour of darkness.

• *Servant of God Padre Pio*

"My Father, if it is possible, let this cup pass from me; yet not what I want but what you want."

• *Matthew 26:39*

- discover more about the grieving process and ways to console those who are grieving;

- reflect on the five stages of death and dying and their connection to your life;

- affirm the worthwhileness of every human life, as well as the redemptive value of suffering;

- study the meaning of the Sacrament of the Anointing of the Sick and the Church's history of caring for the sick.

C•H•A•P•T•E•R

5

The Grieving Process

IN THIS CHAPTER, YOU WILL

- consider different types of loss that inflict suffering;

- understand grief as a reaction to loss;

- appreciate that people's responses to grief vary greatly;

- explore the nature of grief and its accompanying feelings;

- learn about the different phases of the grieving process;

- examine ways to work through grief;

- become more aware of the Church's ministry of consolation;

- see what you can do to help console someone who is mourning.

Journey through Grief

There's a small cross by the side of Highway 128, near the town of Boonville. If this cross could talk, it would tell you this sad story:

Seven years ago my brother, Michael, was at a friend's ranch. They decided to go out for dinner. Joe arrived and volunteered to drive—after just one drink.

Lightheartedly, the four friends traveled the winding road. They didn't know where it would end—nobody did. Suddenly, they swerved into the opposite lane, colliding with an oncoming car.

Back home we were watching *E.T.* on video in front of a warm fire. Then we went to bed. At 2:00 A.M. a police officer woke my mom with the devastating news. Michael had been killed.

In the morning, I found my mother and sister crying. I stood there bewildered. "What's wrong?" I asked, rubbing my sleepy eyes.

Mom took a deep breath. "Come here . . ."

Thus began a grueling journey through grief, where all roads lead to nowhere. It still hurts to remember that day.

—Shortened from "Just One Drink," by Chris Laddish, *Chicken Soup for the Teenage Soul* (Deerfield Beach, FL: Health Communications, Inc.), p. 216.

Types of Loss

Death is the greatest and most obvious loss we can experience. But it is by no means the only cause of human suffering. There are many other types of loss that can inflict pain. Look at the following list. Without writing your responses, reflect on the following questions: How many of these losses have you experienced? How many are you experiencing now? What other losses could be added to the list? ■ ■

Obvious Loss	Loss Due to Change	Unnoticed Loss
Death of loved one or pet	Divorce	Marriage
Breakup of a close relationship	Role reversals	Birth of a child
Incest	Getting involved in a new relationship	End of therapy
Theft	Temporary separation	Achieving a long-term goal
Vandalism or destruction of property	Moving	Promotion
Losing money or a possession	Buying something new	Graduation
Natural disaster	Selling something	Success
Failure	Starting a new job	Finishing a creative project
Being fired	Change in pace	
Rape	Change in schools	
Arrest	Change of teachers	
Chronic illness	Change in stress level	
Temporary illness	Changing roles	
Injury or disability	Disillusionment with a person or ideal	
Miscarriage	Leaving home	
Loss of a limb	Retirement	
	Weaning	
	Puberty	
	Mid-life	
	Menopause	

Discussion

1. Select one example from the **Unnoticed Loss** column. What loss is involved in this example?
2. The teenage years have been described as a time of transition from childhood to adulthood. What losses are a natural part of being a teenager?

Activity

Form small groups, based on a common experience of loss. Allow time for each member to share briefly about the experience and how he or she felt about it. Note similarities and differences in the way members responded to their loss.

Reacting to Loss

It is impossible to get through life without some experiences of loss. As you have just seen, the loss may be very obvious, as in the case of the death of a loved one or the loss of a limb. The loss may be the result of a necessary change—the move to a new house or a transfer to a new school. The loss may also be associated with something positive, such as graduation from high school or reaching a long-term goal.

No matter what the type of loss, all people respond in some way to their losses. Most of us don't like to lose anything. And so we feel an emotional reaction that most psychologists define as *grief*. People, however, experience grief in various ways. The feeling of grief may be short-lived or last for years. It may be overwhelmingly sad or only mildly unpleasant. Whatever its pattern, grieving is a process, something that eventually ends. ▪

In this chapter you will look closer at the grieving process, especially the **mourning** that occurs when a loved one dies, including the customs and rituals that help mourners "get through" their pain. You will also consider various ways that mourners can work through their grief, as well as ways you can support them during this difficult time. ▪

Before proceeding, respond in your notebook to the Attitude Survey. Your answers will give an indication of your present ideas about reacting to loss.

Attitude Survey	I agree	I disagree	I'm not sure
Time heals all losses.			
It is wrong for males to cry at funerals.			
No one experiences grief exactly the way I do.			
Grief shared is grief halved.			
Once a loved one dies, your life is never again the same.			

Psychological Responses to Death

Not all people respond to death in a negative way. If the dying has been particularly long or painful, survivors may feel a great sense of relief when death finally comes. At last, the loved one's suffering has ceased. The ordeal of the survivors is over, too. Their years of struggle, economic drain, and emotional worry have ended. Instead of feeling sad, the survivors may receive death with quiet elation. Now they will have more time for themselves. They can spend their money in other ways. For the first time in years, they may be free to spend time with friends and develop new relationships.

grief Deep and poignant distress, usually accompanied by sorrow.

mourning A process by which people express their grief after the death of a loved one.

*W*hen you find that it is your **destiny** to grieve and suffer, you will have to **accept** your suffering as your single and unique **task**. You will have to acknowledge the **fact** that even in suffering you are **unique** and **alone** in the universe. No one can **relieve** you of your **grief** or suffer in your place. Your unique **opportunity** lies in the way in which you bear your **burden**.

Victor Frankl, Nazi concentration camp survivor

Journal

Think of a time when you grieved over a loss. Was your grief short-lived or did it last for years? Was it overwhelmingly sad or only mildly unpleasant? At this time, has your grief ended, or are you still experiencing it?

Activity

Watch the video *Fried Green Tomatoes*. Then discuss the following questions in a small group.

- While Idgie is still a young child, her older brother is killed in a train accident. How does Idgie mourn his death? How do the other family members express their grief?
- When Buddy, the son of Idgie's friend Ruth, loses his arm in an accident, how does Idgie help him get through his grief?

Grief is a process that involves recognizing feelings and then dealing with those feelings.

disoriented, confused, and unable to function according to their usual patterns. Some people get so numb that they feel nothing. Others feel alienated and wrenched from their ordinary world; the loss seems overwhelming and causes them great pain. ▪

Despite these differences in the way people grieve, several things may be said about grief. First, it is a process, not just a feeling. Grieving takes time. The amount of time and the intensity will vary with each individual. Second, grieving involves the whole person, not just the emotions. Physical aspects of grieving may include nausea, insomnia, weakness, headaches, and increased susceptibility to illness. Third, grieving is hard work. The only way to get over grief is to go through it and actually feel the pain.

The Nature of Grief

Psychologists tell us that grief is the "price" we pay for living a full life and for loving others. When someone we love dies, part of us dies also. In one sense, our lives will never again be the same. Indeed, there are only two ways to avoid grief: (1) die as a baby or young child so that no one we know dies before us, or (2) go through life never loving or caring for anyone else. Needless to say, neither of these alternatives is very appealing. Because love makes life meaningful, we must come to terms with the reality of grief and learn to expect it.

As you have learned, grief is a process rather than just a feeling. It is a process, however, that involves *recognizing* feelings and then *dealing* with them. Grief is not just one feeling, but a mishmash of numerous emotions: sorrow, fear, anger, and guilt, to name a few. To understand the nature of grief, we need to understand something about each of these separate emotions.

Instead of being a callous or selfish response to death, such feelings may culminate years of anticipatory grieving. Grief does not necessarily start when someone dies. For example, a teen whose grandfather has Alzheimer's disease grieves each time the elderly man has a memory loss. As the grandfather's condition gradually worsens, the teen's grieving gradually increases, too. Or consider the case of a teen whose mother has breast cancer. The child mourns with the mother each step along the way—the removal of a breast, the chemotherapy and hair loss, further surgery, her loss of energy and increased pain. Another example would be adults who grieve when they have to admit an aged parent to a care facility.

On the other hand, sometimes death is sudden and unexpected—as in cases involving a car accident, fatal heart attack, stroke, or SIDS (sudden infant death syndrome). One minute the person is alive and healthy; the next minute he or she is dead. In such cases, survivors may feel a sudden beginning to their grief. They are shocked and stunned. They feel that what has happened is not real and are

Discussion
1. Give other examples of how a person might begin grieving before someone dies.
2. Discuss a recent television show or movie in which one of the characters dies. How do the other characters react to the death? Do you think their responses are realistic?

Sorrow

At this grief my heart was utterly darkened; and whatever I beheld was death. . . . Mine eyes sought him everywhere, but he was not granted them; and I hated all places, for . . . they had not him; nor could they now tell me, "he is coming," as when he was alive and absent.

These words were written by Saint Augustine after the death of a close friend. They describe well the depression, emptiness, hopelessness, despair, and pessimism that accompany sorrow. Similar feelings are found in David's lament for his friend Jonathan: "I am distressed for you, my brother Jonathan; greatly beloved were you to me . . ." (2 Samuel 1:26). Mary, the mother of Jesus, also knew such sorrow. As Simeon had once predicted, a sword of sorrow pierced her heart when her son died on the cross.

The sorrow that is part of grieving may be short-lived, as in the case of survivors who feel relieved of a great burden when death finally comes. Or the sorrow may last for years. In some people, the sorrow may come in waves of intense distress and bring on bouts of hysteria. Some people respond to feelings of sorrow by losing motivation and energy. Others may have "a good cry." ■

Fear

During a time of grief, most people also have feelings of fear. Some of these feelings may be unresolved fears about death, the dying process, or dead spirits. Other fears may include those listed in the table at the top of this page.

Fear . . .	Response
Of facing the future alone	"How will I ever live without him/her?" "What is to become of me now?"
Of change and of the unknown	"Nothing will ever be the same because of this."
Of future deaths and separations	"The other people I love are going to die, too. Someday I myself will die."
Of letting go of the past, of forgetting how much the person meant	"I can't even remember his/her face."
Of not surviving the loss	"I'm losing my mind. My heart can't take this."
Of being left emotionally crippled	"I'll never be able to get that close to someone else again."
That what we are feeling is abnormal	"Does anyone else feel this bad for so long? Why can't I get over this?"
Of never being loved again in the same way	"I'll never find anyone to love as much as I loved him/her."

Working through grief means learning not to fear it or fear death. We have to come to accept the fact that both death and grief are inevitable parts of a full life. ■

Of Interest

The Church celebrates the feast of Our Lady of Sorrows on September 15. This day recalls the sorrows in Mary's life due to her love for Jesus:
- the prophecy of Simeon (Luke 2:35);
- the flight into Egypt (Matthew 2:13–21);
- losing the child Jesus in the Temple (Luke 2:41–50);
- the death of Jesus (John 19:26–27);
- the removal of Jesus' body from the cross (Matthew 27:55–60);
- the burial of Jesus (Mark 15:47).

Activity
Read the following psalms. How does each one express the sorrow that is associated with grief?
- Psalm 13
- Psalm 88
- Psalm 31:10–17
- Psalm 102:1–12
- Psalm 77:1–13

Write your own psalm to express a sorrow you have felt.

Discussion
1. Discuss each fear listed in the text. Is it a reasonable or unreasonable fear? Do you have any suggestions about how to deal with this fear?
2. What other fears might be associated with grief?

Anger

Very often, the mourner feels anger—at the deceased for dying, at God for letting this happen, at the doctors for not doing more, at himself or herself for not having seen this coming, and at others for "going on with life as if nothing happened." Accompanying the anger is a sense of helplessness and loss of control. The mourner becomes irritable and restless and may "fly off the handle" at friends and family members. The mourner may also bury himself or herself in a flurry of activity concerning the funeral arrangements in order to regain some sense of control and order. ■ ■

Guilt

Grief is often intermingled with feelings of guilt. "If only I had done something different" and similar thoughts of recrimination may plague the mourner and prolong his or her grieving. Steve, who had loyally nursed his friend Jim for the two years that he struggled with AIDS, was absent only for a brief moment while Jim was in the hospital. During that time, however, Jim died. Now Steve will not forgive himself.

A grown woman with a husband and children of her own took in her elderly mother rather than admit her to a care facility. Rita did everything the doctors told her to do, but one day, without warning, her mother died. Rita is convinced she should have done more and should have been able to prevent her mother from dying. Six months after the death, she still will not forgive herself.

A young woman had an argument with her husband as he was leaving for work. She intended to call him during the day and patch things up, but one thing led to another, and she never got around to calling. On the way home, her husband was killed in an automobile accident. Now she will not forgive herself.

The list could go on and on and on. Some survivors even feel guilty because they don't feel sad after someone has died. The only way to deal with feelings such as guilt, sorrow, fear, and anger, is first to admit that you feel them. The next step involves expressing your feelings—talking about them with a trusted friend, priest, or counselor. The saying "grief shared is grief halved" is a wise one. A sympathetic ear is good medicine for anyone who is mourning. ■

While psychologists differ in their theories regarding the grieving process, all of them agree that it is important for mourners to feel their feelings. Suppressing grief, trying to hold back the tears or the anger, will only make things worse in the long run. The grief

> *I*t's all **suffering**. *Either purposeful or purposeless.* **God**, *one trusts, has a* **purpose**. *The crucial* **question** *is whether each of us finds* **purpose** *in our* **suffering** *or not.*
>
> Father William J. O'Malley, *Redemptive Suffering*

Of Interest

Many survivors of the Titanic disaster later expressed feelings of guilt about surviving when so many others didn't.

 Discussion

What are some reasons a mourner might be angry with the person who died?

 Journal

How do you act when you get angry?

 Activity

1. Role-play this situation: A is a good friend of B, who has just lost a family member. What does A say to B?
2. Role-play this situation: Teenager A tries to comfort child B, whose kitten has just died. What does A say?

The three phases of bereavement include a period of intense grief, a time of transition, and final acceptance of the loss.

will manifest itself later in some worse form—as a behavior disorder (excess drinking, using drugs, and so forth), a serious illness (especially cancer), or a relationship problem. ■ ▪

Grief Does End

People experience grief differently. No single pattern fits everyone. Nevertheless, the grief process does have three major movements or phases that most people experience. The phases together are called the *time of bereavement*.

The first phase is that of intense grief. Such intensity occurs especially in people who don't begin to grieve until after a death occurs. During intense grief, which may last from a month to three months or longer, the person is likely to experience a roller coaster of emotions and thus act very unpredictably.

During the first phase, the mourners may withdraw emotionally from society. There have also been examples in various times and cultures when society itself separated the mourners from the clan, tribe, or village. In Australia, for example, Aborigine widows had to live in a separate hut. During the Victorian era in Europe and America, mourners had to wear special mourning clothes and were forbidden from participating in many social activities.

The second phase in the grieving process is a time of transition. The mourners still feel their loss but are beginning to cope with it. They start to live with the fact that the deceased person is dead, and they become comfortable once more in the environment in which the deceased is missing. Most of the work of grieving takes place at this time. Society has traditionally marked this phase by allowing mourners out of their special huts, letting them change their clothes, and permitting them to talk and visit more with their friends.

In the third phase, the mourners accept their loss and take up their lives again. They allow themselves to form new relationships and have new experiences. Many cultures mark this stage by allowing the widow or widower to date and remarry.

bereavement *The entire grieving process, especially experienced by someone who has lost a loved one to death.*

Discussion

Some psychologists say that mourners are really grieving for themselves and what they have lost rather than for the dead person. Do you agree or disagree? Why?

Journal

What are some things you feel guilty about? Do you think your guilt is reasonable (you really are to blame) or unreasonable (you just feel that you are to blame)?

Of Interest

The socially-mandated mourning period around the time of the Civil War was two years for a spouse, one year for a parent or child, six months for grandparents, and three months for aunts and uncles. On the other hand, rabbis have always discouraged Jews from mourning beyond a year. According to their thinking, to prolong the mourning would appear to question God's goodness. Excessive mourning no longer honors the dead, and further mourning prevents people from fully living their own lives.

Of Interest

Children in mourning were never dressed in black. They wore white in summer and gray in winter, both trimmed with black buttons, ruffles, belt, or bonnet.

How long it takes for someone to reach the third phase depends on each person and each circumstance surrounding the grief. For some people, the grief ends abruptly. They wake up one day and realize that the pain is gone. For other people, grief ends slowly and gradually. Each day is a little better than the last. No matter what the pattern, however, the pain of grieving eventually does end.

Working through Grief

Certain rituals—social and personal—help mourners work through their grief. These rituals help relieve the pain of loss by providing socially-acceptable ways of crying, talking, and acting. Although these rituals may seem contrived or artificial, they actually do help move the mourners through the grieving process. ■

Social Rituals

Every culture has its own social rituals regarding "proper" behavior during mourning. In a Tanala village in Madagascar, for example, mourning takes place on cue. At a given time, the mourners burst out into loud lamentations that continue for some twenty minutes and then stop at a signal. In India, mourners shave their heads. Mourners in China and Korea wear white. New Guinea women cover their faces with ash and wear net headdresses. Australian Aborigines cut themselves. Jews throughout the world have traditionally torn their clothes. Some Jewish men do not shave or cut their hair for the month following the death of a close relative.

The American custom of wearing black as a sign of mourning came from Europe. It stemmed from a fear of the dead. Black was worn to make the living inconspicuous to any evil spirits that might be lingering about.

Sometimes everyone attending a funeral, not just close relatives, would wear black. Men wore black armbands or hatbands; women wore black dresses and veils.

By the nineteenth century, society had definite "rules" that widows were expected to follow during the prescribed two-year bereavement period. For the first year, the widow had to wear a solid black dress with collar and cuffs of folded, untrimmed crepe. She might wear a simple bonnet (not a hat) and a long black veil. Instead of wearing kid gloves, she was allowed to wear only those made from black cotton or silk or crocheted or knit from black thread. Handkerchiefs had to be made of the sheerest white linen with a broad black border.

During the second year of mourning, the widow might wear a lusterless silk dress with black lace on the collar and cuffs. She could then shorten her veil and make it of net. During the last six months of mourning, she was allowed to wear gray, violet, or white. Her bonnet could be trimmed with white or violet lace or flowers. ■

At one time in America, it was the custom for mourners to decorate their homes. Funeral wreaths—hung to let passersby know of the bereavement within—consisted of white or purple flowers or black, white, or purple ribbon streamers. (A black ribbon was used when the deceased was married or elderly; a white ribbon was used when the deceased was young or unmarried.) The doorbell might also be covered, to notify those approaching the house to do so with quiet dignity.

The rituals surrounding the funeral—the notification of friends and family members, the funeral arrangements, the wake and the viewing of the body, the funeral service, the interment, and the reception following—were all social rituals meant to help mourners

Activity
View the movie or read the book *Gone with the Wind*. What mourning customs was Scarlett expected to follow?

Discussion
1. Why do you think most of the social customs regarding mourning have to do with women? Do women grieve differently than men? Does society view women who are mourning differently that it views men who are mourning?
2. The widow's garb became the standard habit for religious women in the Catholic Church. Why do you think this was so?

express their feelings and remove any sense of guilt. At these times, the survivors received support and expressions of sympathy. ▪

Personal Rituals

Most psychologists agree that the real work of grieving begins after the social rituals have ended. The mourner must now, for the most part, deal with grief alone. The work of grieving involves coming to some type of reconciliation with the death, with one's relationship to the dead person, and with one's new future. There are as many ways of going about this work as there are people.

In early America, some people worked through their grief by drawing watercolor mourning pictures, either on paper or silk. The artist painted somberly-dressed family members standing near the tomb. Some women worked through their grief by making mourning quilts. Inscriptions resembling an epitaph were appliquéd or embroidered on the quilt. Other people made mourning wreaths of human hair, which were then framed and put on display. Girls in school often made memorial pictures containing a sampler of different needlework stitches. Such creative expressions allowed the mourner a time for quiet reflection as well as a sense of movement and progression through the grieving process. ▪

Today, some people turn to a professional counselor for help in working through grief. Others seek help from one of the many grief support groups found throughout the country. Still other people turn to prayer and a deepening of their religious faith. ▪

While there is no one "right" way to work through grief, various psychologists do

offer this advice to those who are grieving:

1. **Feel your grief. Don't run away from it.** No one else can feel your feelings for you or know exactly what you are feeling, but others have experienced similar feelings and have gotten through them. Not only can they listen to you, sympathize, and try to understand what you are feeling, their stories can encourage you to face your own grief and work through it with courage.

2. **Review the past in order to own it and then let it go.** Recall the brighter times in your life and embrace those things that have nurtured you through other hard times. Decide what in your relationship with the dead person you want to leave behind and what memories you want to carry with you. Then let go of your resentment and guilt. Realize that life will never be quite the same as before, and move on.

Of Interest

Some people work through grief by seeing, holding, or smelling something that belonged to the deceased. For example, one widow kept her dead husband's shirt under her pillow. One mother would hug the kimono of her dead baby. A young girl would go to the closet and smell her dead brother's shirts. These personal "rituals" helped the mourners find peace in their grieving.

Activity
When a nation grieves the loss of a leader, the social rituals are extensive. Research the social rituals that followed the death of one of the following persons: President Franklin D. Roosevelt, President John F. Kennedy, or Princess Diana of England.

Activity
1. Research the AIDS Quilt Project. If possible, find pictures of the quilt. Where has it been on display? Why do you think this way of mourning has been so popular?
2. Make a class quilt. Decorate one square of the quilt as a memorial to someone who has died. Try to make the square expressive of the dead person. Display the quilt where the entire school can see it.

Activity
Speak with three people about their experience with grieving. Try to include people from different age groups. Ask them to tell about rituals that helped them work through their grief. Report your findings to the class.

Of Interest

For more information on grief support groups, you may wish to contact the following:

• www.griefresourcescatalog.com
• Teenage Grief Incorporated (TAG), 1-818-997-0391

3. **Envision your future. Visualize what might be.** You do not have control over what happened, but you do have a choice about how you will respond to the death. You can withdraw from others, give up on life, and remain embittered and angry. Or you can reach out to others in the community and try to build a loving future. You can make this crisis a turning point, not an endpoint.

4. **Return to the present anew. Enter fully into the present moment.** Your pain can bring you wisdom, strength, compassion, healing, maturity, trust, and hope. ▪

Working through grief can make you more whole and can help you be more in touch with yourself, others, and God. Instead of asking "Why did this happen?" you can now resume life with the attitude found in the following poem of Dag Hammarskjold:

> For all that has been—Thanks!
> To all that shall be—Yes!

The Ministry of Consolation

The Israelites believed that their God was one who sympathized with them and gave them solace in times of sorrow. "You, LORD, have helped me and comforted me" (Psalm 86:17). The Israelites believed in a God who would some day save them from death and from mourning. "He will swallow up death forever. Then the Lord GOD will wipe away the tears from all faces . . ." (Isaiah 25:7–8).

Christians adopted these same beliefs as they developed their concept of God as Trinity. As Paul wrote, "Blessed be the God and Father of our Lord Jesus Christ, the Father of mercies and the God of all consolation, who consoles us in all our affliction . . ." (2 Corinthians 1:3–4). "He will wipe every tear from their eyes. Death will be no more; mourning and crying and pain will be no more, for the first things have passed away" (Revelation 21:4).

Jesus, the Son of God, was also seen as compassionate and consoling. "Blessed are those who mourn," Jesus told his followers, "for they will be comforted" (Matthew 5:4; cf. Luke 6:21). Jesus comforted Mary and Martha at the death of their brother Lazarus (cf. John 11:1–44). Likewise, he consoled the synagogue official whose daughter had died (cf. Matthew 9:18–19, 23–26; Mark 5:21–24, 35–43; Luke 8:40–42, 49–56) and the widow of Nain whose son had died (cf. Luke 7:11–17). These events show not only Jesus' power over death but his ability to change sorrow to joy—something that seems impossible to anyone in the midst of intense grief.

The Holy Spirit is also a God of consolation. On the night before his death, Jesus tells his disciples that he must leave them. But he promises to send the Holy Spirit to support them in their time of mourning. "And I will ask the Father, and he will give you another Advocate, to be with you forever. This is the Spirit of truth . . ." (John 14:16–17). "But the Advocate, the Holy Spirit, whom the Father will send in my name, will teach you everything, and remind you of all that I have said to you" (John 14:26). "It is to your advantage that I go away, for if I do not go away, the Advocate will not come to you; but if I go, I will send him to you" (John 16:7). ▪

Discussion

Edgar Jackson, in his book *You and Your Grief*, offers the following advice to mourners:

• Don't condemn yourself.
• Don't drug yourself or get drunk to ease the pain.
• Don't feel sorry for yourself.
• Don't run away to another place.
• Don't withdraw from others.
• Don't pay too much attention to what others say.
• Don't cross bridges until you come to them.
• Don't underestimate yourself.

What do you think each point means? What is its value in the grieving process?

Discussion

How has God comforted you in times of sorrow?

Not only are we like God when we show sympathy to others; as Christians, we have a responsibility to console those who mourn. This responsibility is listed as one of the spiritual works of mercy. It is also called the Church's *ministry of consolation.*

This ministry of consolation was present from the earliest days of the Church. As Paul told the Corinthians, God comforts us in our sorrow "so that we may be able to console those who are in any affliction with the consolation with which we ourselves are consoled by God" (2 Corinthians 1:4). "Have unity of spirit, sympathy, love for one another, a tender heart, and a humble mind" (1 Peter 3:8). For "if one member suffers, all suffer together with it; if one member is honored, all rejoice together with it" (1 Corinthians 12:26). ▪

This ministry extends to all Church members today. As the *Order of Christian Funerals* asserts:

> . . . when a member of Christ's Body dies, the faithful are called to a ministry of consolation to those who have suffered the loss of one whom they love.

Christian consolation is rooted in that hope that comes from faith in the saving death and resurrection of the Lord Jesus Christ. Christian hope faces the reality of death and the anguish of grief but trusts confidently that the power of sin and death has been vanquished by the risen Lord. The Church calls each member of Christ's Body—priest, deacon, layperson—to participate in the ministry of consolation: to care for the dying, to pray for the dead, to comfort those who mourn.

—General Introduction, *Order of Christian Funerals,* #8

The Church's funeral rite also encourages Catholics to console mourners by writing letters of condolence, sending sympathy cards, bringing food to the family, praying for the dead at the general intercessions at Mass, and participating actively in the Church's death rituals—the vigil service, funeral, interment, and reception. By such actions we show support for others in their time of need; we help them through the grieving process. ▪

Of Interest
One of the titles of Mary is "Comforter of the Afflicted." Another translation of this same title is "Our Lady of Consolation."

Of Interest
Breanne Montgomery, 14, used the experience of her father's death to reach out to other young people undergoing the grief of losing a loved one. When Montgomery's father died of cancer, her mother received gift baskets to help her cope. Montgomery thought that children should receive the same consideration, so she created Bre's Bereavement Box, filled with toys, candy, a photo frame, journal paper, and crafts. Montgomery, a member of Saint Patrick's Parish in Colorado Springs, donates all profits to the local organization S.K.I.P. (Support Kids with Ill Parents). She is training to become a facilitator for the group.

—Adapted from "Keeping Faith," by Teresa Malcolm. *National Catholic Reporter* (April 3, 1998).

 Activity
Read the resurrection narrative in John's Gospel (chapters 20 and 21) from the perspective of the apostles. How does this narrative reflect stages in their grieving process?

 Activity
Find out if your parish has a condolence committee. If so, ask a member to come to your class to explain the ministry of this group and what high school students can do to help. If your parish does not have a condolence committee, discuss the possibility of forming one, and clarify what its purpose would be.

What You Can Do

Most people feel very awkward around someone who is mourning. We want to do something to help, but we aren't sure what to do or what to say. And if the person starts crying, we really feel helpless. Perhaps we say words such as "Call me if you need someone to talk to," but inside we hope the call never comes.

It is difficult to be around someone who is depressed or unpredictable or obsessed with recent death. And yet as Christians, we are challenged to treat others as we would want them to treat us in a similar situation. What can you do to help someone who is grieving? Here is a possible answer: Put yourself in the person's shoes. Think about what would help you most if you were grieving. Then do the same for the other person.

Here are some specific ideas suggested by psychologists:

- Take the initiative. Get in touch with the grieving person rather than wait for him or her to call you.
- Avoid clichés or cold impersonal statements such as:
  —At least N. went fast.
  —At least you have your other family members left.
  —God must have needed N. more than you.
  —It's a blessing; N.'s now out of his/her misery.
  —N. was old and had lived a good life.
  —Cheer up; it was for the best. N.'s in heaven now.
  —Keep busy; it'll help you forget.
  —I know just how you feel.
- Soon after the death, send a sympathy card; include a personal letter of condolence. ▪
- Do something practical for the person. Offer to help clean out the closets, take the deceased's clothes to a charitable organization, address envelopes for thank-you cards, baby-sit, cook a meal, and so forth.
- Continue to stay in touch, both by phone and by visits. Set up a specific time when you will spend time with the person, and then keep the date.
- When you are with the person, make sure you listen to what he or she is saying. Don't attempt to tell the person how he or she is feeling or should feel. And don't think you have to fill moments of silence with trivia about everyone you know. Remember, what is most important is your presence, not what you say. ▪
- Affirm the grieving person as a good person, especially if he or she is feeling guilt.
- Be patient, especially if the person mourns longer than you would like. Try to include the person in an activity you are doing. If the person turns you down, don't take it personally and do remember to ask again later. ▪

> *I*f shedding *each other's* **blood** *makes us enemies,* **sharing** *each other's* **tears** *makes us* **brothers** *and* **sisters**.
>
> Eugene Kennedy, *The Pain of Being Human*

Activity

Look through the sympathy cards at a stationery store. Purchase one you find particularly consoling. Bring the card to class and tell why it would help you in a time of grieving.

Journal

1. Who is someone in your life who is a good listener? How does this person let you know that he or she is truly listening?
2. On a scale of 1 to 10 (with 10 as the highest), how would you rank yourself as a good listener? How might you improve your listening skills?

Discussion

1. Imagine that someone in your family has just died. How would you want your friends to respond? What would you want them to say or do?
2. Discuss each of the clichés given on this page. How would you feel if someone said this to you when you were grieving?

Because many people have difficulty expressing themselves in writing, here are a few tips about condolence letters: When you write a condolence letter, remember that it may be read by several members of the family. It may also be saved and passed down to future generations. But this does not mean that the letter needs to contain perfect spelling or grammar. Nor does it have to be formal. What is important is that you be yourself and express what you are genuinely feeling.

Amy Vanderbilt, in her book on etiquette, says that a good condolence letter has three key ingredients: (1) It expresses understanding and sympathy to the mourner; (2) It praises and says something positive about the deceased, in a personal way; (3) It expresses a sincere desire to be of some help. To explain further, she quotes a condolence letter to a young Jewish widow from an eleven-year-old Catholic girl.

Dear Mrs. Wise,

It's just terrible that God desided to take Rabbi Wise so yung. It's really very meen of Him, because He must have known we wanted Rabbi Wise to stay longer. I don't know if you believ in Purgatory and saints and all that stuff, but I do, and I just happen to know that with all our prayers Rabbi Wise went thru Purgatory awful fast, sort of like a car racer. So he's already in Hevn with God and His Saints (my favrit Saint is Mother Seton). God will take care of Rabbi Wise and you, too, now that youre lone. I'll do your dishes or sit with the baby anytime. Tell Ralfie I have a new rattle for him anyway.

The Amy Vanderbilt Complete Book of Etiquette

The letter is far from perfect grammatically, and yet the young widow treasured it far more than the many purchased sympathy cards she received. ■

Activity

1. Imagine yourself in this situation: Your friend Blanca is mourning the death of her boyfriend, Jorge, who drowned while the two of them were spending the day at the lake. Blanca tried to save Jorge, but she's not a very good swimmer and failed in her attempt. Now she is blaming herself for Jorge's death. Write a condolence letter to Blanca.

2. Imagine yourself in this situation: Mr. and Mrs. Nelson, who are your neighbors, are mourning the sudden death of their two-year-old daughter, Emma. She choked on a grape and died before her mother noticed anything wrong. You used to baby-sit Emma and really liked her. Write a condolence letter that will help the family through their grieving.

Words to Know

bereavement
grief
mourning

Review Questions

1. What are the three types of losses for which people might grieve? Give an example of each.
2. What are three truths about grief that apply to all people?
3. What are four different emotions that are part of grief? Describe each one briefly.
4. What are the three phases of the grief process?
5. What are two social rituals that can help a person work through grief?
6. What are two personal rituals that can help a person work through grief?
7. What are three examples of times Jesus consoled others?
8. What is the ministry of consolation?
9. What are four ways Catholics can become involved in the Church's ministry of consolation?

C•H•A•P•T•E•R

6

The Stages *of* Death *and* Dying

IN THIS CHAPTER, YOU WILL

- consider what death means when it threatens you or a loved one;

- reflect on the traditionally recognized five stages of dying;

- discuss the role of denial, anger, bargaining, depression, and acceptance in your own life;

- examine the synoptic Gospels and how they portray Jesus' attitude toward his own death;

- compare the portrayal of Jesus in John's Gospel with that of the synoptic Gospels's portrayal of him;

- examine the importance of the Sacrament of Reconciliation, both before death and throughout life;

- plan (and celebrate, if you wish) a reconciliation service;

- write (or record) your "last message" to friends and family members.

Living with Cancer

One day, Kristen Drenten was a normal teenager. She was doing okay in school and active in gymnastics and cheerleading. Then Kristen started to feel severe pain in her left leg. A short time later, a biopsy confirmed everyone's worst fears—osteogenic sarcoma (bone cancer). Kristen started chemotherapy right away. Nine months later—after having 123 days of chemotherapy and major surgery to remove the cancer—Kristen got more bad news: There were tumors in her lungs. Here is her story:

When I found out the cancer was back, we all broke down and cried. In May, I had lung resection surgery to remove the tumors. By summer I had pain in my other knee and in my back. Then I learned the cancer was spreading—to my spine, pelvic bone, mouth, right knee. There was nothing the doctors could do.

Two years ago, I would sometimes come home from school and cry because my friends were ignoring me or because I got a low grade. That seems so silly to me now. These days when I cry it's because I know I'm going to die. Probably sometime soon.

Having cancer has taught me a lot about what's important in life. My family has always been there for me, but during the past nine months, we've grown even closer. It's not hard for me to talk about my cancer. What's much harder is to talk about dying. The fact is I won't be here for things most people take for granted: high school graduation, prom, getting married, and having kids. Yet I think it's better to be diagnosed with a terminal illness than to die in a more sudden, tragic way, such as a car accident. At least it gives you time to prepare—to say and do many of the things you want.

I want people to know I'm no different from anybody else—neither is any person with cancer—and that it's important to appreciate what's good in life. I still can. ■ ▪

—Shortened and adapted from "I'm living with cancer," by Kristen Drenten as told to Michelle Sullivan. *Teen Magazine* (January 1998), pp. 60–61.

When Death Hits Home

Unfortunately, Kristen's experience with a terminal cancer is not that rare. Leukemia, another form of cancer, is the leading disease killer of children and teens. Throughout the United States, cancer is the second leading cause of death for the general population. The American Cancer Society reports that more than 564,800 Americans died of cancer in 1998 (1,500 people per day). During that same year, more than 1.2 million new cases of cancer were diagnosed.

For some teens, these facts may seem irrelevant. Death seems unreal. It is something "out there." But what happens when death hits home, when death affects us or someone close to us? What is our "gut" reaction then? How do we feel when death focuses on us or on our loved ones?

Researchers have discovered that people who are faced with life-threatening illness go through five psychological stages—denial, anger, bargaining, depression, and acceptance. These stages are not necessarily sequential. Although people have different patterns in the

Discussion

1. If you could choose how you will die, what would you choose?
2. If you could choose when you will die, what age would you choose?
3. If you knew you were going to die six months from today, what would you do with the time you have left?

Journal

1. How do you think you would react if a doctor said you had a life-threatening illness?
2. How do you think you would react if one of your parents or siblings had a life-threatening illness?

way they go through the stages and how long they spend in each one, these reactions to impending death seem universal.

Before beginning, take a moment to look at the Attitude Survey. Write your responses in your notebook.

Denial

"At first you just don't believe it," said fifteen-year-old Christy, who is suffering from a form of cancer known as Hodgkin's disease. Perhaps these words best sum up similar reactions of other people when they learn they have a serious disease and may be dying: "This can't be happening. God wouldn't do this to me. It's just not possible. I don't feel that sick. Maybe the doctor got my test results mixed up with someone else's."

Such reactions are not unusual. Most people with a potentially terminal illness initially deny their reality. As psychiatrist Dr. Sigmund Freud once taught, each of us subconsciously believes in his or her immortality: Death may take other people, but I am exempt.

Even though people in this first stage of dying may not verbally express **denial**, they may act it out. Frequently, they look for another physician or specialist who can give them better news. Perhaps they continue their regular routine, working and exercising just as hard as before to "prove" that they're not dying.

Denial of serious illness can also take the form of joking. People in denial may put on a brave front to others and even to themselves: "If I don't think about it, it'll go away." "I don't need to deal with this now; I still have plenty of time to deal with it later."

Even though the warning signs of approaching death are there, a person in denial may not take care of unfinished business. He

Attitude Survey	I agree	I disagree	I'm not sure
Many people with a terminal illness refuse to believe they are dying.			
If I had a terminal disease, I would want the doctors to tell me.			
I would get a second opinion before believing I had a terminal disease.			
Hoping to beat a terminal disease is just another form of denying death.			
The death of Jesus makes our dying easier.			

or she may choose not to write a will, buy a cemetery plot, or plan a funeral Mass. The person may never talk to family members about the seriousness of the illness or about how he or she feels.

Denial can take another form as well—desperate hope. At first a person hopes that nothing is seriously wrong. After the doctor's diagnosis, the person in denial may cling to another unrealistic dream—that of finding a cure. While this attitude shows that the person values his or her life, it can also be a form of denying death, of keeping death at bay for as long as possible. ▪ ▪

Anger

Once the defenses of denial weaken, the person who faces the possibility of impending death is likely to become very angry: "Why me? I don't deserve this. It's not fair." The **anger** comes from two sources: a sense of helplessness in the face of death (no longer being in control) and a righteous indignation at the injustice that is being done ("O God, how could you do this to me? Why did you let this happen?").

Of Interest

Psychologists say that denial is a defense mechanism that helps us deal only with as much truth as we can handle at a time. Denial is sometimes needed to survive. But denial can also stop us from making needed changes. For example, many alcoholics and their families spend years denying that anything is wrong.

---

denial *One of the stages of dying, in which a person refuses to admit the truth of his or her condition.*

anger *One of the stages of dying, in which a person is indignant about his or her approaching death and may seek someone else to blame.*

Discussion
Reread the story of Kristen Drenten. Do any of her responses show denial? Which responses indicate she is dealing realistically with death?

Journal
Have you ever had a problem that you refused to acknowledge? (grades in school, weight, a relationship, and so forth) What happened to make you finally face the truth?

When we are angry, it is common to look for someone to blame. You have seen how the writers of the Old Testament blamed human sinfulness for death. All humans are subject to death because of the sin of Adam and Eve. The anger a person may feel about approaching death may also be self-directed. People who have smoked two packs of cigarettes per day for twenty years may indeed be very angry at themselves when they develop lung cancer.

People who are angry very often take their anger out on others. They blame others for their condition. They may be angry at their doctor for not diagnosing the disease earlier. They may be angry at family members for not believing them when they complained about pain or being tired. They may be angry at God for letting this happen. ▪ ▪

bargaining *One of the stages of dying, in which a person tries to buy more time by making a deal with God.*

Because it is impossible for the person to direct his or her anger toward the source of anguish—death itself—he or she may direct it outward, toward others. He or she may treat others with impatience and criticism. Nothing anyone does is right. The family either "never" comes to visit or "never" gives the person any privacy. If the person is in a hospital or nursing home, he or she may complain about the food, the medical care, or the impersonal environment. The rage that the person feels also affects his or her family. Relationships are strained and tension-filled as the people involved struggle to cope with the conflicts thrust upon them. ▪

Bargaining

Bargaining is a natural part of surviving in the world. We bargain for the best price on a car. We negotiate a job contract. And we make trade-off deals with our friends: "If you do this for me, I'll do this for you." Dying people use the same technique: "God, if you just give me one more year, I'll be a good Christian." "If you just let me live to see my sister's wedding, I'll donate my organs to those who need them." "If you miraculously cure me, I promise I'll never smoke again." In this stage, the person tries to buy time. He or she tries to keep death away by promising God new and virtuous behavior.

In the award-winning play *The Shadow Box*, an elderly woman is about to die. Her unmarried daughter takes care of her. But what the woman wants is to see her other daughter one more time before she dies. She is determined to "hold on" until this daughter arrives. (In reality, the daughter died a few years before.) To soothe her mother, the

Of Interest

Sarah Winchester, the widow of Oliver Winchester, believed that the ghosts of all those who were killed by the guns her husband invented were out to kill her. So she struck a bargain with them: as long as her house was unfinished, she would not die. She hired architects and construction workers to add on to her house continuously for thirty-eight years. When she finally died, the house was still unfinished. Today the Winchester Mystery House is a tourist attraction in San Jose, California.

Activity

Search through the Book of Psalms for expressions of anger directed at God or other people. Report your findings to the class.

Journal

1. What are some of the things that make you angry? Have you ever been angry because something seemed unfair? Explain.
2. How do you act toward others when you are angry?

Discussion

1. Why do you think some people die young while others live to old age? Why do some people suffer more than others?
2. Do you think dying people have a "right" to be angry? Why or why not?
3. Do you think dying people have a "right" to take their anger out on others? Why or why not?
4. Do you think it is all right to get angry at God? Why or why not?
5. What are some healthy ways to express anger?

unmarried daughter produces a fake telegram saying the second daughter is on her way from Mexico and not to worry. So the elderly woman continues to refuse to accept death. ■

We find another example of bargaining in a story from the Book of Genesis. According to the story, God is fed up by all the sins that are taking place in the cities of Sodom and Gomorrah. So God decides to level the towns, killing everyone. Abraham knows this means his nephew Lot, who lives in one of the towns, will die. So he tries to strike a deal. "If I find fifty innocent people, will you spare the towns? God agrees. Abraham, however, has second thoughts about being able to find fifty such people, so he tries to lower the number of people he needs to find. "If I find forty-five innocent people, will you spare the towns?" And so the bargaining continues until the stakes are down to ten innocent people.

For all of his wheeling and dealing, Abraham is still unable to meet his part of the bargain. In the end God spares Lot and his family but levels the two cities.

In the bargaining stage, the person finds strength in hope. The person may still be hoping for a cure; in addition, the person now hopes that his or her life will be prolonged so that certain unfinished business can be completed. As long as the business remains unfinished, death can be kept at arm's length. ▨

Depression

Many volumes have been written on clinical **depression** and how to treat it. Depression, for the most part, is seen as a sickness—something abnormal. When a person has a terminal disease, depression may have chemical roots in the disease itself. But psychological depression may also be a normal response to a bad situation. Think about it: The dying person will soon leave behind everything he or she has ever known. The person needs time to "mourn" this separation.

Often, a dying person who is depressed does not want to talk with or have visitors. The person may brood a lot or start crying quietly. During this stage, death as a loss becomes real. The person acknowledges that he or she will not live to see another birthday, marriage, or future children and grandchildren. Whatever life he or she had, whatever relationships have been developed, whatever jobs still need to be done—all this will soon be over.

In depression, the person begins to separate himself or herself from life. The battle against death is now seen as futile. The person stops fighting for more life and grows weaker. An interior battle, however, is raging. The person struggles between despair and a final ray of hope—that God will find him or her worthy, that his or her life has been meaningful, and that life somehow continues on past death.

This stage is a time of personal assessment. The person looks back on his or her life, on its strengths and its weaknesses. The final battle is perhaps the struggle to accept oneself with all one's imperfections. Such self-acceptance may be difficult to achieve in the midst of the indignities sometimes associated with dying—the loss of good looks, the amputation of a limb, possible bowel and bladder incontinence, and increasing helplessness. ▨

depression *One of the stages of dying, in which a person becomes sad about his or her approaching death and begins to assess his or her life.*

Discussion

1. Do you know of any situations in which someone "held on" to life until after an important event? Do you think the person's mental state really affected the time of death, or was the timing just coincidental? In other words, is there a specific time when each person is destined to die, no matter what he or she does?

2. If you were told that you had cancer and would probably only live three more months, what would you try to bargain for?

3. Which do you think bargaining expresses most: fear of death, denial of death, or the need to remain in control of one's own destiny?

Journal

What would you leave unfinished if you died right now?

Journal

1. Have you ever been depressed? What was the reason for the depression? What helped get you out of your depression?

2. If you had to assess your life right now, what would you list as its strengths? Its weaknesses? How would you "judge" yourself?

The warm touch of a hand can help a dying person through the stage of depression to the final stage in the dying process—acceptance.

At this time, the dying person may seek reconciliation with God, with the Church, and with others. The person may view such reconciliation as a necessary prerequisite to self-acceptance. During reconciliation, it is important for friends or family members to affirm the dying individual as worthy and lovable. The warm touch of a hand and a simple prayer may mean a great deal. They can help the depressed person reach the final stage in the dying process.

Acceptance

Once the dying person has found reconciliation with self, God, and others, there is a final "yes." During this last stage, the person accepts death and waits for it calmly and peacefully. The person may even be willing to talk about his or her life and approaching death. ▪

This attitude of **acceptance** is not the same as giving up. Acceptance is a good

feeling. "I have now finished my unfinished business. I've said everything I want to say. I'm ready to go." For the religious person, the desire to be united fully with God becomes more important than remaining with family and friends. Instead of looking at the past or even the present moment, the dying person looks forward to the future. ▪

Saint Ignatius of Loyola captured the essence of the dying person's final surrender to God in this prayer from his *Spiritual Exercises*:

> Take, O Lord, all my liberty. Receive in their entirety my memory, intellect, and will. And since whatever else I have or hold you have given to me, so I give everything back to you to be managed entirely according to your preference. To me give only your love and your grace, and with these I am rich enough and want nothing more.

acceptance *The last stage of dying, in which a person accepts death and looks forward to future life after death.*

Activity

1. Research a famous painting, poem, song, or novel that deals with the psychological aspects of dying. What does the author have to say about the experience of dying? Is it depressing or not?
2. Express your feelings about death by some type of artistic creation (drawing, poem, song, sculpture, dance, and so forth). Share with the class what you have created.

Discussion

How is acceptance different from giving up? Try to give examples to explain your response.

As Paul explains in his First Letter to the Corinthians, at death the faithful person shall know God fully as he or she is known. "Faith, hope, and love abide, these three; and the greatest of these is love" (1 Corinthians 13:13). In this last stage, the dying person already begins to experience the surety of love, God's total and unconditional acceptance. He or she looks forward to a complete experience of this love in death. For this reason, the dying person can say with Jesus: "It is finished" (John 19:30) and "Father, into your hands I commend my spirit" (Luke 23:46). ■

Jesus' Attitude toward His Own Death

As Christians, we believe that we are not alone in our dying. Step by step, stage by stage, Jesus goes with us toward, and then through, death. As one who died himself and then conquered death, he is a savior who is both role model and companion to those who are dying. Jesus truly understands what death means and what the dying person goes through. For this reason, it is important to study the Gospels and learn more about Jesus' attitude toward his own death.

The four Gospels give us different views of Jesus, depending on when they were written and the audience for whom they were intended. John's Gospel, which was the last Gospel to be written, tends to be a theological reflection on Jesus as the Son of God. Because this Gospel emphasizes Jesus as

divine, it is very difficult to catch glimpses of Jesus' human personality or feelings. Throughout the Gospel, Jesus is not only aware of his approaching death; he is always in control of it.

The Gospels of Matthew, Mark, and Luke, which are known as the *synoptic Gospels,* stand in contrast to John. They more clearly present Jesus as both divine and human. In these Gospels, we find a Jesus who goes through stages—much like those presented in this chapter—before accepting his own death. The following pages present a brief summary of the synoptic Gospels. ■

Of Interest

The Catholic Church recognizes Saint Joseph as the patron of a happy death. Although the Bible says nothing about his death, tradition tells us that he died at home in the company of Jesus and Mary.

Activity

1. Look up each of the following Scripture passages. How does each one relate to acceptance, the final stage of dying?
   • Matthew 10:37–39
   • Luke 2:25–32
   • Philippians 3:7–14
2. Read the Book of Job. Identify passages that reflect Job's experiences of the five stages of dying.

Discussion

Does knowing about the death of Jesus make dying any easier for a Christian?

Of Interest

The seven last phrases spoken by Jesus are sometimes the focus of reflection on Good Friday. These last phrases are:

- "Father, forgive them; for they do not know what they are doing" (Luke 23:34).
- "Woman, here is your son. . . . Here is your mother." (John 19:26–27).
- "I am thirsty" (John 19:28).
- "Today you will be with me in Paradise" (Luke 23:43).
- "My God, my God, why have you forsaken me?" (Matthew 27:46; Mark 15:34).
- "It is finished" (John 19:30).
- "Father, into your hands I commend my spirit" (Luke 23:46).

Although both Matthew and Luke write about the infancy of Jesus, only Matthew prefigures Jesus' death at this time. He does this in mentioning the Magi's gift of myrrh, the spice used to anoint corpses (cf. Matthew 2:11). The second prefiguring of death is found after Jesus' baptism, when he is tempted in the desert. The devil takes Jesus to Jerusalem and stands him on top of the parapet of the Temple. "If you are the Son of God, throw yourself down" (cf. Matthew 4:5–6; Luke 4:9). Similar words are spoken later to Jesus as he hangs on the cross (cf. Matthew 27:40; Luke 23:37, 39). Both temptations are the temptation to deny the reality of death. In both cases, Jesus rejects the temptation. ▪

Early in Luke's account of Jesus' ministry is the reference to Isaiah's suffering servant (cf. Luke 4:18–19; Isaiah 61:1–2, 58:6). As you have already learned, most Jews expected the Messiah to live forever. Only the prophet Isaiah wrote about a savior who would have to suffer and die to save others. By including the quotation from Isaiah, Luke is telling us that Jesus already had knowledge that he would die.

Although Matthew and Mark do not quote Isaiah, they contain the same message. Not once, but three times Jesus predicts his own suffering, death, and resurrection (the first prediction—cf. Matthew 16:21; Mark 8:31; Luke 9:22; the second prediction—cf. Matthew 17:22–23; Mark 9:31; Luke 9:44; the third prediction—cf. Matthew 20:17–19; Mark 10:33–34; Luke 18:31–33). He tells his followers that they, too, must lose their lives for his sake in order to find them again (cf. Matthew 10:39, 16:25; Mark 8:35; Luke 9:24). ▪

Midway through Luke's Gospel, the Pharisees warn Jesus that Herod wants to kill him. Despite their warnings, Jesus deliberately proceeds toward Jerusalem, where he knows that he will be killed (cf. Luke 13:31–33). As the time of death grows closer, Jesus knows that one of his disciples will betray him, yet he does nothing to stop him (cf. Matthew 26:21; Mark 14:18; Luke 22:21). At his Last Supper, Jesus again predicts that his blood will be "shed on behalf of many" (cf. Matthew 26:28; Mark 14:24; Luke 22:20).

Perhaps better than any other episode in the Gospels, the account of the agony in the garden shows us the psychological struggle Jesus went through to accept his own death. Both Matthew and Mark record Jesus as saying, "I am deeply grieved, even to death" (Matthew 26:38; Mark 14:34). Luke elaborates further: "In his anguish he prayed more earnestly, and his sweat became like great drops of blood falling down on the ground" (Luke 22:44). Jesus seems to be going through the stage of depression.

All three synoptic Gospels say that Jesus needed his friends to pray with him at Gethsemane and that they let him down. Instead of keeping watch, they fell asleep—not once, but three times. How Jesus responds to them could be interpreted as anger (cf. Matthew 26:40–41; Mark 14:37–38; Luke 22:46).

The bargaining stage also seems to be found in the garden. "My Father, if it is possible, let this cup pass from me" (cf. Matthew 26:39, 42; Mark 14:36; Luke 22:42). Finally, there is acceptance of death. "Not my will but yours be done" (cf. Matthew 26:39; Mark 14:36; Luke 22:42). "See, the hour is at hand" (cf. Matthew 26:45–46; Mark 14:41).

Activity

Read Luke's account of the infancy of Jesus (Luke 2:1–40). Is the death of Jesus prefigured in any way in this gospel account?

Discussion

What do you think Jesus meant when he said that we must lose our lives in order to find them? What do you think this means in today's world? Give examples.

Both Matthew and Mark record that while Jesus was dying on the cross, he said: "My God, my God, why have you forsaken me?" (Matthew 27:46; Mark 15:34). While these words may be interpreted as those of an angry or despairing person, it is important to know the Jewish custom of praying. By praying the first line of a psalm, the person was actually praying the entire psalm. These words of Jesus are the first line of Psalm 22. Only a reading of the entire psalm reveals what Jesus was expressing through these words.

Luke gives us a different glimpse of Jesus' frame of mind when he was on the cross: "Father, forgive them; for they do not know what they are doing" (Luke 23:34) and "Today you will be with me in Paradise" (Luke 23:43). Both of these statements seem to indicate that Jesus' focus was on reconciliation. The final words of Jesus, "Father, into your hands I commend my spirit" (Luke 23:46), seem to be those of a man who has reached the final stage of acceptance.

Meditation on the death of Jesus can affect the way we approach our own deaths. Jesus did not sin, so death could not be God the Father's way of punishing him. Instead of asking why he had to die at all or why he had to die at such a young age, Jesus approached death with faith, hope, and love. He believed in the Father's love for him, and this was enough for him. These same sentiments are found in Jesus' advice to us: "Do not worry about your life. . . . Can any of you by worrying add a single hour to your span of life? . . . Strive first for the kingdom of God and his righteousness, and all these things will be given to you as well" (Matthew 6:25, 27, 33). ▪ ▪

The Sacrament of Reconciliation

Paul taught that by Jesus' suffering and death, Jesus reconciled the world with God (cf. 2 Corinthians 5:18) as well as all things on earth with those in heaven (cf. Colossians 1:20). The Church, in turn, shares in Christ's ministry of reconciliation and forgiveness. The first sacrament that brings about this reconciliation and forgiveness is Baptism. But because people, out of weakness, continue to sin after Baptism, there is a sacrament for the pardon of sins committed after Baptism (cf. John 20:21–23). We call this sacrament *Reconciliation*.

The Church calls people to conversion and renewal throughout their lives. We are encouraged to admit our sins against God and others, to feel sincere contrition for these sins, and to celebrate the Sacrament of Reconciliation from time to time. The Church especially encourages Christians to celebrate the Sacrament of Reconciliation at the time of approaching death. The sacrament may be celebrated during communion of the sick, during the Sacrament of Anointing of the Sick, or during the celebration of viaticum. There are four parts of the Sacrament of Reconciliation. ▪

The Four Parts of the Sacrament of Reconciliation

Contrition on the part of the dying person for all sins committed against God and others
Confession of these sins to the priest, who acts as the representative of God and the Church
Acceptance of an act of penance that shows the desire to change one's life and repair any injury that was done by the sin
The receiving of absolution, or pardon

Activity
1. Read Psalm 22. How does this psalm reflect the different stages of death and dying? What stage is represented at the end of the psalm?
2. Analyze the scene of the death of Jesus in *Godspell*. How does the figure of Jesus in this musical accept his own death? What meaning does the death have? Present your analysis to the class, using examples from the soundtrack of the production to illustrate your points.

Discussion
What do you think Jesus meant when he said that a person should seek first God's kingdom? How does this relate to the way Christians should approach death?

Journal
1. What does the Sacrament of Reconciliation mean to you? How important is it in your life?
2. If you knew you were going to die soon, with whom would you first like to be reconciled?

Of Interest

Here is a traditional Act of Contrition:

My God, I am sorry for my sins with all my heart. In choosing to do wrong and failing to do good, I have sinned against you, whom I should love above all things. I firmly intend, with your help, to do penance, to sin no more, and to avoid whatever leads me to sin. Our Savior Jesus Christ suffered and died for us. In his name, my God, have mercy.

The four parts of the Sacrament of Reconciliation may be seen in the following outline of the Rite of Reconciliation for someone who is dying.

Invitation to trust. The priest invites the dying person to trust in God by saying one of the following prayers:

A. May the grace of the Holy Spirit fill your heart with light, that you may confess your sins with loving trust and come to know that God is merciful. Amen.

B. May the Lord be in your heart and help you to confess your sins with true sorrow. Amen.

C. The Lord does not wish the sinner to die but to turn back to him and live. Come before him with trust in his mercy. Amen.

Revelation of state of life. If the dying person does not know the priest, the person gives the priest some background information about himself or herself.

Confession of sins. The dying person confesses his or her sins. The priest may then give suitable counsel.

Acceptance of satisfaction. If appropriate, the priest suggests an act of penance, which the dying person accepts as a sign of amendment and reparation.

Penitent's prayer of sorrow. The dying person may say a familiar Act of Contrition or one of the following prayers:

A. Lord, Jesus, you opened the eyes of the blind, healed the sick, forgave the sinful woman, and after Peter's denial confirmed him in your love.

Listen to my prayer, forgive all my sins, renew your love in my heart, help me to live in perfect unity with my fellow Christians that I may proclaim your saving power to all the world.

B. Father of mercy, like the prodigal son I return to you and say:
"I have sinned against you and am no longer worthy to be called your son/daughter."
Christ Jesus, Savior of the world, I pray with the repentant thief to whom you promised Paradise:
"Lord, remember me in your Kingdom."
Holy Spirit, fountain of love, I call on you with trust:
"Purify my heart, and help me to walk as a child of light."

Absolution. The priest extends his hands over the head of the dying person and says:

God, the Father of mercies,
through the death and resurrection of his Son,
has reconciled the world to himself and sent the Holy Spirit among us for the forgiveness of sins;
through the ministry of the Church may God give you pardon and peace,
and I absolve you from your sins in the name of the Father, and of the Son, and of the Holy Spirit. Amen.

The Lord has freed you from sin
May he bring you safely to his kingdom in heaven.
Glory to him for ever. Amen. ■

—From the *Roman Ritual*:
Pastoral Care of the Sick

Activity

Look up one of the following Scripture passages mentioned in the prayers of the Rite of Reconciliation. How does the passage relate to forgiveness of sin and reconciliation with others?

- Matthew 9:1–8
- Luke 23:39–43
- Luke 7:36–50
- John 9
- Luke 15:11–32
- John 21:15–19

Your Last Words

Imagine for a moment that you are dying right now and that ten of your closest friends or family members are with you. What would you want to say to each person?

Person 1: _____

What I would like to say:

Person 2: _____

What I would like to say:

Person 3: _____

What I would like to say:

Person 4: _____

What I would like to say:

Person 5: _____

What I would like to say:

Person 6: _____

What I would like to say:

Person 7: _____

What I would like to say:

Person 8: _____

What I would like to say:

Person 9: _____

What I would like to say:

Person 10: _____

What I would like to say:

Sometimes death takes us by surprise. We don't get a chance to prepare for it or to say good-bye to those we love. Are there any reasons you cannot say your "last words" to these people now? ■

Activity

Instead of writing your "last words," prepare an audiotape or videotape of your messages.

Words to Know

acceptance
anger
bargaining
denial
depression

Review Questions

1. What are the traditionally-recognized stages of dying? Do all people go through these stages in the same way?
2. What are some indications that a person may be denying the fact of his or her approaching death?
3. How might a person express anger about the fact that he or she is dying?
4. What is a typical bargain a dying person might make?
5. What kind of "work" does a person do during the depression stage of dying?
6. How is acceptance of death different from giving up?
7. Why is it important to study the Gospels and to reflect on Jesus' attitude toward his own death?
8. How are the different stages of death found in the agony of the garden and the crucifixion?
9. What are the four parts of the Sacrament of Reconciliation? Why does the Church encourage people who are dying to celebrate this sacrament?

C•H•A•P•T•E•R

7

The Dignity *of* Every Human Life

IN THIS CHAPTER, YOU WILL

- explore some of the effects suffering has on a person's self-concept and sense of worth;

- embrace the Christian belief that all human life has dignity and is worthwhile;

- see that suffering can be redemptive—something that benefits us and others;

- reflect on New Testament passages that call us to unite our sufferings with the passion of Christ;

- learn why the Church disapproves of direct forms of killing, such as voluntary active euthanasia and physician-assisted suicide;

- understand how terminal sedation and the voluntary stopping of eating and drinking differ practically and morally from euthanasia and physician-assisted suicide;

- study excerpts from official Church documents dealing with human dignity and bioethical issues;

- understand the importance of having a living will and a durable power of attorney for health care.

"Will I Live to Be Seventeen?"

Physical suffering doesn't just affect your body. It also affects your feelings and self-concept as well as your relationships. Here is the ordeal one high school student went through when she found out she was seriously ill.

While my classmates looked forward to graduation and wondered "Will I get asked to the prom?" I had a bigger question to deal with: "Will I live to be seventeen?"

I was a junior in high school when a bump on my leg was diagnosed as chrondrosarcoma, cartilage cancer. No chemotherapy or radiation could make it go away; the only hope was for it to be removed before it could spread. The next step was a bone transplant.

My doctor had opened a bone bank six years before. When people die, they can choose to donate their bones to a bone bank. Doctors usually use the bone bank for pieces or chips of bones to fill in spots where bone is needed. My right leg needed a whole new fibula bone, the narrow, outer bone in the lower leg. There was a small chance I could contract HIV from the donated bone. There was also a possibility that my body would reject the new bone, which would mean that I would have to get a new bone and undergo surgery again.

I had a week to spend with my boyfriend and family before the surgery. I feared that it might be the last week of my life. During that week, I went back to school to get my assignments. Some of my friends stopped talking to me, as if they thought I could give them cancer by hanging out with them. Word had spread around school that I had "a disease." I was devastated. I felt like I wanted to die. Everywhere I went, people stared. I didn't look different; but in their minds, I was sick, and talking to me was dangerous.

The surgery lasted six hours. The doctor took out my fibula, disconnected my muscles, and moved my nerve in order to remove the tumor. He implanted the donated bone and a steel plate with eleven screws. I was in the hospital for eight days. My "best friends" never visited me.

I went through three and a half months of physical therapy and spent six months on crutches. I missed the whole second semester of my junior year. Today, I'm seventeen and the cancer is in remission. I have no feeling on the top of my right foot, but I'm able to walk short distances. What will happen next in my life? I don't know for sure, but I try to live each day completely. Life is too remarkable to give up without a fight. ■

—Shortened from "I was diagnosed with cancer," by Jennifer Skinner. *Teen Magazine* (August 1996), p. 72+.

Discussion

1. Would you donate (after death) your body organs and bones for transplants? Why or why not?
2. Would you accept a body organ or bone from an unknown donor if it offered you hope of staying alive? Why or why not?
3. Why do you think Jennifer's "friends" avoided her and never visited once she got sick?
4. How did the cancer affect Jennifer's self-concept and self-esteem?

How Much Is Too Much?

People like Jennifer Skinner know what severe physical suffering is like. They also know that the toll suffering can take on their self-esteem and relationships can be even worse than the suffering itself. According to Church teaching, no one suffers in a vacuum. And yet, from a psychological point of view, often that is exactly the situation suffering creates. It isolates us from others. It threatens to make us feel worthless.

Many people place their personal value on what they can do physically. We get affirmed by our accomplishments and by being useful. When we get seriously sick, however, we can't contribute to our families or social settings as we once did. Because we have become physically incapable, we are tempted to think that we, as people, are useless, too. We hate being a burden to others. Even worse, we hate being the object of other people's pity or rejection due to fear.

As Jennifer discovered, severe physical suffering can be accompanied by feelings of great helplessness, defeat, and loneliness. We are trapped within the physical limitations of our body, and we're not sure if tomorrow will be better or worse. Fortunately, Jennifer came through her experience as a stronger, wiser person. Some people who face relentless pain don't fare as well. What about you? How much suffering do you think you could handle before you wondered if your life was still worth the effort? That is one of the questions you will be considering in this chapter.

The chapter you are about to begin deals with several **bioethical** issues raised by severe suffering. Specifically, you will look at the

Attitude Survey	I agree	I disagree	I'm not sure
We never receive more suffering than we can handle.			
Humans have a right not to suffer.			
Personal suffering means that we are favored in the eyes of God.			
We have a right to die with dignity.			
We have a right to die when and how we want.			

morality of various terms found with more frequency in today's news: "pulling the plug" on life support, euthanasia, physician-assisted suicide, and terminal sedation.

Before proceeding, respond in your notebook to the above survey. ■

What's the Point?

You have learned in this course how suffering is not necessarily all evil but not exactly all good, either. It certainly is a fact of life. Still, when severe suffering happens to us, it's difficult to believe that our suffering has value and that we are still worthwhile human beings.

Fourteen-year-old Grace, in the movie *The Horse Whisperer*, knows how worthlessness feels. After she loses a leg in a horrific riding accident, she feels ugly—that her whole life is ruined. "Who will want to marry me now?" she sobs. It's a similar question to the one Job asks in the Bible after he becomes terribly sick with festering sores. He is so ugly he can't even look at himself. He curses the day he was born (cf. Job 3:3–6) and wishes that he were dead (cf. Job 7:1–10; 9:21; 10:1). ■

bioethics *The discipline that deals with the moral implications of biological research and its applications to humans, especially in medicine.*

Journal

1. How do you think each of the following situations would affect your self-concept and sense of worth? Why?
   - being diagnosed with a serious disease
   - being diagnosed with a terminal disease
   - being in the hospital for a prolonged period of time
   - losing all your hair due to chemotherapy and radiation
   - losing an arm or leg
2. How much suffering do you think you could handle before you wondered if your life was still worth the effort? Explain.

Activity

Look up the passages from the Book of Job cited on this page. Then, in a small group, discuss the following questions:
- How did suffering affect Job's self-concept and sense of worth?
- How do you think you would feel in a similar situation?
- If you were one of Job's friends, what would you say or do to convince him that he is a worthwhile person?

Anyone who has faced great suffering can identify with Grace and Job. And yet the gospel continually calls us to a different reality: Jesus suffered and died for us. As disciples, we are to identify with him, not with Grace or Job. For the truth is, if suffering were pointless, Jesus would not have accepted it.

Indeed, the passion and death of Jesus affirm two basic points of faith: (1) all human life has **dignity** and is worthwhile; and (2) great good can come out of suffering. Suffering can be redemptive, something that benefits us and benefits others. It is important to explore these two points further.

Human Dignity

Throughout his life, Jesus taught that all human life has dignity. Human life is sacred. Every person has been created in the image and likeness of God. Human dignity does not depend on our physical appearance. Nor does it rely on our capacity to DO anything, to be useful, or even to take care of ourselves. We have dignity and worth simply because God made us and loves us. This dignity continues even in sickness and suffering.

Belief in human dignity means that we all are stewards of the gift of life. We have a

*We find **peace** of mind and heart precisely when we come to **terms** with the fact that **life** is a **mystery**, a **gift** from God, a **blessing** over which we **do not** have complete **control**.*

Seven Michigan Bishops, "Living and Dying According to the Voice of Faith"

responsibility to treat ourselves and others with respect and to never give up on life. As people of faith, we are challenged to accept suffering when it comes and to deal with it in ways that are brave, dignified, and unselfish. Furthermore, we are called to respond with genuine care toward those who are sick, not as people to be pitied, but as people who share in the passion of Christ.

Redemptive Suffering

Suffering is a pointless waste of time only if we let it be. People of faith hold firm to the belief that great good can come out of suffering when this suffering is joined with the suffering of Jesus. To understand what this means, it is important to see how Jesus suffered, how he reacted to the suffering and accepted it. Only

dignity *The belief that all people have an intrinsic worth because they are made in the image and likeness of God. Because of human dignity, all people have a right to respect and to whatever is needed for life (shelter, food, clothing, medical care).*

Catholics Believe
. . . "By freely uniting themselves to the passion and death of Christ," [the sick] "contribute to the good of the People of God." [Lumen gentium 11§2.] . . . The sick person . . . contributes to the sanctification of the Church and to the good of all . . . (Catechism, #1522)

Jesus taught that every person, created in the image and likeness of God the Father, has dignity. We all are stewards of the gift of life.

then can we find God in the midst of our pain. Only then will our suffering become bearable.

When we read the gospel accounts of the Last Supper, the garden of Gethsemane, and the crucifixion, it is not difficult to imagine the suffering Jesus went through. In this experience of suffering, Jesus found the will of God the Father and attained interior peace. Furthermore, he was able to redeem others. Suffering is not the enemy of God. Rather, God is present to us in our suffering. God participates in every second of our lives. As Jesus once explained, "The kingdom of God has come near" (Luke 10:11).

Unshakable belief in the redemptive power of suffering is what motivated Paul and the other apostles to endure hardships for the sake of Christ. This belief is the foundation of their resilience, their courage, and their hope. It is the basis of their advice to the first Christians and to us:

> For you were bought with a price; therefore glorify God in your body.
>
> —1 Corinthians 6:20

> We are afflicted in every way, but not crushed; perplexed, but not driven to despair; persecuted, but not forsaken; struck down, but not destroyed; always carrying in the body the death of Jesus, so that the life of Jesus may also be made visible in our bodies. For while we live, we are always being given up to death for Jesus' sake, so that the life of Jesus may be made visible in our mortal flesh . . . because we know that the one who raised the Lord Jesus will raise us also with Jesus, and will bring us with you into his presence.
>
> —2 Corinthians 4:8–11, 14

> I appeal to you therefore, brothers and sisters, by the mercies of God, to present your bodies as a living sacrifice, holy and acceptable to God, which is your spiritual worship.
>
> —Romans 12:1

> For just as the sufferings of Christ are abundant for us, so also our consolation is abundant through Christ.
>
> —2 Corinthians 1:5

> May I never boast of anything except the cross of our Lord Jesus Christ, by which the world has been crucified to me, and I to the world.
>
> —Galatians 6:14

> . . . we are . . . joint heirs with Christ— if, in fact, we suffer with him so that we may also be glorified with him. I consider that the sufferings of this present time are not worth comparing with the glory about to be revealed to us.
>
> —Romans 8:16–18

> But rejoice insofar as you are sharing Christ's sufferings, so that you may also be glad and shout for joy when his glory is revealed.
>
> —1 Peter 4:13

> . . . we also boast in our sufferings, knowing that suffering produces endurance, and endurance produces character, and character produces hope, and hope does not disappoint us, because God's love has been poured into our hearts through the Holy Spirit that has been given to us. ▪
>
> —Romans 5:3–5

Catholics Believe

. . . By his passion and death on the cross Christ has given a new meaning to suffering: it can henceforth configure us to him and unite us with his redemptive Passion. (Catechism, #1505)

Activity

Read one of the following Scripture passages about the suffering Jesus went through.
- The Last Supper (Matthew 26:20–35)
- The garden of Gethsemane (Matthew 26:36–56)
- The crucifixion (Matthew 27:15–50)

Then write a prayer in which you ask God to help you share in Christ's sufferings and develop the attitudes found in the New Testament passages quoted above.

> *The authentic Christian **doctrine** of the **cross** is not that Christ . . . **spared** us from having to suffer, **but** rather that Christ . . . gives **ultimate**, saving **meaning** to our own personal and corporate **suffering**.*
>
> Peter Bernardi SJ, "The hidden engines of the suicide rights movement." *America* (May 6, 1995), p. 14+.

conversion in Saint Francis of Assisi and Saint Ignatius of Loyola. Suffering due to tuberculosis propelled Saint Thérèse of Lisieux to spiritual greatness. Lifelong struggles with asthma and poor health strengthened the faith of Saint Bernadette and caused it to overflow in the healing waters of Lourdes. In their suffering, these saints discovered the redemptive value of suffering—not just for themselves but for others. Through their suffering, they became new people, transfigured into the very Body and Blood of Christ. ▪

euthanasia *The painless putting to death of someone who is terminally ill; sometimes called mercy killing. In voluntary active euthanasia, the physician not only provides the means of death but actually administers the lethal injection at the patient's request. The Church considers euthanasia to be murder and thus immoral.*

Throughout the centuries, many Christians have taken to heart the New Testament message concerning suffering. For example, the experience of mental and physical suffering brought about genuine

Every year millions of Catholics make a pilgrimage to the healing waters of Lourdes, France, where, in 1858, the apparition of the Blessed Virgin Mary appeared eighteen times to fourteen-year-old Bernadette Soubirous.

Voluntary Active Euthanasia (VAE)

It is in light of human dignity and the belief in the redemptive value of suffering that Catholics must approach present day issues concerning suffering, life, and death. The first of these issues we will discuss here is voluntary active **euthanasia**. The word *euthanasia* means "good death." Another term often used is *mercy killing*. The term commonly refers to the direct taking of human life in order to relieve suffering. *Voluntary euthanasia* means that the killing is done with the patient's consent. *Active euthanasia* means that the doctor not only provides the means of death but actually administers the lethal injection at the patient's request. Cases of voluntary active euthanasia usually involve someone who is elderly or who is suffering terribly.

Activity

1. Read about the life of one of the saints mentioned on this page. Be prepared to report to the class about this saint and how he or she became a new person through suffering.

2. Write a poem or short essay that explains your understanding of the redemptive value of suffering. Be prepared to share with the class what you have written.

Some people, such as members of the **Hemlock Society USA** and the Euthanasia Society, argue that simply being alive is not a good in itself, especially when someone can seemingly no longer live with meaning and dignity or live without pain. According to the philosophy of these societies, each person should have the right to choose the time of his or her death, especially if a truly human life seems no longer possible. So they encourage those with a terminal illness to plan their own death. They also urge doctors and family members to exercise "compassion" by helping those with terminal illnesses to die.

The only country in the world that permits voluntary active euthanasia is the Netherlands. There, the practice of euthanasia involves sedating the patient to unconsciousness and then giving a lethal injection of a muscle-paralyzing agent, such as curare. Currently in the United States, euthanasia is against the law. It is also forbidden by the Catholic Church. If a doctor or family member intentionally causes a suffering person to die, it is considered to be murder.

In June 1998, members of Not Dead Yet, a group representing disabled people who oppose voluntary active euthanasia, protested at the national conference of the Hemlock Society USA. "Basically, this is legalized killing of anybody with any type of disability." Tom Cagle said as he sat in his motorized wheelchair. Sue Butte, another member of Not Dead Yet, agreed: "The very first right we are offered is the right to die. We want the right to live."

Indeed, there are many ethical problems associated with euthanasia. Some people fear that voluntary euthanasia would quickly deteriorate into involuntary euthanasia— killing without the patient's consent. They also fear that life-and-death decisions would be based on cost effectiveness rather than on the value of human life. Euthanasia is wrong because it violates human dignity and the value of human life. If we are truly people who affirm life, then we have a moral obligation to protect the vulnerable members of our society, prevent unscrupulous and unethical medical practices, and guarantee the best possible medical care for all. ▪

Physician-Assisted Suicide (PAS)

If active euthanasia is wrong, what about a situation in which a doctor or family member "assists" a person in committing suicide? The physician or family member provides the means but does not actually administer the lethal injection or dose. For example, the physician prescribes a lethal dose of barbiturates; the patient actually takes the pills. Such situations are known as **physician-assisted suicide**.

One of the problems with physician-assisted suicide is that it is not always effective. Families may be left with a patient who is vomiting, aspirating, or cognitively impaired but not dying. Furthermore, PAS is illegal. Aiding and abetting a suicide is a felony in twenty-six states. Most importantly, PAS is immoral. It is still suicide; it is still killing— intentionally taking a human life.

Hemlock Society USA
A modern-day society that believes each person should have the right to choose the time of his or her death. The society advocates suicide, especially in circumstances of advanced age and terminal illness.

physician-assisted suicide
A type of mercy killing in which a physician or family member assists a person in committing suicide. The physician provides the means of death but does not administer the lethal injection or dose. The Catholic Church considers physician-assisted suicide to be murder and thus immoral.

> *T*rue **compassion** *does not* **eliminate** *the* **sufferer**, *but seeks to* **relieve** *the* **suffering**.
>
> Seven Michigan Bishops, "Living and Dying According to the Voice of Faith"

Discussion

1. Why do some people think that a person has a right to choose when he or she will die?
2. Why do you think the Church says that this decision rightfully belongs to God alone?

Dr. Jack Kevorkian burns a cease-and-desist order in April 1997 in Detroit. The order, issued by the state of Michigan, warns Kevorkian to stop assisting in suicides or face charges of practicing medicine without a license.

terminal sedation *An ethical course of treatment intended to relieve the pain of a dying patient rather than intentionally kill the patient. In terminal sedation, a physician gives the dying patient medications (usually barbiturates or benzodiazepine) that cause unconsciousness. Life supports are removed, including intravenous food and water, while the disease runs its final course. The patient usually dies in a few days or a week.*

voluntary stopping of eating and drinking *(a) A situation in which a dying patient voluntarily decides not to eat or drink. Death eventually is caused by dehydration or starvation. (b) A situation in which an unconscious dying patient (who has previously given his or her consent) is taken off life-support and disconnected from feeding tubes.*

Situations involving physician-assisted suicide in the United States have been rising since 1990. In June 1990, Dr. Jack Kevorkian of Michigan used a machine he had built to assist in the suicide of a 54-year-old Oregon woman named Janet Adkins, who had Alzheimer's disease. Because the action was illegal in Oregon, the woman traveled to Michigan, where she committed suicide using Kevorkian's machine. Kevorkian's actions provoked loud cries of alarm and disapproval from both the Catholic Church and the American Medical Association. Both groups were adamant: No reason can ever justify the causing of one's own or another's death. No one has the right to decide when a person, terminally ill or not, should die. Dr. Kevorkian, however, was not deterred. By 1998, despite persistent court challenges, he had assisted in more than 100 suicides.

In 1994, the state of Oregon passed a bill allowing physicians to prescribe lethal drugs to terminally ill patients. The bill was affirmed in 1997. In 1998, United States Attorney General Janet Reno upheld the law, saying that the federal government would not prosecute doctors who assisted suicides in that state. As a result of the ruling, Oregon produced a detailed manual on how doctors can end a life. The Oregon Health Service Commission included physician-assisted suicide on the list of health services that are paid for through Oregon's Medicaid program; the taxpayers are paying for the suicide of those who are poor. On March 24, 1998, a woman in her mid-80s with cancer became the first known person to die under the Oregon law.

In November 1998, a similar bill legalizing physician-assisted suicide was on the ballot in Michigan; the proposal failed as 71 percent of voters voted against the bill. However, it is likely that similar ballots will soon be found in other states. ▪

Allowing a Person to Die

Morally, there is a big difference between active forms of killing—such as voluntary active euthanasia and physician-assisted suicide—and allowing a person to die. VAE and PAS involve actions or omissions that intend to cause death. "Allowing a person to die" involves withholding or withdrawing useless or disproportionately burdensome treatment, thus allowing the person to die from the fatal disease or condition. The most common forms of allowing a person to die are known by the terms **terminal sedation** (TS) and **voluntary stopping of eating and drinking** (VSED).

Terminal Sedation (TS)

In terminal sedation, a physician gives the dying patient medications (usually barbiturates or benzodiazepine) that cause unconsciousness. Life supports are removed, including intravenous food and water, while the disease runs its final course. The patient usually dies in a few days or a week and, presumably, without pain or the tortures of hunger or thirst.

Activity
Find out if assisted suicide is a felony in your state. Then prepare a class debate arguing for or against physician-assisted suicide.

The primary intention of terminal sedation is to stop the pain, not kill the patient. It is a way to make the patient as comfortable as possible throughout the dying process. Terminal sedation is used as a last resort—when everything else fails. In almost all cases, the patient is not involved at this time in this life-and-death decision. The illness has progressed to the point where the person is unable to make rational decisions.

In short, terminal sedation is a compassionate way to relieve a dying patient's pain; however, there are ethical problems to consider. For example, it is not right to carry out terminal sedation without the patient's explicit knowledge or approval. Why would a dying person reject terminal sedation? Some terminally ill patients believe their dignity would be violated if they had to be unconscious for a prolonged time before they die or that their families would suffer unnecessarily while waiting for them to die. Furthermore, some patients prefer to die at home rather than in the hospital where terminal sedation is available. ▪

In 1997, the United States Supreme Court explicitly endorsed terminal sedation while quashing an effort to create a constitutional right to physician-assisted suicide. The court stated that no one should die in pain or suffer for lack of medication even if it has to be given in doses that might hasten death. The United States bishops agreed. ▪

Voluntary Stopping of Eating and Drinking (VSED)

In this situation, the dying patient voluntarily decides not to eat or drink. Death eventually is caused by dehydration or starvation. In other words, the patient is allowed to die. The process, which takes one to three weeks, may increase the patient's suffering due to hunger and thirst. Ethical problems concerning VSED arise when the patient is unconscious. Should water and food be considered "extraordinary means" of life support or a normal part of health care?

The landmark case of a young Catholic named Karen Ann Quinlan (1954–1985) brought the issue of VSED to the attention of the world. On April 14, 1975, Karen lapsed into an irreversible coma after taking a combination of tranquilizers and alcohol. The lower court in New Jersey refused to give her parents permission to remove her respirator. This decision was later reversed by the Supreme Court. With the support of their local pastor, Karen's parents had the respirator removed. To everyone's surprise, Karen continued breathing on her own. For nine more years, she was kept alive on antibiotics and high-nutrient feedings through a tube. Her father visited her daily; her mother visited two or three times a week. When Karen died of pneumonia in 1985, she weighted only sixty pounds.

In Karen's case, a distinction was made between the respirator (extraordinary means) and assisted nutrition and hydration (an ordinary form of health care). In the years following Karen's death, families involved in similar situations have taken a closer look at the definition of "extraordinary." The issue was again raised in the case of Nancy Cruzan (1957–1990), a young woman from Missouri. On January 11, 1983, Nancy was injured in a car accident that left her with irreversible brain damage. For eight years, she lay in a coma in a hospital. The hospital refused to let the family stop life-sustaining treatment without court approval. In June 1990, the United States Supreme Court upheld the Missouri court's insistence that the state had the right to require Nancy's family to produce "clear and compelling evidence" that she would not want to continue treatment. After the family did this, a Missouri judge allowed doctors to remove Nancy's feeding tube. She died twelve days later.

Of Interest

In April 1998, the *New England Journal of Medicine* published the results of a survey that asked family practitioners, general internists, cardiologists, and others who regularly care for the dying whether they had ever given lethal injections or had written prescriptions so patients could kill themselves. Eighteen percent had gotten such requests. Five percent said they had given at least one lethal injection, and 3 percent had written a prescription. Some had done both, and overall, about 6 percent said they had done one or the other. The doctors said most of the patients asked for help ending their lives because of discomfort, pain, loss of dignity, and fear of uncontrollable symptoms.

Of Interest

For more information about Karen Ann Quinlan, read the book *Karen Ann* or view the TV movie *In the Matter of Karen Ann Quinlan*.

 ### *Discussion*
What is the difference between terminal sedation and euthanasia or physician-assisted suicide?

 ### *Journal*
1. If a person in your family was in great suffering and was about to die, would you want him or her to be terminally sedated? Explain your position.
2. If you were in great suffering and were about to die, would you want to be terminally sedated? Explain your position.

Nancy Cruzan (1957–1990) died on December 26, 1990, twelve days after doctors removed her feeding tube.She had been in a coma for eight years.

Was the removal of the feeding tube moral or immoral? The answer is not clear. The Missouri bishops issued a statement about Nancy's death, in which they said the following:

> We believe that no person has the right to directly take his or her own life or to take the life of another innocent person. On the other hand, in light of modern medical technology, it is not always necessary to use every possible measure to prolong life indefinitely. Pope Pius XII has taught that "extraordinary means" need not be taken to prolong life when such means offer no real benefit and when such extraordinary means are onerous to the patient or even to others (for example, the family).

—Missouri Bishops, *Statement on Ending Nancy Cruzan's Nutrition and Hydration*

living will *A legal document in which people make known their wishes about what medical or health care treatment they would or would not want if they became seriously ill. The purpose of the document is to ask that one's dying not be unreasonably prolonged.*

The bishops' words could be interpreted to mean that they considered assisted nutrition and hydration as extraordinary means in Nancy's case. They did state that the decision about cases such as hers should be made in light of moral principles and "should be taken with great deliberation." ▪

As you can see, the moral dilemmas surrounding suffering and death are complicated. Undoubtedly the Catholic Church will continue to issue statements as further reflection occurs and future situations arise. Regardless of that reflection on the specifics of these situations, however, the Church's stance will always reflect a recognition of the sanctity of life and the belief that the life of a person who has physical or psychiatric disabilities is no less important than that of a person without such a handicap. ▪

Advance Directives for Health Care

Both the Karen Quinlan and the Nancy Cruzan cases made people aware of some of the moral and legal dilemmas that modern medicine and medical technology create. As a result of these cases, people began making what are now called **living wills**. In a living will, people make known their wishes about what medical or health care treatment they would or would not want if they became seriously ill.

A living will usually expresses the person's wish not to receive extraordinary means of life support if he or she becomes physically or mentally disabled and there is no reasonable expectation of recovery. A living will may also state that the person is to be given medication to lessen pain, even if it hastens the moment of death. The purpose of the document is to ask that one's dying not be unreasonably prolonged.

Discussion

1. Do you think assisted nutrition and hydration are "extraordinary means" or an ordinary form of health care? Explain your position.

2. A fair number of people *do* recover from a coma. How should this affect one's attitude toward withdrawing food and water from people who are comatose?

Activity

Role-play the following situation: Family member A has been in a coma for eight months. Discuss the "pros" and "cons" of continuing treatment or stopping it.

Despite its good intentions, a living will has shortcomings. It does not name anyone to see that those wishes are carried out. In addition, a living will may be too general to speak to every situation that may arise in a given case. Thus, problems can arise. For example, whose wishes does a doctor honor if a patient's family is not in agreement about what is to be done? Furthermore, there is the question of whether the doctor may legally honor the wishes of any family member.

Over the past ten years, the wording of living wills has evolved so that they will stand up in court should they be put to the test in a particular case. This refinement process has created not only better living wills but a second document known as a ***durable power of attorney for health care.*** A durable power of attorney is a legal document authorizing someone else to make medical decisions in the patient's best interest if he or she is unable to make such decisions. It legally authorizes someone by name (the agent) to make medical or health care treatment decisions for another. Thus, the decisions of the agent have the same legal force as if it were the patient speaking on his or her own behalf.

On December 1, 1991, a federal law known as the *Patient Self-Determination Act* went into effect in the United States. Under this law, any adult who is admitted to a hospital, care facility, or health care program is to be asked if he or she has any advance directives for health care. The response is to be noted on his or her records. The Patient Self-Determination Act also mandates that a patient must receive written information concerning his or her rights under state law to make decisions about treatment options. A patient must also be told about a program's or health care facility's policy in matters of advance directives.

Church Teaching

The **magisterium** of the Catholic Church consists of the pope and the bishops in union with him. The magisterium has the duty to guide Catholics and to maintain truth in all

*H*ealth care **professionals** *must* **never forget** *that fundamentally they are* **involved** *with* **persons**, *not diseases.*

Vincent J. Genovesi, "To suffer and die in Christ." *America* (March 23, 1996), p. 10+.

teachings of faith and morality. The bishops and the pope do this by issuing periodic statements, called encyclicals and pastoral letters, about moral principles and specific faith topics. What follows are excerpts from various statements and documents that reflect the Church's teaching regarding terminal suffering and death.

durable power of attorney for health care *A legal document authorizing someone else to make medical decisions in the patient's best interest if he or she is unable to make such decisions. The authorized person (agent) has the same legal force as if it were the patient speaking on his or her own behalf.*

magisterium *The highest teaching authority in the Catholic Church. The magisterium is composed of the bishops in union with the pope. The magisterium has the responsibility of teaching and defending the principles of Catholic faith and morality.*

Of Interest

Anyone who decides to execute an advance directive for health care should be sure to do the following:

- discuss it with one's physician and one's family members;
- place a copy of the directive in one's medical records;
- give copies to family members, close friends, and neighbors;
- keep a reduced-size copy in a purse or wallet;
- in the case of a durable power of attorney, give a copy to the agent and the alternate agent, if there is one.

Human Dignity and Suffering

Suffering has a special value in the eyes of the Church. It is something good, before which the Church bows down in reverence with all the depth of her faith in the redemption.

—*The Christian Meaning of Human Suffering.*
Apostolic letter written by Pope John Paul II
on February 23, 1984.

Suffering contains a special call to the virtue . . . of perseverance in bearing whatever disturbs us or causes us harm. In doing this, we unleash hope, which maintains the conviction that suffering will not get the better of us, that it will not deprive us of our dignity as human beings, a dignity linked to awareness of the meaning of life.

—Pope John Paul II, *The Christian
Meaning of Human Suffering*

Redemptive Suffering

In bringing about the redemption through suffering, Christ has also raised human suffering to the level of the redemption. Thus each person in his or her suffering can also become a sharer in the redemptive suffering of Christ.

—Pope John Paul II, *The Christian
Meaning of Human Suffering*

Terminal Sedation

When death is clearly inevitable and close at hand, a patient or caregiver can make the decision to forgo aggressive medical treatment which would impose an excessive burden on patient and family. In such cases, the Church particularly encourages pain management and hospice care for the dying. Further, patients and their caregivers have a legitimate right to insist on the best and most effective pain management and treatment to minimize suffering. One may even legitimately choose to relieve pain by use of medications which may have the unfortunate side effect of decreasing consciousness or shortening one's life, if this is done with the intent of relieving pain and no other means are available to serve this goal.

—*Living and Dying According to the Voice
of Faith.* Pastoral letter written
by the Michigan Bishops.

As individuals and as a society, we can assure dying persons that their lives retain meaning and that their continued presence is not a burden to us. We can be more open and candid about the fact that dependency does not diminish our humanity.

—*Assisted Suicide: Bad Public Policy.*
Pastoral letter written by Archbishop
Rembert Weakland.

Extraordinary Means

While euthanasia or direct killing is gravely wrong, it does not follow that there is an obligation to prolong the life of a dying person by extraordinary means. At times the effort to do so is of no help to the dying and may even be contrary to true compassion. People have a right to refuse treatment which offers no reasonable hope of recovery and imposes excessive burdens on them and perhaps also on their families. At times it may even be morally imperative to discontinue particular medical treatments in order to give the dying the personal care and attention really needed as life ebbs.

—*To Live in Christ Jesus: A Pastoral Reflection on
the Moral Life,* #58. Issued by the National
Conference of Catholic Bishops in 1976.

We are not the owners of our lives and, hence, do not have absolute power over life. We have a duty to preserve our life and to use it for the glory of God, but the duty to preserve life is not absolute, for we may reject life-prolonging procedures that are insufficiently beneficial or excessively burdensome.

—*Ethical and Religious Directives for Catholic
Health Care Services.* National Conference
of Catholic Bishops (1995).

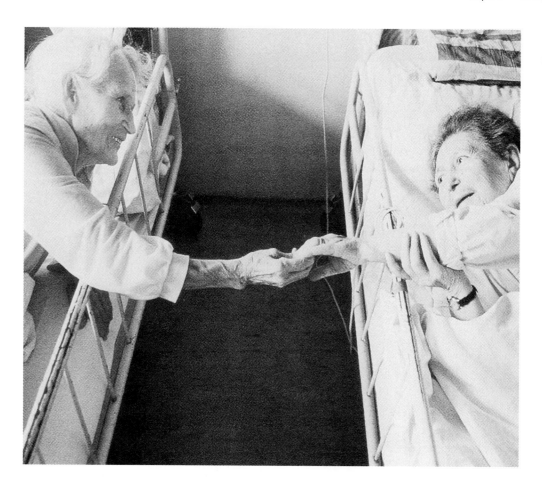

Euthanasia

Nothing and no one can in any way permit the killing of an innocent human being, whether a fetus or an embryo, an infant or an adult, an old person, one suffering from an incurable disease, or a person who is dying. Furthermore, no one is permitted to ask for this act of killing, either for himself or herself or for another person entrusted to his or her care, nor can he or she consent to it, either explicitly or implicitly.

—*Declaration on Euthanasia*, #19. Issued by the Sacred Congregation for the Doctrine of the Faith, 1980.

As Catholics, we believe euthanasia is morally wrong because it is the destruction of life. It also opens the door to other potential crimes against life, especially against those who are chronically ill or disabled. Euthanasia is unnecessary as well as wrong, because suffering and pain can be relieved in many morally acceptable ways.

—The Michigan Bishops, *Living and Dying According to the Voice of Faith.*

Physician-Assisted Suicide

Suicide—the conscious choice to destroy one's own life—is always morally wrong. Concurring with someone's intention to commit suicide and cooperating in the process can never be condoned. Such assisted suicide is a perversion of genuine mercy. It is especially tragic when undertaken by physicians, whose very professional code charges them never to harm but always to respect life.

—The Michigan Bishops, *Living and Dying According to the Voice of Faith.*

Your Advanced Directives for Health Care

If you are under eighteen, your parents or guardians already have legal authority to make decisions regarding your health care. If you are eighteen or older, it is important to execute an advanced directive for health care. Here is a durable power of attorney for health care prepared by the Catholic Health Association. The document is applicable in most states but does not assure that it includes every state's technical requirements.

1. Creation of a Durable Power of Attorney for Health Care

To my family, doctors, and all those concerned with my care:

I, _____ (name), residing at

_____ (street address)

in _____ (city or county), _____ (state), being of sound mind, intend by this document to create a durable power of attorney for health care. My executing this durable power of attorney for health care is voluntary. I expect, despite the creation of this durable power of attorney for health care, to be fully informed about and to make any health care decision for myself whenever I am able to do so. For purpose of this document, "health care decision" means an informed decision in the exercise of my right to accept, maintain, discontinue, or refuse any care, treatment, service, or procedure to maintain, diagnose, or treat my physical or mental condition.

2. Designation of Health Care Agent

If I am unable to make health care decisions for myself, due to my incapacity, I hereby designate my

_____ (relationship), _____ (name), residing at

_____ (street address) in

_____ (city or county), _____ (state)

(home telephone: _____-_____-_____), to be my health care agent for the purpose of making health care decisions on my behalf. If he/she is ever unable or unwilling to do so, I hereby designate my

_____ (relationship), _____ (name), to be my first alternate health care agent for the purpose of making health care decisions on my behalf. In the event that neither of these people is able or willing to be my health care agent, I then designate my _____ (relationship),

_____ (name), to be my second alternate health care agent for the purpose of making health care decisions on my behalf.

3. General Statement of Authority Granted

Unless I have specified otherwise in this document, if I ever am unable to receive and evaluate information effectively or to communicate decisions to such an extent that I lack capacity to manage my health care decisions, I instruct my health care provider to obtain the health care decisions of my health care agent for all my health care. I have discussed my desires thoroughly with my health care agent as well as those named as alternates and believe that they understand my philosophy regarding the health care decisions I would make if I were able to do so. I desire that my wishes be carried out through the authority given to my health care agent under this document.

My health care agent is instructed that if I am unable, due to my incapacity, to make a health care decision, he/she shall make a health care decision for me. My health care agent shall base his/her health care decision on any health care choices that I have expressed prior to the time of the decision. If I have not expressed a health care choice about the health care in question, my health care agent shall base his/her health care decision on what he/she believes to be in my best interest.

4. Admission to Nursing Homes or Long-Term Care Facilities

My health care agent may admit me to a nursing home or other long-term care facility as he/she may deem appropriate.

5. Provision of Non-Orally Ingested Nutrition and Hydration

My health care agent may have non-orally ingested nutrition and hydration withheld or withdrawn from me. This includes nutrition and hydration supplied through tubes entering anywhere in my body.

_____ (initials) Yes, my agent has specific authority regarding non-orally ingested nutrition and hydration.

If I have not initialed "yes," my agent does NOT have authority to withhold non-orally ingested nutrition and hydration.

6. Statement of Desires, Special Provisions, or Limitations

In exercising authority under this document, my health care agent shall act consistently with my following stated desires, if any, and is subject to any special provision or limitations that I specify.

_____

_____

_____

_____

7. Inspection and Disclosure of Information Relating to My Physical or Mental Health

Subject to any limitations in this document, my health care agent has the authority to do all of the following:

(a) Request, review, and receive any information, verbal or written, regarding my physical or mental health, including medical and hospital records.

(b) Execute on my behalf any documents that may be required to obtain this information.

(c) Consent to the disclosure of this information.

8. Signing Documents, Waivers, and Releases

Where necessary to implement the health care decisions that my health care agent is authorized by this document to make, my health care agent has the authority to execute on my behalf any of the following:

(a) Documents titled or purported to be a "consent to permit treatment," "refusal to permit treatment," or "leaving hospital against medical advice."

(b) A waiver or release from liability required by a hospital or physician.

_____ Dated: _____

Statement of Witnesses

The foregoing document was declared by _____ (name) to be his/her grant of a Durable Power of Attorney for Health Care and was signed in our presence, all being present at the same time, and we, at his/her request and in his/her presence and in the presence of each other, have subscribed our names as witnesses on the date above written.

_____   _____

_____   _____

* Notary affidavit is optional in most states but is recommended.

 Words to Know

bioethics

dignity

durable power of attorney for health care

euthanasia

Hemlock Society USA

living will

magisterium

physician-assisted suicide

terminal sedation

voluntary stopping of eating and drinking

 Review Questions

1. What does the Church mean when it says that all human life has dignity?
2. What is redemptive suffering? How can our suffering be redemptive?
3. What advice does the New Testament give us regarding suffering?
4. How did suffering affect saints such as Francis of Assisi, Ignatius of Loyola, Thérèse of Lisieux, and Bernadette of Lourdes?
5. What is the difference between voluntary active euthanasia and physician-assisted suicide?
6. Why does the Church consider euthanasia and physician-assisted suicide to be immoral?
7. What is terminal sedation? How does this action differ from euthanasia or physician-assisted suicide?
8. What is the Church's position regarding extraordinary means of life support?
9. What is the difference between a living will and a durable power of attorney for health care?

C•H•A•P•T•E•R

8

Care *for* *the* Sick *and* Dying

- see how fear of the sick can sometimes express itself in prejudice and discrimination;

- consider your own stereotypes regarding people who are elderly, sick, physically disabled, psychologically disabled, or dying;

- examine the underlying reasons for fear of the sick;

- review how Jesus and the apostles healed the sick;

- explore the Church's history regarding care of the sick;

- reflect on excerpts from the bishops of the United States about the sick, elderly, disabled, and people with AIDS;

- study the meaning and revised rite of the Sacrament of the Anointing of the Sick;

- receive tips about what to say and do when you visit someone who is sick or elderly.

A Brighter Life

The hallways of the Veterans Administration Medical Center are painted orange and brown, colors that absorb most of the light that shines in. Seventeen-year-old Tirzah Orcutt has been tearing down those walls, sort of.

"Little by little, I want to change the colors of the walls," Orcutt said. "The environment needs to be uplifting."

For the past four years, the high school senior has spent more than five hundred hours volunteering at the hospital, a place she calls her second home. She even left a permanent mark by helping organize the painting of a mural in a gated, outdoor patio space known as the hospital's "wandering area."

With its magenta mountains and desert landscape, the mural was a meticulous project. Orcutt spent hours preparing a grant proposal, then had to weigh each detail down to which shade of blue to use. "Different colors produce different feelings," she said. "We had to go to the veterans and get their opinion, to know what they like."

Only sixteen at the time, Orcutt worked with artist Jim Covarrubias to make the project a success.

Her efforts have earned various awards and scholarships, but it's her interaction with the veterans of the hospital that Orcutt values most out of her experience.

Such as the friendship with Joe Courtney, a veteran of the Korean and Vietnam Wars. The two met after Courtney was admitted to the hospital last July. He takes part in recreation therapy, an area in which Orcutt volunteers.

On a recent day at the hospital, the two chatted away like old friends, Orcutt explaining her idea for another mural—a scene of a lake per Courtney's request. "He's like my grandpa," Orcutt said, "Especially after my own grandfather passed away."

In addition to her volunteer work, she has supported her own family members who faced death. She recalled spending nights finishing homework at the bedside of her grandfather and both of her older brothers, one of whom died of a rare terminal illness.

"I don't look at it as tragedy," she said, repeating a philosophy that guides her life: Do well in spite of something and not poorly because of it.

"I know there's a need to volunteer for the veterans," she said. "Just visiting them once a week makes a difference in their lives." ▪

—Adapted from "Teen leaves lasting mark on veterans,"
© *The Arizona Republic* (April 27, 1998). Article by
Lisa Wilson. Used with permission. Permission
does not imply endorsement.

Activity

Find out what care facilities (hospitals, veterans hospitals, convalescent homes) are located in your city or area. Choose one of these facilities to research further. Contact the facility's director of volunteer services. Find out what volunteer programs are available for teens. Report your findings to the class. If possible, get involved in one of these programs.

Fear of the Sick

Sickness is part of life. In 1997, over 61 million people were treated for illnesses in the United States, and that number only reflects those who were served by Catholic hospitals. Although people frequently get sick, society tends to treat the sick as "untouchables." Our fear of the sick is just as strong as our fear of the dead, especially when the disease is infectious and fatal. When the sick person is someone who is also dying, our fears multiply. ■

Unfortunately, these fears often express themselves as prejudice and discrimination against the sick, the elderly, the terminally ill, or those who are physically or psychologically disabled. Consider, for example, the case of Ryan White. At age 13, he contracted HIV as the result of a contaminated blood transfusion for hemophilia. Parents and students alike protested his presence in school. Hardly anyone would talk to him. Ryan's case is not isolated. We ban the "unwanted" sick to institutions because we don't want to deal with them or face what they represent. ■

Attitude Survey	I agree	I disagree	I'm not sure
I like to visit friends who are sick.			
Hospitals are depressing places; in addition, they smell bad.			
I would prefer to stay away from someone who is HIV-positive (infected with the AIDS virus).			
I wouldn't mind volunteering at a convalescent home.			
The Sacrament of the Anointing of the Sick is only for those who are dying.			

In this chapter, you will explore the social dimensions of dealing with and caring for the sick. You will see how care of the sick has always been an important part of the Church's history and social teaching. You will also explore the meaning of the Sacrament of the Anointing of the Sick and learn some tips about how to relate to people who are sick.

Before beginning, complete the survey above. Write your answers in your notebook.

Although over 61 million people were treated for illnesses by Catholic hospitals in the United States in 1997, society tends to treat the sick as "untouchables."

In Memory

Ryan White was born on December 16, 1971, in Kokomo, Indiana. He died of AIDS on April 8, 1990. His life was dramatized in the television movie, The Ryan White Story, and in the book, Ryan White: My Own Story (New York, NY: Dial Books, 1991). Both the movie and the book document the prejudices Ryan encountered because of AIDS.

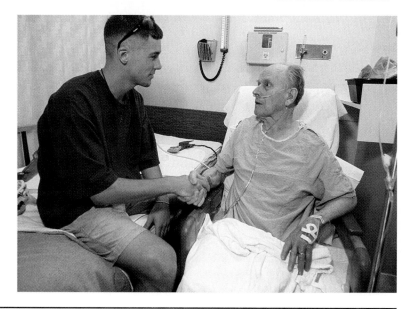

 Activity
Write an essay that supports or refutes the following statement: "Dying people are the most discriminated against and dehumanized minority in our culture."

 Discussion
1. Do you think employers, school officials, and other people have a right to know the names of persons who are HIV-positive? Or do you think test results should be kept confidential?
2. Do you think students who are HIV-positive should be allowed to stay in school as long as possible?
3. Suppose someone who is HIV-positive has unprotected sex without telling the other person about his or her condition. Do you think this person should be prosecuted for endangering the life of another? Why or why not?

Of Interest

According to the National Center for Injury Prevention and Control (NCIPC), the leading causes of death in the United States in 1995 were:

1. heart disease
2. cancer
3. cerebrovascular diseases, such as stroke and hypertension
4. pulmonary diseases, such as chronic bronchitis, emphysema, and asthma
5. accidents
6. pneumonia and flu
7. diabetes
8. HIV
9. suicide
10. liver disease

Stereotypes

We often fear what we do not know. When someone becomes sick or disabled, our fear increases. The person no longer seems human; instead, he or she has become a giant label: "sick" or "disabled" or "terminally ill." At best, we relate to the label and our perceived stereotypes of it rather than relating to the individual person. At worst, we shy away from the people we have labeled, or we refuse to relate to them at all. Then, because we have isolated ourselves from these people, we fear them even more. Stereotypes and prejudice become a vicious circle.

Think about the stereotypes you or other teenagers have regarding the following groups of people. List the stereotypes here or in your notebook. ■ ■

*Suffering is a **grace** not only to the one **invited** into it but to those **around** the person as well: relatives, friends, health care workers. Human **suffering** can evoke **compassion** and **respect** in those sensitive enough to **resonate** to it.*

Father William O'Malley, *Redemptive Suffering*

Facing Our Fears

Stereotypes and prejudice reflect underlying fears. Some people fear those who are sick because they are afraid that they, too, will contract the same disease. In cases of contagious diseases, such fears are justified. In most cases of sickness, however, the fears have no basis in reality.

Some people fear the machines, tubes, needles, pills, and other paraphernalia that go along with being sick—especially if the person is in a hospital or convalescent home. The strange sights, sounds, and smells of the sick person's room can be frightening to those who are not used to them.

Other people fear the sick because sickness is a reminder of death. If you look at the major causes of death in the United States today, this fear seems appropriate. In 1995, for example, eight of the ten leading causes of death were some type of sickness. (The other two leading causes of death were accidents and suicide.)

Group	Stereotypes
the elderly	
the sick	
the psychologically disabled	
the physically disabled	
the dying	

Discussion

1. What prejudices are reflected in each of these stereotypes?
2. What behaviors flow from these stereotypes?
3. How could you and others begin to change the way you think about certain groups of people?

Journal

1. Do you know anyone in the stereotyped groups listed? What is the person like? Does he or she fit the stereotype? How does your experience affect the way you perceive other people in the same group as this person?
2. If you were in one of these groups, how would you want people to treat you?

Another reason we fear sickness is that we aren't as close to it as past generations. In former times doctors made house calls, and the sick were treated at home. Now people are treated in doctor's offices or in hospitals. The elderly are sent to live in retirement communities and care facilities. The physically and psychologically disabled attend separate "special education" classes. Sickness has been removed from our ordinary experience of life; hence, we tend to fear what we do not know. ▪

These fears are not new. The Old Testament tells us that people hid their faces from the sick, spurned them, and held them in no esteem (cf. Isaiah 53:3). In the time of Jesus, most people considered the psychologically disabled and epileptics to be possessed by evil or unclean spirits. Lepers were avoided at all costs and had to live apart from others. The deaf, blind, and crippled were thought to be sinners. Because they were not accepted by society, they lived on the streets as beggars. ▪

Jesus and the Sick

Jesus countered the prevailing fears of his day with tangible action. He cared for those who were sick in ways that were compassionate and healing. He treated the sick as individual people who had dignity rather than as stereotyped labels.

Indeed, caring for the sick was an important part of Jesus' ministry; examples of it can be found in all four Gospels. Despite the prejudices of his day, Jesus reached out in love to heal all who came to him. ▪

Catholics Believe
. . . [Christ's] compassion toward all who suffer goes so far that he identifies himself with them. . . . His preferential love for the sick has not ceased through the centuries to draw the very special attention of Christians toward all those who suffer in body and soul. It is the source of tireless efforts to comfort them. (Catechism, #1503)

Jesus Cared for and Healed . . .

Lepers	Romans	The physically disabled	The sick	Those possessed by demons
Matthew 8:2–4	Matthew 8:5–13	Matthew 9:2–8	Matthew 4:23–24, 8:16, 10:8, 14:14	Matthew 8:28–34
Mark 1:40–45	Luke 7:1–10	Matthew 9:27–31	Matthew 8:14–15	Matthew 9:32–34
Luke 5:12–16	John 4:46–53	Matthew 12:9–14	Matthew 9:20–22	Matthew 12:2
Luke 17:11–18		Matthew 20:29–34	Mark 1:29–31	Matthew 15:21–28
		Mark 2:1–12	Mark 5:25–34	Mark 1:21–28
		Mark 3:1–6	Luke 4:38–39	Mark 5:1–20
		Mark 7:31–37	Luke 8:43–48	Mark 7:24–30
		Mark 8:22–26	Luke 9:2, 10:9	Mark 9:14–29
		Mark 10:46–52	Luke 14:1–6	Luke 4:31–37
		Luke 5:17–26		Luke 8:26–39
		Luke 6:6–11		Luke 9:37–43a
		Luke 13:10–17		Luke 11:14–15
		Luke 18:35–43		
		John 5:1–9		
		John 9:1–7		

Discussion
1. If you have any elderly relatives, where do these people live? Do you have very much contact with them? Why or why not?
2. If another member of your family were dying, would you want that person to die at home or in a hospital? Why?

Journal
Do you have any fears about being around the sick or visiting a hospital, care facility, or hospice? If so, try to identify the reasons behind your fears. What can you do to overcome these fears?

Activity
Choose one of the categories of people for whom Jesus cared. Read the cures Jesus worked for these people. Choose one story. Retell it—from the perspective of Jesus, of the sick person, or of bystanders—as a song, skit, poem, cartoon, or news story.

One of Jesus' many healings was the healing of the blind man of Jericho, depicted in this painting by Nicolas Poussin.

Such actions were to be expected from Isaiah's "suffering servant" savior. Thus Matthew includes the following dialogue in his gospel:

When John [the Baptist] heard in prison what the Messiah was doing, he sent word by his disciples and said to him, "Are you the one who is to come, or are we to wait for another?" Jesus answered them, "Go and tell John what you hear and see: the blind receive their sight, the lame walk, the lepers are cleansed, the deaf hear, the dead are raised, and the poor have good news brought to them."

—Matthew 11:2–5

In addition to his own actions of care toward the sick, Jesus gave his apostles the power to heal (cf. Matthew 10:1; Mark 3:14–15). This power continued in full force after Pentecost. Peter and John cured a crippled beggar (cf. Acts 3:1–10). The apostles cured the sick and those disturbed by unclean spirits (cf. Acts 5:12–16). Philip cured the paralyzed and crippled (cf. Acts 8:4–8). Ananias cured Saul of his blindness (cf. Acts 9:17–19). Peter healed a paralyzed man named Aeneas (cf. Acts 9:32–35) and raised a woman who fell sick and died (cf. Acts 9:36–42). By their actions, the apostles called all members of the Church to pray for the sick and show compassion toward them. ■ ■

Discussion

1. What do you think about present-day faith healers? Can prayer really cure a person?
2. Some people say that the gift of healing ended with the apostles. Do you think this is true or not? Are there ways that we, too, have the gift of healing?

Activity

Read the following Bible passages. What does each one say about how we are to treat the sick? What is to be our motivation?

• Matthew 25:31–46   • Luke 10:30–37   • 1 Corinthians 12:12–26

Church History and Care of the Sick

The early Christians became so good at caring for the sick that Constantine abolished all other **hospitals** in A.D. 331, thus making care of the sick the sole responsibility of the Church. The first Christian hospitals were in monasteries. In A.D. 370, for example, Saint Basil of Caesarea established a monastery in Cappadocia that included a hospital and a separate **leprosarium**. Early in the sixth century, Saint Benedict founded the monastery of Monte Cassino, where care of the sick was placed above every other Christian duty. Later in the same century, Saint John the Almsgiver built monastic hospitals for the poor in Alexandria. The manner in which monks cared for their own sick became a model for the laity. The monasteries had an **infirmary** and a **pharmacy** and frequently grew their own medicinal plants.

In 1099, the Catholic Church built a hospital in Jerusalem for sick pilgrims. The hospital was capable of treating two thousand patients. Throughout the Middle Ages, the Benedictine order founded more than two thousand hospitals in Europe so that the sick could find help and the dying could die in peace and dignity.

In 1540, King Henry VIII dissolved all Catholic monasteries in England. As a result, the loss of hospitals in England forced secular authorities to provide for the sick, the injured, and the disabled. From that time on, two systems of hospitals developed side by side—private hospitals, sponsored primarily by the Church, and public or government-run hospitals.

Throughout the centuries, the Church has continued to be a worldwide leader in the care of the sick. Some noteworthy people involved in this work include the following:

- *Saint John of God* started a hospital in Granada in the early sixteenth century. This foundation marked the beginning of the Brothers Hospitaller of Saint John, an order devoted solely to the care of the sick. Today Saint John of God is the patron saint of nurses, hospitals, and the sick.
- *Saint Martin de Porres*, a Dominican lay brother, first worked with the sick in the monastery's infirmary in Lima, Peru, in the early seventeenth century. Later he served those who were sick and poor throughout Lima.
- *Saint Vincent de Paul* laid the foundations for a system of hospitals in Paris in the seventeenth century. He also started professional nursing.
- *Rose Hawthorne Lathrop* founded the Servants of Relief for Incurable Cancer in Hawthorne, New York, and opened the first cancer hospital there in 1900.
- *Mother Teresa of Calcutta* founded the Missionaries of Charity to work with the sick and the dying poor in Calcutta, India. Gradually her communities spread throughout the world, taking care of the sick and the terminally ill. In 1979, Mother Teresa received the Nobel Peace Prize.

In the second half of the nineteenth century, the Church also became the leader in establishing mission hospitals throughout the world. ▪

Saint John of God

hospital *An institution staffed and equipped for the diagnosis and treatment of the sick or injured. Most hospitals today have both inpatient and outpatient facilities.*

leprosarium *A hospital for leprosy patients.*

infirmary *A place where the sick are lodged for care and treatment.*

pharmacy *A place where medicine is dispensed.*

Activity

1. Find out more about the Catholic hospital(s) in your area. When was it founded? How many patients does it treat? Does the hospital have a particular focus or specialty?

2. Find out more about the Medical Missionary Sisters or Maryknoll Missionaries. How do they help care for the sick throughout the world? How can lay people join in the work of these religious communities?

3. View one of the following videos.
   - *Entertaining Angels*   - *Marvin's Room*   - *Lorenzo's Oil*

   Discuss the conflicts and problems the caretakers faced in the movie. What personality traits did they have to have and what actions did they have to take in order to be good caretakers of the sick?

Of Interest

Since 1915, the Catholic Health Association of the United States has existed as a national organization serving Catholic hospitals and long-term care facilities, their sponsoring organizations, and other health and related agencies and services.

---

hospice Originally a guest house for travelers. Today hospices serve as care facilities for individuals who are terminally ill.

prognosis A doctor's forecast of the probable course and termination of a disease.

dispensary A place where medical aid is dispensed.

Anointing of the Sick One of the seven sacraments of the Catholic Church, to be received by a sick or elderly person or by someone who is dying. The three parts of the sacrament include the general inter-cessions for all the sick, the laying on of hands, and the anointing with the Oil of the Sick.

The Hospice Movement

Hospices were originally guest houses or "way stations" intended for pilgrims. Like hospitals, they were sponsored by religious communities. The most famous of these early hospices, the hospice of Saint Bernard, continues to offer shelter for modern-day travelers passing over the Pennine Alps.

Today, hospices are retreats where the dying can live out their last days in a non-institutional, homelike atmosphere. Patients are usually admitted only after they have received a **prognosis** of months or weeks to live. Friends and family can gather around the dying person to help give as much support, comfort, and affection as possible. The hospice team includes doctors, nurses, social workers, consultants, and trained volunteers. Hospices may be in individual homes, hospitals, nursing-care facilities, or separate facilities.

In 1905, the Sisters of Charity founded the Saint James Hospice in London to care for the dying. The modern hospice movement, however, did not really begin until 1967, when Dr. Cicely Saunders founded Saint Christopher's Hospice in London. ▪

The Church Today

Health care is an important part of the Church's social ministry today. Throughout the world, the Catholic Church runs 5,482 hospitals, 16,226 **dispensaries**, 857 leprosariums, and 12,077 homes for the aged. In the United States, there are 587 hospitals, 363 health care centers, and 1,234 homes for special care that are operated by the Catholic Church.

Visiting the sick is considered one of the corporal works of mercy and is thus an important part of the life of every parish. When a person is confined by illness and is unable to go to church for reception of the sacraments, the parish priest, deacon, or Eucharistic minister visits the person. In addition to talking with the sick person, the minister also brings Holy Communion.

Parishes remember their sick each week in the general intercessions at Mass and periodically in celebrations of the Sacrament of the **Anointing of the Sick**—either in the parish or on an individual basis.

The Church's Social Teaching

The Catholic bishops of the United States periodically publish statements and pastoral letters to advise Catholics of the Church's social teaching. The following excerpts from some of these documents deal with four topics related to this chapter: the sick, the elderly, the disabled, and persons with AIDS. As Catholics, we have a responsibility to put the bishops' teachings into practice.

The Sick

- . . . we wish to call all Catholics to a fuller acceptance of their responsibility for their own health and for their share in the healing apostolate of the Church. (#3)
- Because all human beings are created according to God's image, they possess a basic human dignity which calls for the utmost reverence. On the individual level this means a special responsibility to care for one's own health and that of others. On the societal level this calls for responsibility by society to provide adequate health care, which is a basic human right. . . . (#10)
- The works of mercy call Christians to engage themselves in direct efforts to alleviate the misery of the afflicted. . . . (#12)
- . . . we must embrace every chance to help and to liberate, to heal the wounded world as Jesus taught us. Our hands must

Activity

Find out if there are any hospices near you. How does the hospice help patients and their families? Is there any program where members of the community can volunteer at the hospice?

be the strong but gentle hands of Christ, reaching out in mercy and justice, touching individual persons, but also touching the social conditions that hinder the wholeness which is God's desire for humanity. (#13) ■ ■

—United States Bishops, *Health and Health Care* (November 19, 1981).

The Elderly

• Society has come to take a negative view of the elderly. This can be seen in the increasing tendency of families to rely on institutions to care for their elderly members, and in repeated efforts by some government officials to cut services and benefits for the elderly in order to ease the burden of inflation on the rest of society. (#3)

• In rejecting the elderly, we do more than perpetuate injustice. When we reject any stage of human life, we are in effect rejecting a part of ourselves and our connections with the human community. . . . (#5)

• The biblical commandment to "Honor your father and mother" (Dt. 5:16) reminds us that, above all else, the family ought to be a place of love, respect, and caring for the aging members of society. . . . (#6)

• . . . Our first task is to restore to the elderly the dignity and sense of worth which they deserve. (#8) ■

—United States Bishops, *Society and the Aged: Toward Reconciliation* (May 5, 1976).

The Disabled

• It is not enough merely to affirm the rights of persons with disabilities. We must actively work to realize these rights in the fabric of modern society. Recognizing that persons with disabilities have a claim to our respect because they share in the one redemption of Christ, and because they contribute to our society by their activity within it, the Church must become an advocate for and with them. It must work to increase the public's sensitivity toward the needs of [persons with disabilities] and support their rightful demand for justice. Moreover, individuals and organizations at every level within the Church should minister to . . . persons [with disabilities] by serving their personal and social needs. . . . (#11) ■

—United States Bishops, *Pastoral Statement of the United States Bishops on Persons with Disabilities* (November 15, 1978).

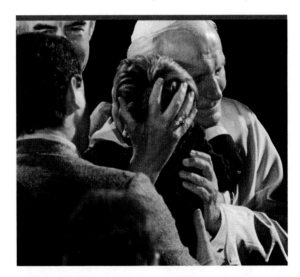

Of Interest

Pope John Paul II graphically demonstrated the call to compassion and care for the sick when he embraced four-year-old AIDS sufferer Brendan O'Rourke at Mission Dolores in San Francisco on September 17, 1987.

 ### Discussion
What are ways that teenagers can share in the healing apostolate of the Church?

 ### Activity
The bishops say that health care is a basic human right, and yet many people in the United States cannot afford health care. Find out whether or not your family has medical insurance and how much it costs per year. Then compare the United States' system of private health care and HMOs to the Canadian system of socialized medicine. Which system seems more in keeping with human dignity?

 ### Discussion
What are possible ways that we—as individuals and as a society—can restore to the elderly their dignity and sense of worth?

 ### Discussion
1. Why are special ramps, parking places, and bathroom facilities for persons with disabilities a matter of justice? How would a person with disabilities fare at your school?

2. How would you react if you saw: (a) non-disabled people parking in a handicapped parking space because they have an unneeded handicapped sticker? (b) non-disabled people sitting in the handicapped companion seats at the movie theater?

Of Interest

In the past, when the priest arrived for the last rites, a bell was rung. The original purpose of this "passing bell" was to keep away any evil that might be lurking about the dying person. The bell was also rung at death, to announce the passing of the soul from this world to the next, and to invite the faithful to pray for its safe passage.

Oil of the Sick Oil blessed by the bishop at the Chrism Mass on Holy Thursday. The oil used is usually olive oil, unless it cannot be obtained. Then another oil derived from plants may be substituted.

The Sacrament of the Anointing of the Sick offers the sick and the elderly the possibility of healing and helps prepare them for death. If possible, this sacrament should be celebrated in the presence of the Christian assembly within Mass.

Persons with AIDS

- Persons with AIDS are not distant, unfamiliar people, the objects of our misled pity and aversion. We must keep them present to our consciousness as individuals and as community, and embrace them with unconditional love. The Gospel demands reverence for life in all circumstances. Compassion—love— toward persons infected with HIV is the only authentic Gospel response. (Part 2, #3)
- Our response to persons with AIDS must be such that we discover Christ in them and they in turn are able to encounter Christ in us. Although this response undoubtedly arises in the context of religious faith, even those without faith can and must look beyond suffering to see the human dignity and goodness of those who suffer. (Part 6, #1) ■

—United States Bishops, *Called to Compassion and Responsibility: A Response to the HIV-AIDS Crisis* (November 30, 1989).

Anointing of the Sick

For many centuries, Catholics perceived the Sacrament of the Anointing of the Sick as the "last rites" of the Church. Known as *Extreme*

Unction, the sacrament was thought to prepare a person for death. Thus, only a person who was in immediate danger of death took part in this sacrament. It was usually celebrated in private, far away from the eyes and participatory prayers of the Church community.

The bishops of Vatican II called for a closer examination of this sacrament and for a revision that reflected its true meaning. The result was the 1972 revised rite, which called the sacrament by a new name: *Anointing of the Sick*. This name reflects the sacrament's dual purpose from biblical times: to offer the sick person the possibility of healing and to prepare the person for death.

According to the revised rite, the following people may receive the Sacrament of the Anointing of the Sick:

- Those whose health is seriously impaired by sickness or old age
- Those about to undergo surgery because of a serious illness
- Elderly people weakened by age, even if no serious illness is present
- Sick children who are sufficiently mature to be comforted by the sacrament

If possible, the sacrament is to be celebrated in the presence of the Christian assembly within Mass—either in church, in the home of the person who is sick, or in the hospital. The liturgy of the sacrament includes the litany of the faithful for the sick, the laying on of hands, and the anointing with the **Oil of the Sick**. Under normal circumstances, the sick person is anointed both on the forehead and on the hands. In case of necessity, however, a single anointing can be given on the forehead (or another part of the body, depending upon the person's physical condition). The sacrament may be repeated if the sick person recovers and falls sick again. ■

 Activity
Find out ways in which your local Church is responding with compassion and love to (a) the elderly, (b) persons with disabilities, and (c) persons with AIDS.

 Activity
Read James 5:14–15. What does the passage say is the purpose of Anointing of the Sick?

Liturgy of Anointing

Litany

(The people respond: "Lord, have mercy.")

Let us pray to God for our brothers and sisters and for all those who devote themselves to caring for them.

Bless [the sick people] and fill them with new hope and strength: Lord, have mercy. (R.)

Relieve their pain: Lord, have mercy. (R.)

Free them from sin and do not let them give way to temptation: Lord, have mercy. (R.)

Sustain all the sick with your power: Lord, have mercy. (R.)

Assist all who care for the sick: Lord, have mercy. (R.)

Give life and health to our brothers and sisters on whom we lay our hands in your name: Lord, have mercy. (R.)

Laying on of Hands

(The priest silently lays his hands on the head of each sick person.)

Prayer over the Oil

(The priest either blesses the oil or, if it has already been blessed, says a prayer of thanksgiving.)

Anointing

Priest (while he anoints the person's forehead): Through this holy anointing may the Lord in his love and mercy help you with the grace of the Holy Spirit.

Person: Amen.

Priest (while he anoints the hands): May the Lord who frees you from sin save you and raise you up.

Person. Amen.

Prayer after Anointing

(The priest chooses one.)

A. General

Father in heaven, through this holy anointing grant our brothers and sisters comfort in their suffering. When they are afraid, give them courage, when afflicted, give them patience, when dejected, afford them hope, and when alone, assure them of the support of your holy people. We ask this through Christ our Lord. Amen.

B. In terminal illness

Lord Jesus Christ, you chose to share our human nature to redeem all people and to heal the sick. Look with compassion upon your servants, whom we have anointed in your name with this holy oil for the healing of their body and spirit. Support them with your power, comfort them with your protection, and give them the strength to fight against evil. Since you have given them a share in your own passion, help them to find hope in suffering, for you are Lord for ever and ever. Amen.

C. In advanced age

God of mercy, look kindly on your servants who have grown weak under the burden of years. In this holy anointing they ask for healing in body and soul. Fill them with the strength of your Holy Spirit. Keep them firm in faith and serene in hope, so that they may give us all an example of patience and joyfully witness to the power of your love. We ask this through Christ our Lord. Amen. ■ ■

—International Committee on English in the Liturgy, *Pastoral Care of the Sick: Rites of Anointing and Viaticum* (Collegeville, MN: The Liturgical Press).

Discussion

1. What are ways that people in your parish minister to the sick?
2. Have you ever attended a celebration of the Sacrament of the Anointing of the Sick that took place in church? What impressed you about the rite?

Activity

Find out when your parish will next celebrate the Sacrament of the Anointing of the Sick. Volunteer to help in one or more of the following ways: drive a person who is sick to church, provide music, help decorate the church, act as an usher or greeter, help with refreshments after Mass.

Visiting the Sick and the Elderly

Hospitals and convalescent homes always need volunteers to provide a variety of personal services. Here are just a few ideas of how you can minister to those who are sick or elderly:

- Help with music and crafts.
- Read to the patients letters from their friends or relatives.
- Read to the patients a short story, the newspaper, or passages from the Bible.
- Take a patient (who is able) out for a drive.
- Talk with the patients about their families and about events that are going on in the world.
- Escort patients to an event at the facility.
- Bring a birthday cake on a patient's birthday.
- Bring useful or silly presents.
- Bring in a pet for the patients to hold. (You must first make sure this is allowed.)

If you feel uncomfortable in the hospital or convalescent setting or if you can't think of anything to say to a person who is sick or elderly, here are some tips that might help:

- Learn the patient's condition in advance. This "homework" will prepare you for what to expect.
- Be sure the person is not too tired to have visitors. (Don't wake up someone in order to talk.)
- Show the patient that you intend to spend some time. Take off your coat, put down your school books, and so forth.

- Sit down so that you are on the same eye level as the sick person. (This position will help you talk to the person as an equal rather than talking down to or treating the person like a child.)
- If you think you may feel awkward talking with the person, bring a bouquet of flowers or balloons, a card, a magazine, or a book to give to the patient. This gift will give you something to talk about right away.
- Encourage the patient to talk. Focus on him or her, not on yourself. Ask questions that need more than a "yes" or "no" answer.
- Talk loudly enough to be heard. (Many elderly people cannot hear as well as they once did.)
- Be responsible for keeping the conversation going. Don't wait for the person to entertain you.
- Communicate nonverbally as well as verbally. Maintain eye contact to show that you are genuinely interested. If appropriate, touch the person's hand or shoulder.
- Don't give advice unless it's asked for.
- Allow the patient to be honest about how he or she is feeling. If patients are grumpy, don't tell them to cheer up.
- Ask if you can do anything for the patient, such as write a letter, make a phone call, water the plants, or get him or her a drink.
- Leave when you see the patient is getting tired. ■

If the patient has a terminal illness, here are some tips that might help you during your visit:

- Accept the person's impending death as well as your own eventual death. If you can do this, you can help the person reduce his or her anxiety about death.

> *The most* **redemptive** *thing one* **can do** *for another is just to* **understand**.
>
> Father Richard Rohr, *Job and the Mystery of Suffering*

Activity

1. Role-play the following situation: Teenager A goes to visit patient B in the hospital. The two people know each other from school.
2. Role-play this situation: Teenager A spends two hours a week at a convalescent home. Teenager A has been assigned to elderly person B. The two are strangers.
3. Role-play this situation: Teenager A finds out that older brother B is HIV-positive.
4. Role-play this situation: Two adults, brother A and sister B, must decide what to do with their father C, who is 86 but still in relatively good health.

- Allow the person to accept the reality of the situation at his or her own pace. Do not withhold or force information upon the person.
- Be available (don't rush right off) and supportive. Use eye contact and physical touch.
- Remember to pay attention to family members you meet. They also need support before and after death occurs. Listen actively to what they say. If you feel comfortable doing so, express your own faith but do not impose your religious beliefs on them. ▪

*W*hen we **feel** another person really **cares**, it's surprising how the **problem**, for the most part, can **fade**. We don't need the answers any more. The mere fact that **someone** is **carrying** the **burden** with us, **walking** with us on the **journey**, for some unbelievable reason—it's not logical at all— **takes care** of much of the **problem**.

Father Richard Rohr, *Job and the Mystery of Suffering*

Journal

Volunteer two hours each week at a local hospital, care facility, or hospice. Keep a record of your experiences in your notebook. What did you give those who were sick or elderly? What did they give you in return? What are some of the things you learned from your experience?

Words to Know

Anointing of the Sick	leprosarium
dispensary	Oil of the Sick
hospice	pharmacy
hospital	prognosis
infirmary	

Review Questions

1. What are reasons some people fear the sick?
2. How can a stereotype and an act of discrimination toward the sick form a vicious circle? Give an example.
3. How did Jesus and the apostles treat others who were sick? Give three examples.
4. What has been the Church's involvement in health care throughout history?
5. What is the purpose of hospices?
6. What are ways the Catholic Church cares for those who are sick today?
7. What are the main parts of the Sacrament of the Anointing of the Sick?
8. What are three suggestions to keep in mind when visiting those who are sick?

Dealing *with* Death

- learn about ancient customs and beliefs, as well as their connection to present-day burial customs;

- study how the early Christians approached death and venerated the martyrs and saints;

- explore America's civil customs surrounding death;

- understand the social rituals (visitation, wake, funeral, and committal service) that accompany death in our society.

Apart from the cross there is no other ladder by which we may get to heaven.

• *Saint Rose of Lima*

C•H•A•P•T•E•R

9

Ancient
Customs
and Beliefs

IN THIS CHAPTER, YOU WILL

- appreciate the importance of respect for the human body, alive or dead;

- make connections between present-day burial customs and those of the past;

- learn about the six ways ancient peoples disposed of their dead;

- explore the reasons behind Egyptian mummies and pyramids;

- study the beliefs and burial customs of the ancient Chinese, Greeks, Etruscans, and Romans;

- learn why the Israelites preferred burial to cremation;

- examine the history of the Church's teaching on cremation;

- consider what being a "temple of the Holy Spirit" means today.

A Question of Respect

Each day Jason and Eddie took public transportation to get to school. They rode the "E-line" to Mason Street, walked two blocks, and then caught the "32" bus, which would drop them off at Mid-City High.

The highlight of the trip was the two-block walk. One of the buildings there had been torn down, and a taller one was going to replace it. Bulldozers and construction crews were busy digging deeper for the new foundation. Jason and Eddie always liked to stop for a minute to see how things were progressing. This particular morning, however, the bulldozers were silent. The only sounds were those of angry protesters standing outside the fence.

"What's going on?" Jason asked Eddie as they approached the scene.

"I guess you didn't watch the news last night," Eddie replied. "The bulldozers uncovered an old Native American burial ground. Members of an Indian Rights Group went to city hall and got an order to halt construction. They, with anthropologists from the university, will excavate the site and then recommend what to do with the skeletons and remains."

Jason, whose father was in construction, could not believe the amount of money the company would lose each day its crew and equipment sat idle. "Can't they just dig up the bones and donate them to the university or to the museum?" he asked.

"It's a question of respect," Eddie answered. "How would you like it if your grandparents' remains were on display in a museum or being studied by students?"

Jason thought about this for a moment. "It's not the same," he argued. "These people died hundreds of years ago. No one, not even the Indian Rights Group, knows who was buried here. In fact, no one even knew this was a Native American burial ground."

"But now that they know, things are different," Eddie said. "The Native Americans believe a burial ground is always sacred. They are the descendants of those people, even if they can't put names on them. Proper tribal procedures have to be followed. And then the bones need to be reburied in the closest Native American burial ground."

Jason shook his head as they kept on walking. It still seemed ridiculous to disrupt the present and to hold up the future, all because of the distant past. ▪

Discussion

1. Elaborate on Jason's position: Human remains have no right to halt progress or interrupt our lives today. Then tell whether or not you agree with this position.

2. Elaborate on Eddie's position: The dead and their remains have a right to be treated with respect. Then tell whether or not you agree with this position.

True Progress

Some people believe that progress means marching ever forward and forgetting about the past. Others think that we should study history to learn from it and to avoid making the same mistakes. Death itself seems to be the "Great Divide" between the past, present, and future. Those who die no longer have a future on this earth, nor do they belong to our present reality. Their remains (regardless of what we believe about an afterlife) are now relegated to history.

Respect for the remains of one's loved ones may be found in most cultures throughout history. Some cultures based this respect on fear of the dead; some based it on love for the person and the person's memory. Nevertheless, the concept that we should have respect for human remains continues into our century. Throughout the United States, it is a misdemeanor to vandalize a **cemetery**; it is a felony to dig up a grave without a permit.

Although our lives today are very different from those of ancient people, in some ways they are the same. Despite our modern-day technology and scientific achievements, there is nothing new about the way we dispose of our dead. All our present methods of **interment** have their roots in the past. Thus it is important to understand the history of funeral rites and burial customs. Hopefully such knowledge will lead you to a greater appreciation and respect for the humans who have come before us.

What are your views on funeral rites, cemeteries, and human remains? In your notebook, write your responses to the survey above. ■

Attitude Survey	I agree	I disagree	I'm not sure
Most ancient peoples didn't care what happened to their dead.			
The people who came before us are not important.			
Modern-day funeral customs have nothing to do with those of ancient peoples.			
If a person is cremated, his or her body will not rise on the last day.			
Respect for dead bodies begins with the respect we show our own body and the bodies of others.			

cemetery Means "land of those who are sleeping." According to the law, a cemetery is any place that contains six or more human bodies. It may include a burial park for earth interments, a mausoleum for crypt or vault interments, or a crematory and columbarium for cinerary interment.

interment Disposition of human remains by inurnment, entombment, earth burial, or burial at sea.

Respect for the remains of those who have died may be found in most cultures throughout history. Today, throughout the United States, it is a misdemeanor to vandalize a cemetery; it is a felony to dig up a grave without a permit.

Activity
What do you know about the people who once lived where you live now? Go to the library or city hall, and see what you can find out.

burial *Placement of human remains in a grave.*

tomb *A grave or space for the burial of the dead.*

grave *Space of ground, usually in a burial park, used for burial.*

cremation *Burning the body of a deceased person; reducing the body of a deceased person to ashes.*

cremains *Human remains after incineration by fire.*

ossuary *A container for the bones of the dead.*

embalming *The process of preparing a dead body for burial. During the embalming process, body fluids are replaced with preserving chemicals.*

coffin *Another term for casket.*

entombment *Placement of human remains in a crypt or vault.*

A Practical Problem

For people of every age, death was not just a topic for philosophical discussion. It was an immediate, practical problem. What, for example, should be done with the dead body? How should it be disposed of?

Archaeological evidence tells us that ancient people disposed of their dead in a variety of ways. The oldest form of interment was cave **burial**. Forty-four thousand years ago, Neanderthal peoples buried their dead in the same cave in which they lived. With the dead they buried food and flint tools. They laid out the bodies in an east-west orientation, with the feet toward the rising sun.

Before burial, Cro-Magnon peoples (35,000–10,000 years ago) covered their dead with red ocher. They buried shells, necklaces, clothes, tools, and animals with the dead. Sometimes the head of the person was buried in a place separate from the body. This practice may have been meant to discourage the dead from returning.

The second form of interment was earth burial. Before 4000 B.C., massive stone **tombs** were built throughout Spain, the British Isles, Scandinavia, Germany, Holland, and France. These tombs were communal **graves**, containing anywhere from five to one hundred bodies buried over many years. Some archaeologists have proposed that these tombs

represented the womb of an earth goddess. The people may have believed that if the dead were put inside that womb, they would be reborn.

A third method of disposing of the dead consisted of burning the body. **Cremation** seems to have begun in Europe during the Stone Age. Cremation did not completely dispose of the dead; often the remaining ashes and bones (**cremains**) were placed in **ossuaries** and then buried.

The simplest way of disposing of the dead was to leave the corpse exposed to the elements. The body may have been left on the ground, in trees, on rocks, or on special platforms. The ancient Persians, for example, exposed their dead to scavenger birds. The ancient Chinese left the dead in rock caves or in the jungle, protecting them only slightly with a covering of leaves or brush.

Water burial was perhaps the second easiest way to dispose of the dead. Sometimes the corpse was thrown in a river or lake. In some cultures that practiced water burial, the dead were wrapped to protect them from fish and then weighted with stones. Water burial was prevalent among island peoples and those who had to deal with death while at sea.

The most elaborate forms of disposal involved preservation of the entire body or parts of the body. Methods included smoke-drying, treatment of the body with mineral or vegetable preservatives, and **embalming**. After preservation, the body was usually placed in one or more **coffins**. The coffin was then laid to rest in a house-like tomb. Both the ancient Egyptians and the Aztecs of Mexico **entombed** deceased rulers in elaborate pyramids.

The Great Pyramid, just outside Cairo, contains 2,300,000 blocks of stone, each weighing about two and one-half tons. The pyramid measures 750 feet per side and is as high as a fifty-story building. In the Mexican temple town of Teotihuacán, the tombs below the mammoth pyramids contain painted walls, realistic clay figures, flowers, fruits, and other burial gifts.

Pyramids in Mexico and ancient Egypt, such as those pictured above in Giza, held the entombed remains of deceased rulers.

The last form of disposal of the dead was endocannibalism—the ritualistic eating of the dead person, usually including the brain. The eating was regarded as an act of piety toward the dead. It was thought to be a way for the living to absorb and carry on the dead person's power and personality.

Sometimes an entire culture would dispose of its dead by only one of these six methods. Some cultures used more than one method simultaneously. Still other cultures practiced one method for a while and gradually switched to another one. The method chosen by a particular society almost always reflected its belief system concerning the afterlife or fear of the dead. To get a better understanding of the connection between death customs and beliefs, we must take a closer look at specific cultures. Among those you will study in this chapter are the Egyptians, Chinese, Greeks, Etruscans, Romans, and the peoples of the Old Testament. ▪

The Egyptians

The elaborate efforts of the Egyptians to preserve the dead stemmed from their beliefs about death and the afterlife. They thought that at death, a person's *ka* (spirit) left the body. For a person to be reborn in the afterlife, the spirit and body had to be reunited. Reunion would only take place if the spirit could recognize the body; thus it was imperative that the body be preserved from decay. If the body had decomposed, the spirit would roam forever, searching for a body that no longer existed.

Not everyone in Egyptian society, however, was destined for immortality. Only the rich "merited" preservation by an elaborate mummification procedure. The bodies of the poor were not embalmed. Instead, they were merely washed and then buried directly in the sand.

Mummification was a religious ritual that lasted seventy days. While a priest chanted, embalmers used hooks (somewhat like crochet hooks) to draw out the brain, bit by bit, through the nostrils. Then the embalmers cut open the left side to remove the stomach, liver, intestines, pancreas, and genital organs. (The heart remained with the body.) They rinsed out the abdominal cavity with palm wine and filled it with myrrh and cassia. Then they shaved the body and dehydrated it in natron, a natural soda. After washing and anointing the body with scented oils, the embalmers wrapped it tightly in hundreds of yards of resin-soaked linen. Between the layers, they put amulets inscribed with magical incantations to protect the wearer during his or her journey in the afterlife.

On top of the wrappings, the embalmers then placed a stylized mask that resembled the face of the deceased and that would allow the spirit to recognize its body. Such masks were commonly made of cloth covered with stucco or plaster, which was then painted. The mummy was placed in an elaborately decorated coffin. If the person was important, three coffins, fitted together each inside one another, were used. These coffins were then carried in procession to the place of burial.

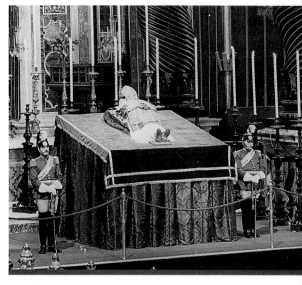

Of Interest

The Vatican has some similar burial customs regarding a dead pope. When a pope dies, his body is placed in a cypress coffin along with medals struck during his pontificate. This coffin is placed inside a second coffin made of lead, which contains the death certificate and the pope's coat of arms. Then this coffin is placed inside a third coffin, made of oak. Pictured above is the public viewing of the body of Pope John XXIII (1881–1963) after his death.

Of Interest

Today, the Dayak of Borneo believe it is essential to treat the dead body with great respect until the flesh has completely decayed. Only then will the soul detach itself from the body and go to its afterlife. When someone dies, the Dayak wash and prepare the body. Then they place it on a funeral platform near the village. The body remains there until the flesh has decayed. As people see the body decompose, they gradually become separated from the deceased.

Discussion

How do each of the six methods of disposition show (or do not show) respect for the dead body?

Of Interest

sarcophagus An ornate and elaborate outer casket, usually made of marble, granite, or heavy metal. The body may be placed directly inside it, or the entire casket may be placed inside the sarcophagus.

The funeral procession varied, depending upon the location of the pyramid. Sometimes oxen pulled a boat carrying the coffin up the river (or a specially built canal) to the pyramid. Behind the mummy's boat came another boat with a chest containing the preserved vital organs. On other occasions, servants carried the coffin and its organ chest in a procession. Heading the procession were other servants who carried flowers and trays of food, oils, jars of water and wine, embalmed pets, furniture, swords, and necklaces—indeed, everything the person would need for the afterlife. Directly in front of the coffin and organ chest came hired mourners, dressed in the blue-gray color of mourning. According to custom, they smeared their faces with dust and mud, beat their heads, and wailed loudly during the procession.

When the mummy arrived at the tomb, a jackal-masked priest (impersonating Anubis, the divine embalmer) held the coffin upright. He ritually opened the mouth of the dead person, thus symbolically restoring its ability to move, talk, and eat.

The mummy, along with food, furniture, and so forth was placed in a **sarcophagus** in a multichambered, richly decorated tomb that was tunneled underground. Next to the coffin were placed papyrus scrolls containing verses from the *Egyptian Book of the Dead*. These verses were meant to act as a road map, guiding the soul past any obstacles on its journey in quest of reunion with the *ka*, or spirit.

Usually animals were sacrificed at the tomb. Sometimes, for an important ruler, his wives and favorite slaves were also killed and buried with him so his every need in the afterlife would be met. After the burial ceremonies were completed, people stayed outside the tomb and had a feast celebrating the creation of a new god.

The tomb of King Tutankhamen (1340 B.C.), a minor pharaoh who died when he was eighteen, gives us a tantalizing hint of the elaborateness of Egyptian funerary rites. Tutakhamen's embalmers wrapped each toe and finger separately. His funeral mask and one of his coffins were made of gold. Buried with him were 143 different amulets and an astonishing treasure of diadems, rings, necklaces, bracelets, and pendants. ■

Archaeologist Howard Carter, after discovering the tomb of King Tutankhamen in 1922, carefully removes the wrappings and exposes the body of the minor pharaoh. Found in the burial chamber were treasures of jewelry, furniture, clothes, weapons, a chariot, and paintings on the walls, such as the one pictured here of King Tut between Anubis, the jackel-headed god of embalming, and Hathor, the goddess of West. Perhaps the greatest treasure was that of the solid gold funerary mask, found on the king's head.

Journal
If you could take three things with you to the afterlife, what would you take? Why?

The Chinese

The ancient Chinese consistently buried their dead. Wealthy families also buried dogs, horses, and other humans with their dead. Some emperors went to their graves with 300 servants. These customs stemmed from a belief that dead ancestors should be worshiped. Neglect of the ancestors could cause sickness or disasters to living family members.

When a member of a family died, mourners dressed in white. The coffin was elaborately decorated with gold and flowers and then placed on a litter and carried through the streets. After the burial, the family kept a memorial shrine to the dead person in the house and worshiped there daily. ■

The Greeks

The ancient Greeks considered earth burial important; otherwise, the dead spirits would never find peace. Around 1000 B.C., however, the Greeks began to cremate their dead. This practice may have been a health measure; it also may have been a way to protect the body from putrefying or from being desecrated as the body of Hector was dishonored by Achilles. Not all Greeks merited the "right" of cremation. Suicide victims, infants who did not yet have teeth, and persons struck by lightning (a sign of disfavor with the gods) could not be cremated. This prohibition suggests the Greeks may have thought that cremation and burial affected the dead differently.

The Etruscans

Outside Caere, Italy, the Etruscans built an elaborate City of the Dead in the fifth century B.C. Because they thought life after death was similar to life on earth, they constructed each tomb as a house, with rooms and elaborate wall paintings. People brought food daily for the dead to eat. On special days, people sacrificed animals, letting the blood sink into the earth. This practice was based on the belief that the dead needed blood in order to live on in the afterlife. The Etruscans also staged "funeral games" to honor the dead. The losers of these chariot races, wrestling matches, discus throws, and so forth were killed to provide enough blood to appease the dead.

The Romans

The ancient Romans buried some of their dead and cremated others. The Laws of the Twelve Tables (mid-fifth century B.C.) forbade both the burial and the burning of bodies within the city, showing that both customs were then practiced.

In ancient Roman burials, often a death mask resembling the deceased was placed over his or her face. Such masks, made of wax, were usually fashioned right on the face of the corpse to assure their likeness to the dead person. Sometimes the mask was worn by a hired actor, who accompanied the funeral procession to the site of burial. Patrician families saved the masks as ancestral portraits and displayed them on ceremonial occasions. During the last month of the Roman calendar, the people held a state funeral, known as *Parentalia*, which honored deceased ancestors. One of the rites performed on that day was the repairing and decorating of ancestral graves.

Romans probably received the custom of cremation from the Greeks. Roman poet Virgil said it was used before the foundation of Rome; another poet, Ovid, mentioned that the body of Remus (one of the founders of Rome) was cremated. Cremation reflected Roman belief that the soul alone lived on after death. Cremation was a way to release the soul from the body. Often a bird was released as the body burned, to symbolize the upward flight of the spirit. The ashes were preserved in decorated urns. Final **inurnment** took place in specially built **columbaria**.

Of Interest

Sometimes the Romans disposed of their dead by a practice called *os resectum*. Before cremation, they cut off a finger from the corpse. The body was burned, but the finger was saved. Funeral rites were held for the finger, which was then burned.

inurnment *Placing cremated remains in an urn and placing it in a niche.*

columbarium *A building, room, or other space containing niches for inurnment of cremated remains.*

Activity

How many of your ancestors can you name? Trace your family lineage back three generations. Try to include all children, where these people lived, and where they are buried or inurned.

The Romans held a similar belief to that of the Etruscans about the need to appease the dead with blood. At the funeral of Brutus in 264 B.C., three pairs of gladiators (professional combatants) competed in the amphitheater. During the time of Julius Caesar (d. 44 B.C.), the wild popularity of these funeral games swelled the ranks of the gladiators to 300 pairs. Gladiators were chiefly slaves and criminals. Most gladiators fought with shields, armor, and swords. Some fought with short swords, lassoes, and tridents. The battles were fought on foot, on horseback, or in chariots. If a gladiator survived several funeral games, he became famous and could be discharged from further service. If a gladiator was wounded, the spectators themselves decided whether he should die or be granted mercy.

Old Testament peoples

The Israelites regarded death as the ultimate enemy of God. Death was the climax of all earthly pain and sorrow, the final estrangement from God. Death was seen as punishment for original, as well as personal, sin. Thus sin was to be avoided at all costs. A person who died early was thought to have sinned. Israelites could save themselves from early death by practicing virtue, doing good deeds, and giving alms to the poor. Indeed, they believed that long life was the most tangible proof of God's favor. ▪

Beliefs about death and the afterlife (or lack of it) were related to the Israelites' understanding of the human person. A human being was thought to be an animated body, not a composition of material body and immaterial soul. As long as the body (or the bones) remained, the soul continued to exist in a land of the dead called *Sheol*. In Sheol, the soul continued to feel what happened to the body but was incapable of any living response. Once the body decayed completely, the soul, too, became extinct.

These beliefs made it important for the Israelites to inter the dead properly. Proper interment meant earth burial or entombment, not cremation (as was practiced by many of their neighbors, who did not believe in the same God). As a rule, the

Of Interest

As people converted to Christianity, gladiator shows began to fall into disfavor. Emperor Constantine tried to abolish the games in A.D. 325, without much effect. The shows, which were often held in places such as the Coliseum in Rome, were finally abolished by Honorius (A.D. 393–434).

Activity

Search through the Book of Genesis to find out how old Abraham, Isaac, Jacob, and Joseph are reported as being when they died. What message were the authors of Genesis conveying by these ages?

Israelites did not embalm their dead; the exceptions to this were Jacob and Joseph, who both died while the Israelites were in Egypt (cf. Genesis 50:2–3, 26).

Immediately after death, the nearest relatives closed the dead person's eyes and embraced the body. The corpse was washed and then dressed in the clothes he or she had used in life. A soldier, for example, was buried in armor, with his sword under his head and his shield under his body. The body was laid out in the best room in the house; friends and professional mourners came to grieve with the family members.

The Israelites rarely used coffins. Instead, the corpse was carried to the tomb or grave on an open **bier**. The corpse was placed in the grave or tomb, either drawn together in a fetal position and laid on the left side or stretched out straight on its back. Interment took place either in burial sites outside the city walls, in tombs in family gardens, or in caves carved in hillsides.

The oldest graves were single or connected caves. The entrance to such a cave was blocked by a stone. During the Bronze Age, people of the Old Testament used shaft graves. Entrance to the underground cave was a perpendicular shaft or tunnel, which, after the burial, would be filled with rubble. Later, burial caves had burial ledges for the dead. Previous remains were swept away into a bone pit to make room for the recent dead. During the Greco-Roman period, underground tombs had several chambers which were provided with niches or shelves. If a niche was reused, the previous remains were put into an ossuary and labeled with the name of the dead person.

Sometimes the Israelites buried their dead with articles used in life: dishes, bowls, perfume containers, lamps, weapons, and jewelry. This practice may have come from the neighboring Canaanites, who equipped their

The oldest graves were single or connected caves. The entrance to such a cave was blocked by a large stone.

dead for the afterlife. In one tomb found by archaeologists in Canaan, a rich woman had been buried with bronze cauldrons, carnelian beads, cosmetic and perfume containers, lamps, incense boats, and drinking bowls. There is no evidence that the Israelites followed this custom to express belief in an afterlife; rather, they were merely following the customs of the area in which they lived.

The Israelites believed firmly that cremation was a form of sacrilege. Only animals, enemies, and criminals could be cremated. The only example of cremation in the Old Testament is found in 1 Samuel. After Saul and his sons died in battle, the Philistines mutilated and displayed their bodies. To prevent further dishonor to the remains, the men of Jabesh-Gilead burned them. ▪ ▪

bier *A moveable platform or framework upon which a casket is placed for easy movement.*

Activity
Compare the two accounts of the disposition of Saul's body. Why do you think the accounts differ?
- 1 Samuel 31:8–13
- 1 Chronicles 10:8–14

Discussion
Review the burial customs of each culture presented in this chapter. How did the burial customs of each reflect its beliefs about death and the afterlife?

Of Interest

Across the United States, cremation has become an increasingly popular choice in funerals. According to 1990 statistics from the Cremation Association of North America, 20 percent chose cremation. According to the same source, cremation was used in up to 40 percent of the funerals in some states.

Of Interest

To show its disdain for the condemned heretic John Wycliffe, the Church Council of Constance (1414–1418) ordered that his body be dug up (forty-four years after his death) and cremated and the ashes thrown into a river.

ecclesiastical burial
Interment according to the rites of the Church. All Catholics in good standing have the right to ecclesiastical burial, as do catechumens, unbaptized children whose parents intended to have them baptized, and baptized members of other Christian Churches (unless it is considered to be against their will).

The Church and Cremation

The early Christians tended to dispose of their dead according to local custom. Around Jerusalem, the Christians followed the Jewish custom of earth burial or entombment. In Egypt, the Christians practiced mummification. But the Christians in Rome never adopted the practice of cremation.

There are perhaps two reasons for this. First, cremation was a practice of those with non-Christian beliefs (for example, the belief in many gods). Burial, on the other hand, was a common Jewish practice, and many early Christians had been Jews before. Second, cremation was thought to show disrespect for the dead body. According to Origen, a Greek theologian and biblical scholar, burial gave the body "due honors." From the viewpoint of Tertullian, cremation was a cruel "punishment," something the body of a Christian did not deserve.

Many people have erroneously thought that the Catholic Church opposed cremation because of its belief in the resurrection of the body. In times of persecution, the enemies of Christianity made sure the bodies of Christian martyrs were cremated. Church historian

Eusebius described a second-century persecution in Lyon in his book *Ecclesiastical History*:

> After torture and execution the bodies of the martyrs were guarded by soldiers, so that their friends could not bury them. Finally after some days the bodies were burned and reduced to ashes and swept into the Rhine so that no trace of them might appear on the earth. And this they did as if able to conquer God and prevent their new birth, "that," as they said, "they may have no hope of a resurrection."

The early Christians, by and large, never believed that destruction of the body by fire would prevent resurrection.

While the early Church resisted cremation as a practice of those with other beliefs, the Catholic Church of the Middle Ages and the nineteenth century opposed it because of the anticlerical and anti-ecclesiastical beliefs of some of those who practiced cremation. Because cremation was thought to be a means of subverting the faithful, the Church legislated against it. In 1300, Pope Boniface VIII supported burial as normative Catholic practice and threatened to excommunicate anyone who did otherwise. In 1886, Pope Leo XIII forbade Catholics to join cremation societies and to request cremation for themselves or others. Catholics who violated these decrees were to be denied burial by the Church. In 1892, the Church officially excluded violators from receiving the last sacraments.

The 1917 *Code of Canon Law* forbade cremation in its Canon 1203. Other canons stated that any person requesting cremation could not receive **ecclesiastical burial** or have a requiem Mass celebrated on his or her anniversary of death.

In 1963, the Church modified its position on cremation. The "Instruction with Regard to the Cremation of Bodies" (issued by the Congregation for the Doctrine of the Faith) upheld the traditional practice of Christian burial but said that cremation could be permitted for serious reasons, provided it did not involve any contempt of the Church or any attempt to deny the doctrine of the resurrection of the body. A person who was cremated could receive the Last Rites and be given ecclesiastical burial. A priest could say prayers for the dead at the crematorium but not conduct full liturgical ceremonies there. The cremains were to be treated with respect and placed in consecrated ground. ■

This new opinion is expressed in the *Code of Canon Law* (1983).

> The Church earnestly recommends that the pious custom of burying the bodies of the dead be observed; it does not, however, forbid cremation unless it has been chosen for reasons which are contrary to Christian teaching.
>
> —Canon 1176.3, *Code of Canon Law, Latin-English Edition* (Washington DC: Canon Law Society of America, 1983)

The new opinion is also found in the *Order of Christian Funerals* and the *Catechism of the Catholic Church*. In 1997, the Vatican granted permission for funeral Masses to be celebrated in the presence of cremains, provided the local bishop approves of the practice. ■

Temple of the Holy Spirit

Respect for a dead person's body is a logical extension of Catholic teaching that one's body is holy. The body is holy, first, because God created us "in the divine image" (Genesis 1:27). Second, the body is a dwelling place of God. We are filled with God's own life and presence.

For the Jewish people, the dwelling place of God on earth was the Temple in Jerusalem. Jesus used the analogy of the Temple when speaking about his own death and resurrection. "I am able to destroy the temple of God and to build it in three days" (Matthew 26:61). The same destiny awaits all followers of Jesus. As Saint Paul writes, "Do you not know that you are God's temple and that God's Spirit dwells in you? If anyone destroys God's temple, God will destroy that person. For God's temple is holy, and you are that temple" (1 Corinthians 3:16–17).

Catholics Believe

The Church permits cremation, provided that it does not demonstrate a denial of faith in the resurrection of the body. (Cf. CIC, can. 1176 § 3.) (Catechism, #2301)

The human body is a temple of the Holy Spirit.

Journal

When you die, do you want your body to be buried in the ground, entombed in a mausoleum, or cremated? Why?

Activity

1. Obtain a copy of the *Order of Christian Funerals*. Look up each of the following sections concerning cremation. Then prepare a summary of your findings.
   - General Introduction, #19
   - #204
   - #207
   - #212
2. Consult the *Catechism of the Catholic Church* or a Catholic encyclopedia to find out more about the doctrine of the resurrection of the body. What does this belief mean?

Catholics Believe

The human body shares in the dignity of "the image of God": it is a human body precisely because it is animated by a spiritual soul, and it is the whole human person that is intended to become, in the body of Christ, a temple of the Spirit. (Cf. 1 Cor 6:19–20; 15:44–45.) (Catechism, #364)

For these reasons, the Catholic Church teaches that the human body is the temple of the Holy Spirit. We strengthen God's life within us whenever we receive the sacraments and participate in the life of the Christian community. So what does this teaching have to do with you? Simply this: you need to treat your own body and the bodies of others with respect. This respect should not start after death but should begin now.

Respect is an attitude. But it is also expressed through actions. In addition to dressing modestly, we have a responsibility to keep ourselves strong and healthy. We have a Christian duty to eat the right foods, get enough sleep and exercise, and have regular medical checkups. We also have a responsibility to protect the safety of others and help them maintain their health. In particular, four areas involving respect for the body deserve additional mention.

The first area that may be disrespectful of the body is hazing, or the initiation rites that some older teenagers force on younger teens. Although meant to be fun, hazing sometimes includes hitting, kicking, public ridicule, humiliation, getting someone drunk, stuffing people into trash cans or automobile trunks, or pulling down someone's pants. Such behavior, even when it is physically harmless, shows disrespect and may hurt someone psychologically. When hazing gets out of hand, the result can be bodily pain, even death.

The second area is eating disorders. Many teenagers dislike their bodies and try, through eating or not eating, to change them. Anorexia is a habit in which someone eats little or nothing. In essence, the person starves his or her body. Bulimia is a pattern of stuffing oneself and then vomiting in order not to gain weight. Compulsive overeating is a pattern of eating too much all the time. These behaviors show disrespect for one's body and can lead to death. ▪

Drug abuse is the third area that shows disrespect of the body. Despite national campaigns to the contrary, more and more teenagers are trying marijuana, cocaine, and other types of illegal drugs. Almost no one thinks that he or she will get "hooked" but often that is what happens. Soon the person needs higher doses to get the desired effect. Sometimes the dosage taken becomes lethal. Even where no addiction occurs, "recreational" drug use can lead to death. Many people are killed each year in drug-related fights and shootings.

We need to treat our bodies and the bodies of others with respect. We have a responsibility to keep ourselves strong and healthy.

Journal

1. On a scale of 1 to 10 (with 10 as the highest), how do you feel about your body? Do you like the way you look? Are you satisfied with how much you weigh?
2. On a scale of 1 to 10, how well do you treat your own body with respect?
3. On a scale of 1 to 10, how well do you treat the bodies of others with respect?

The fourth area is abuse of sex. The Catholic Church teaches that full sexual expression belongs only in marriage. Therefore, the Church has always opposed premarital sex, seeing it as, among other things, disrespectful of the body. But both promiscuous sex and date rape take disrespect a step further. In promiscuous sex, a person has sex with many different people in a short period. There's no love involved and no consideration for the feelings of the other. In date rape, one "friend" forces sex on the other. There's no respect for the person's right to say "no." ▪

Activity

1. Search through newspapers and news magazines for recent examples of hazing, eating disorders, drug abuse, or abuse of sex that led to death. Present your findings in class. Then discuss what could have been done to prevent each situation from going so far.
2. Make a list of practical ways that teenagers can grow in respect for their own bodies.
3. Make a list of practical ways that teenagers can grow in respect for the bodies of others.

Words to Know

bier	embalming
burial	entombment
cemetery	grave
coffin	interment
columbarium	inurnment
cremains	ossuary
cremation	sarcophagus
ecclesiastical burial	tomb

Review Questions

1. What are the six ways ancient peoples disposed of their dead?
2. Why did the Egyptians mummify their dead?
3. What beliefs and customs did the Chinese have regarding dead ancestors?
4. Why did the Etruscans and Romans stage bloody funeral games and gladiator fights?
5. Why was it important to the Jews of the Old Testament to bury the dead properly?
6. Compare the burial customs of the Jews and those of the early Christians. How were they the same? How were they different?
7. What are two reasons the Church opposed cremation?
8. What does present Canon Law say about cremation?
9. Why does the Catholic Church teach that the human body is the temple of the Holy Spirit?

C•H•A•P•T•E•R

10

Christian Customs *and* Beliefs

IN THIS CHAPTER, YOU WILL

- realize the importance of remembering the dead through mementos and keepsakes;

- study the burial of Jesus and the customs of the Jews at that time;

- learn how the early Christians approached death;

- explore the underground world of the catacombs and what they meant to Christians of the third through fifth centuries;

- examine the origin and history of the Church's cult of relics;

- appreciate the art related to death;

- consider ways that modern parish churches remember the dead;

- articulate ways you want to be remembered by others after your death.

The Steamer Trunk Mystery

Of Interest

Father Damien (Joseph de Veuster) went to the Molokai leper colony as a missionary in 1873. For sixteen years, he served as priest, doctor, carpenter, priest, and undertaker to the lepers. In 1884, he contracted leprosy himself; five years later he died. He was proclaimed "venerable" by Pope Paul VI in 1977.

Mornings always seemed to bring something new to the Castañeda household.

"Hey, listen to this," Maritza said, her eyes glued to the morning paper. "The county coroner found a musty old trunk in the basement of his office. It had just been sitting there for 26 years."

"Yeah, so?" Isabel replied sleepily as she took some milk out of the refrigerator.

"Well, the coroner found out that the trunk was part of the estate of Godwin Swift, a lawyer who died without a will. Actually, the trunk belonged to the lawyer's father, Dr. Sidney Swift, the doctor who had treated Father Damien."

Isabel came to the table and sat down. "Wasn't he the priest who went to Molokai to help the lepers?"

"That's him, all right," Maritza affirmed. "He's a candidate for sainthood, and the coroner thought the trunk might contain some of his things."

"Did it?"

"It says here he found a guava wood walking stick, a hand-carved pipe, a shiny black lului nut watch fob, and glass-plate negatives showing Father Damien on his deathbed."

"Then the mystery's solved," Isabel said, taking a bite of cereal.

"Nope," Maritza said. "Here's the real mystery: No one knows who has the right to the trunk and its contents."

"If Father Damien's almost a saint, shouldn't his things belong to the church in Hawaii?"

"The coroner thinks so, but the lawyers involved say they have a legal duty to locate possible heirs. Meanwhile, the auction house wants to sell the things to the highest bidder. It says here the trunk and its contents might be worth thousands."

"Maybe so, but I don't think they should be sold. They're an important part of Church history. They should be preserved, or something, for posterity."

"I agree," Maritza said as she put aside the paper. "But we'll just have to see what the court says." ▪

Discussion

What do you think should be done with Father Damien's things? Why?

Important Keepsakes

Death often changes the value we place on things. A simple watch, a photograph of the deceased, a piece of clothing—suddenly these items become important keepsakes. While the monetary value of these items may be insignificant, their sentimental value is priceless. After all, they are mementos of our loved one who has died; they help us hang on to the past and keep the dead close. ■

No one can study the history of Christian burial customs without noticing the importance of preserving the memory of those who have died. Just think of some of the memorial customs in your own life. Perhaps your family has written the name of its dead members in a Bible. Was your town library or a branch of your local hospital built "in memory" of someone who died? Perhaps you have a painted portrait of an ancestor or a locket of that person's hair. ■ ■

In this chapter, you will see how these customs were handed down to us from the Christians of earlier centuries. Before beginning, write down in your notebook your responses to the Attitude Survey.

Early Christian Burial Customs

Much of what we know about the burial customs of the Jews in the time of Jesus comes from the New Testament. For example, after John the Baptist was beheaded, his disciples came and buried his body (cf. Matthew 14:12). When someone died, the family hired wailers and instrumentalists to gather around the deathbed (cf. Matthew 9:23). Burial took place the same day the person died (cf. Acts 5:5–6, 10), unless that day was the Sabbath.

Attitude Survey	I agree	I disagree	I'm not sure
We should not forget those who have died.			
Artistic expressions have always been an important way to remember and honor the dead.			
It is important to visit the graves of dead family members.			
I like churches that have many different statues and paintings of the saints.			
Relics of the saints should be treated with respect.			

Of Interest

Christians are not the only ones who memorialize the dead. The Taj Mahal outside Agra, India, is a seventeenth-century mausoleum built by Mughal Emperor Shah Jahan in memory of his wife, Arjumand Banu Begam, who died in childbirth. The building, with its bulbous double dome, parapets, pinnacles, and domed kiosks is considered one of the seven most beautiful buildings in the world.

 Discussion
Audio and video recordings have made it possible for us to see and hear people long after they are dead. Name some of your favorite songs that are associated with a composer or singer who is dead. Name some of your favorite movies or TV shows that are associated with a director, actor, or actress who is dead. In what way do these people "live on" after death?

 Journal
What items do you have that remind you of someone who has died? How do you feel when you see these items? How valuable are they to you?

 Activity
Make a list of the ways the dead are remembered in your town or city (statue, plaque, painting, name on building, street name, and so forth). Then prepare a short report about one of these people.

Of Interest

The Basilica of the Holy Sepulcher, located in the Christian quarter of Jerusalem, is visited frequently by pilgrims. Under the basilica is the tomb where Christ is said to be buried. Originally a cave in a small hillside, it had an outer chamber and an inner burial chamber. In the second chamber, pilgrims can see a slab covered by a piece of marble, where the body of Jesus is said to have lain.

shroud *A white sheet or robe-like garment that may be worn by the deceased.*

wake *A watch kept over the dead, which may take the form of visitation, calling hours, or shiva. The new Order of Christian Funerals calls for a vigil service as part of the wake, including prayers and Scripture readings.*

pallbearer *A person who helps carry the casket to and from its place in church and at the cemetery. An honorary pallbearer escorts the casket but does not actually carry it.*

eulogy *A speech that praises an individual who has died.*

The Jews had no undertakers or formal cemeteries. Family or friends would wash the body, anoint it with oils and perfumes, bandage the hands and feet, wrap the corpse in a linen **shroud,** and cover the face with a cloth. Entombment might be in a family garden or in one of Palestine's abundant caves. (The law said that human burial had to be at least twenty-five yards from a house and not along a main road.) The corpse was carried to the tomb or grave on an open bier, accompanied by family members and spectators (cf. Luke 7:11–12). Inside the tomb, the person was laid on his or her back, in the posture of sleep.

The burial of Jesus followed the same customs. All four Gospels agree that Joseph of Arimathea came and took Jesus' body for burial. The Gospels of Matthew, Mark, and Luke tell us the body was merely covered with a linen cloth and placed in the tomb, which was then sealed with a stone. The women had to wait until after the Sabbath to anoint the body with spices. John's Gospel, however, tells us that Nicodemus brought a mixture of myrrh and aloes (a fragrant resin from India). Jesus' body was wrapped in the linen, along with the spices, and then laid in Joseph's tomb. ▪

Christians continued the Jewish practice of closing the dead person's eyes and mouth after death. Next, they washed the body (cf. Acts 9:36–37) and anointed it with myrrh and spices to preserve it before burial. The body was wrapped in white linen (a symbol of the white cloth at Baptism) and then dressed with clothes the person wore during his or her life. The outer garment was usually violet.

During the second century, a **wake** was sometimes held in the home of the deceased before burial. When burial occurred on the same day as death, a three-day watch took place at the grave. When burial took place the day after death, the wake took the form of a night vigil, sometimes in church. Friends consoled relatives and prayed for the deceased; the body was surrounded by candles; a priest read Scripture passages dealing with death and resurrection.

In the funeral procession, the body was placed on an open bier with the head exposed. Young men, frequently relatives, acted as **pallbearers**. Acolytes led the processions, and deacons carrying torches escorted the corpse. Instrumental music, hired mourners, and actors and buffoons were all excluded because these were practices of those who did not believe in the Judeo-Christian God. Instead, during the procession the Christians sang psalms (most frequently Psalms 22, 31, 100, 114, and 115). ▪

The Eucharist was celebrated either at the grave or in the church. During the Mass, the body was anointed again (a reminder of baptismal anointing) to signify that the deceased had persevered in the faith to the end. At the grave, a funeral oration, or **eulogy**, was given by a relative or friend (if this had not already been done in church). The speech praised the virtues of the deceased and offered consolation to the family members.

Activity

Read the gospel accounts of the burial of Jesus. How are the accounts similar? How do they differ? How do they reflect traditional Jewish burial customs and beliefs?

- Matthew 27:57–61
- Mark 15:42–47
- Luke 23:50–56
- John 19:38–42

Activity

Read one of the psalms listed in this section. Rewrite the psalm in your own words, or set the actual verses of the psalm to music. Be prepared to discuss how the psalm helps us remember the dead.

After the eulogy, relatives approached the corpse to give it a final kiss. Then the body was wrapped in linen and placed in the grave as if sleeping. The hands were either extended alongside the body or folded across the chest. Usually the body was buried with the feet to the east, to await the Second Coming of Christ. Before leaving the cemetery, the priest offered farewell prayers, called *vivas*, that the departed might live in God and intercede for the living.

Christians made frequent visits to the graves of their loved ones, especially on the third day, seventh or ninth day, thirtieth or fortieth day, and one-year anniversary. The entire Christian community remembered the dead during prayer offerings at the Eucharist. Special Masses were said on the annual feasts of death, in memory of the dead and for the benefit of their souls. ■

The Catacombs

At the end of the second century, most Christians of Rome were poor; thus they tended to live in the "suburbs." The Church owned only one cemetery, called Saint Callixtus. It was named after the deacon Callixtus, who was appointed head of the cemetery under Pope Zephyrinus (199–217) and who, when he himself was pope (217–222), greatly enlarged it. Eventually, the cemetery had five levels underground, spread over six miles.

By the third century, a number of wealthy people had converted to Christianity. Their homes became *tituli*, or church centers much like parishes today, where Christians could gather to celebrate the Eucharist and the sacraments, to receive religious instruction, and to assist the needy. The wealthy Christians donated land to the Church for private burial grounds. In turn, these cemeteries were named after their benefactors: Priscilla, Comitilla, Maximus, Thraso, Commodilla, Agnes, and so forth.

Halfway through the third century, Pope Fabian (236–250) divided Rome into seven districts. He appointed seven deacons to supervise these districts. Among their duties was funeral organization, a task that the state did not provide. Each district was allotted a burial zone outside the walls of the city, with a certain number of cemeteries. These underground cemeteries are what we now call the **catacombs**.

Despite popular belief, the catacombs were not secret places built by the Christians to flee persecution. Instead, the Romans had built the subterranean tunnels as part of a vast network for waterworks. When the Romans abandoned the tunnels, Christians found in them a solution for the space they needed for burials. The Christians simply dug ledges or shelves, one on top of the other, along each side of the narrow walkways. Thus they were able to provide burial for the poor in great numbers.

The Christians wrapped each corpse in a sheet before placing it on a shelf, which often contained two or more members of the same family. The name of the deceased, along with the date of death, was painted or sculpted on the slab that served as its door. Small terra-cotta lamps and vases for perfume were often placed above the tomb.

Of Interest

In Jewish funerals, closing the eyes was the time for loud wailing. Christians curbed this practice by singing psalms. In his book *On the Care of the Dead*, Saint Augustine mentioned Psalm 100, which speaks of God's mercy and judgment.

---

catacombs Underground burial sites of many early Christians, especially around Rome.

The Catacombs of Saint Callixtus in Rome had five levels underground, spread over six miles.

Discussion

Why do you think three, seven, nine, thirty, and forty days were important times to remember the dead? What might these numbers have symbolized?

Of Interest

Nine popes (also saints) are buried in the catacomb of Saint Callixtus:

Saint Pontian (230–235)
Saint Anterus (236)
Saint Fabian (236–250)
Saint Lucius I (253–254)
Saint Stephen I (254–257)
Saint Sixtus II (257–258)
Saint Dionysius (259–268)
Saint Felix I (269–274)
Saint Eutychian (275–283)

---

relic A sacred object associated with a saint. A first-class relic is the saint's body or part of the saint's body. A second-class relic is a part of clothing or an article used by a saint. A third-class relic is any object touched to the first-class relic.

reliquary A container for safeguarding and exhibiting the relics of saints.

Periodically throughout the maze of catacomb tunnels were small rooms that the Christians used as chapels. While these rooms were much too small to accommodate an entire community, family members and friends could gather there to celebrate the Eucharist for their dead loved ones. On the walls of these chapels were painted frescoes that reminded the mourners (who, for the most part, couldn't read) of biblical stories that expressed belief in the resurrection.

Among the frescoes that can still be seen today in the catacombs are Abraham's sacrifice of Isaac, Moses and the spring in the desert, three youths in a fiery furnace, the rooster (the story of Saint Peter's denial), the Good Shepherd, bread and fish (the miracle of the loaves and fishes), bread and wine or people around a table with bread and wine (the Eucharist), the healing of the paralytic, and the baptism of Jesus. ■

The fourth century brought more religious persecutions and martyrs for Christ. After more and more martyrs were buried in the catacombs, Christians sought *depositio ad sanctos*, the privilege of being buried near the graves of the martyrs. Those considered most holy—virgins, monks, and priests—were buried closest to the martyrs.

The catacombs were used as cemeteries until the early fifth century. Then a new custom took over, that of burying the dead beneath the floors of cemetery basilicas. At first, Christians continued to visit the tombs of martyrs and saints in the catacombs. During the next four centuries, the remains of most martyrs and saints were transferred to churches within the city walls. After that, the catacombs fell into disuse; many of their entrances were covered over with buildings or vegetation. They were forgotten until the sixteenth century, when Antonio Bosio located about thirty catacombs beneath Rome.

Relics

When Bishop Polycarp was martyred in the mid-second century, the citizens of Smyrna began public veneration of his remains. Each year, on the anniversary of his martyrdom, Christians honored his bones because of his holiness in following Christ. This practice spread quickly among Christian communities as more and more of their members were martyred. By the fourth and fifth centuries, this practice had grown into a liturgical cult known as the *veneration of* **relics**.

Under this practice, the tombs of martyrs were opened and the relics were distributed to Christians in the form of objects that had touched the actual body or bones. These objects were enclosed in little cases, called **reliquaries**, and hung around a person's neck. Saint John Chrysostom and Saint Basil of Caesarea defended the cult of relics, saying that relics reminded people of saints who were Christian role models. Saint Augustine also defended the cult of relics, pointing to the miracles worked by God through them and to their origin in Scripture (cf. Acts 19:12).

Eventually people developed the notion that the more extraordinary the miracles

Of Interest

Three nonbiblical symbols may be seen in catacomb artwork as well:

• the dolphin, a symbol of redemption, which was thought to carry the souls of the saved "across the sea" to heaven;

• the peacock, whose glorious tail symbolized the new and glorious life of those who died in Christ;

• the phoenix rising from flames, a Roman myth that symbolized the resurrection of the dead.

Activity

The following Bible passages were depicted in catacomb art. Look up one of the passages. Then tell how it related to Christian belief in the resurrection.

• Genesis 22:1–19
• Exodus 17:1–7
• Matthew 3:13–17
• Matthew 26:31–35, 69–75; John 21:15–23

• Mark 2:1–12
• Mark 6:30–44
• John 10:11–18
• 1 Corinthians 11:23–24

The relic of Saint Clare of Assisi, Santa Chiara, Assisi, Italy

associated with the relic, the holier the person who had died. Thus the Church began to require the working of miracles through the intercession of a dead person before that person could be **canonized**. One miracle had to be worked in answer to prayers to that person in order for the person to be declared "blessed"; two miracles had to be worked before the Church declared the person a "saint."

Before beatification, the person's body had to be **disinterred** and examined, to make sure the remains were truly those of the person and also to obtain relics.

In the Eastern Church, the bodies of saints were exhumed, dismembered, and transported from place to place for the edification of the people. In the Western Church, such plundering of graves was against the law. It was not until the eighth century that Pope Paul I and Pope Paschal I authorized the dismemberment and dispersal of the bodies of the saints. During the Middle Ages the cult of relics became so popular (and so economically profitable) that many relics were falsified.

During the Crusades, commerce in relics reached a new peak. After Crusaders sacked Constantinople, Antioch, and Jerusalem, they sent back many relics to churches and cathedrals in Europe. Because so many fraudulent relics appeared in circulation at this time, the Council of Lyons (1274) prohibited the veneration of new relics without the pope's prior authentication of them.

By the late Middle Ages, most churches displayed bodies or relics of the saints close to the altar. According to Church law, an altar could not be dedicated unless it contained the sealed relics of two martyrs. The pastor of a new church had to request from Rome the relics of the saint in whose honor the church was named.

Because many superstitions arose regarding relics and because some Christians erroneously began to worship the relics themselves, theologians restated the Church's teaching. Thomas Aquinas noted that every relic is a record, or a reminder, of a saint. Relics themselves have no sanctifying or miraculous powers; rather, it is God who works miracles through them. God is to be the principal object of worship, not the saints or their relics.

A first-class relic is a body or a body part (skin, bones, eyes, hair, and so forth) of a saint. One example of a first-class relic is the body of Saint Ambrose, which is preserved in a glass coffin under the altar of Saint Simpliciano's Basilica in Milan. A second-class relic includes any part of the saint's clothing, an article used by the saint, or instruments of a martyr's imprisonment or death. A third-class relic is any object touched to the body or grave of a saint. ■

Today, the authentication and use of relics comes under the jurisdiction of the Vatican's Congregation of Rites. According to the present Code of Canon Law, the Church may buy relics but not sell them. ■

Catholics Believe
. . . The honor paid to sacred images is a "respectful veneration," not the adoration due to God alone: Religious worship is not directed to images in themselves, considered as mere things, but under their distinctive aspect as images leading us on to God incarnate. The movement toward the image does not terminate in it as image, but tends toward that whose image it is. (St. Thomas Aquinas, STh II–II, 81, 3 ad 3.) (Catechism, #2132)

---

canonization *The process by which the Church officially declares a dead person to be a saint. If the Church can prove that the person led a life of heroic virtue, it confers the title "venerable." If one miracle is worked through the person's intercession, the Church confers the title "blessed." If two miracles are worked through the person's intercession, the Church confers the title "saint." The miracle requirements can be and have been waived in some cases.*

disinterment *To dig up a grave for the purpose of identifying or moving human remains; to exhume.*

Activity
1. Ask your pastor about any relics the parish may have. See if you can find out (a) which saints are represented, (b) when the saints lived and some information about their lives, (c) how the saints died, (d) whether the relics are first-class, second-class, or third-class relics, and (e) how the relics were obtained.
2. Role-play a conversation with someone from a different denomination or religion. How would you explain to this person the history and meaning of relics in the Catholic Church?

Discussion
1. Do you have any relics, or have you seen any? Describe them. What feelings do they invoke in you?
2. Why do you think Canon Law permits the Church to buy relics but not to sell them?

Of Interest

On November 14, 1987, Church officials exhumed the remains of Father Junipero Serra (founder of the California missions) as a requirement for his beatification. He was buried in a grave below the stone floor of the Carmel Mission in Monterey, California. Physicians and forensic anthropologists identified Serra's remains by comparing bone measurements with information listed on Serra's Spanish passport and from information recorded about him by fellow Franciscans. Serra was beatified by Pope John Paul II on September 25, 1988. His feast day is July 1.

mausoleum A structure or building for entombment of casketed human remains in crypts or vaults.

crypt A space in a mausoleum in which casketed remains may be placed and sealed; the lower part of a church used for worship and/or burial.

Saint Peter's Basilica

Hundreds of thousands of Catholics visit Saint Peter's Basilica in Rome each year to hear the pope speak and to attend liturgical celebrations. But not all of these pilgrims realize that the present church (built in the seventeenth century) lies over a first- to fourth-century burial place, once used by non-Christians and Christians. Non-Christians called this place the necropolis or "city of the dead." Christians referred to it as the *ceometerium* or "land of sleeping people." ▪

The burial place was situated close to the Circus of Gaius and Nero where, according to tradition, the apostle Peter was martyred between A.D. 64 and 67. Non-Christians used the necropolis to inter the bodies or ashes of their dead along the north side of the circus. During the first and second centuries, some Christian tombs were built on the south side. The burial place consisted of rows of **mausoleums** or family chapels decorated with paintings and mosaics. It contained places for the ashes of the cremated and sarcophagi for those who were buried. Christian art—the shepherd, the fisherman, the anchor, the vine, Jonah and the whale—decorated the walls.

A church was erected by Constantine and Pope Sylvester between A.D. 321 and 329 to preserve what was believed to be the tomb of Saint Peter. In order to create a platform for the church, Constantine's workers had to bury the necropolis and dig out part of the hill to the north. They built a monument, called the *Trophy of Gaius*, over what was thought to be the tomb of Saint Peter. The church had various functions. It was used as a civic assembly hall, a church and place of pilgrimage, a covered cemetery, and a hall for banquet and funeral receptions. There was no fixed altar until the time of Gregory the Great, who raised the sanctuary and concealed the tomb of the

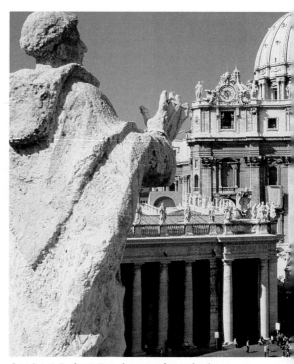

Saint Peter's Basilica in Rome lies over a first- to fourth-century burial place.

apostle in the **crypt** below. The altar was thought to be placed directly above the tomb.

The twentieth-century search for the tomb of Peter was by no means a simple one. Archaeologists digging beneath Saint Peter's were able to find a place in the necropolis-cemetery, which they labeled as "Camp P." According to tradition, Saint Peter was buried at the foot of the red brick wall along Camp P. But when archaeologists dug up the spot, there were no remains.

In 1953, archaeologist Margherita Guarducci spent time studying the graffiti that covered a low wall on the right of Camp P. One of these statements read "Peter is here." Further research led her to discover the bones and fragments believed to be those of Saint Peter. On the other hand, there are a number of arguments against this belief. Today, visitors

Discussion

How do the terms *necropolis* and *cemetery* and their meanings reflect different beliefs about death and the afterlife?

to the necropolis-cemetery can see these remains behind a sheet of glass in a modest irregular niche.

Between the ancient necropolis and the floor of the present basilica are the remaining parts of the Constantine church and the crypt built later by Gregory the Great. This area, known as the Vatican Grottoes, was restored during the twentieth century and is open to visitors. Many popes are interred in the Grottoes. Among them are Pius XII, John XXIII, Paul VI, and John Paul I, who was only pontiff for thirty-three days.

Next to Saint Peter's Basilica is the Vatican Museum, which houses the richest collection of Christian sarcophagi in the world. In the first centuries of Christianity, the sarcophagus represented the most luxurious form of burial. It was a rectangular- or oval-shaped **casket** covered by a lid, either pitched in two directions like a roof or flat with a tablet for inscriptions in the center. Often, biblical scenes, such as the raising of Lazarus, healings performed by Christ, and the miracle of the loaves and fishes, were sculpted on the lid and sides.

Remembering the Dead Today

If you walk into a church that was built before the Second Vatican Council, you are likely to find many physical mementos of the dead. The church may house statues of Jesus, Mary, Joseph, and other saints. You may see paintings or carvings of particular saints or scenes of Jesus' life. Most likely, there is some type of artistic rendering of the stations of the cross. Subtler forms of mementos might be stained-glass windows purchased "in memory of" a deceased parishioner or memorial plaques on the organ, pews, and pulpit, acknowledging the financial donation of or in memory of someone who died.

The bishops of Vatican II, in revising the liturgy, wanted to maintain a connection to tradition while also making sure Catholics understood the difference between worship and veneration. Only God may be worshiped; the saints and any relics pertaining to them may only be venerated. *Worship* refers to the respect we owe a divine being. *Veneration* refers to the respect we owe people who are particularly wise, heroic, virtuous, and so forth. For this reason, the bishops advised the following:

> The practice of placing sacred images in churches so that they may be venerated by the faithful is to be firmly maintained. Nevertheless, their numbers should be moderate and their relative location should reflect right order. Otherwise they may create confusion among the Christian people and promote a faulty sense of devotion.

—*Constitution on the Sacred Liturgy*, #125

Of Interest

To visit the necropolis-cemetery beneath Saint Peter's you must get advance reservations by writing to:

Reverenda Fabbrica di S. Peitro
00120 Citta del Vaticano

casket *A receptacle in which the dead body is placed for burial.*

Discussion

Have you ever visited Saint Peter's in Rome? If so, what impressed you most? If not, is it a place you would like to visit someday? Why or why not?

Activity

1. After doing further research, make a drawing that compares the present floor plan of Saint Peter's to that of the church built by Constantine and the earlier necropolis-cemetery.

2. Research the life and accomplishments of one of the popes interred at Saint Peter's. How can this person be a role model for us today?

Of Interest

Among the canons of the *Code of Canon Law* dealing with the veneration of saints, sacred images, and relics are the following:

- **Canon 1186:** To foster the sanctification of the people of God the Church recommends to the particular and filial veneration of the Christian faithful the Blessed Mary ever Virgin, the Mother of God, whom Christ established as the Mother of the human race; it also promotes true and authentic devotion to the other saints by whose example the Christian faithful are edified and through whose intercession they are sustained.

- **Canon 1187:** Veneration through public cult is permitted only to those servants of God who are listed in the catalog of the saints or of the blessed by the authority of the Church.

- **Canon 1188:** The practice of displaying sacred images in the churches for the veneration of the faithful is to remain in force; nevertheless they are to be exhibited in moderate number and in suitable order lest they bewilder the Christian people and give opportunity for questionable devotion.

In churches built after the Second Vatican Council, it is likely that there are fewer statues, pictures, and artistic representations of saints and martyrs so as not to distract the faithful from the actual celebration.

The 1970 edition of the *Roman Missal* elaborated on the bishops' point by saying:

> In accord with ancient tradition, images of Christ, Mary, and the saints are venerated in churches. They should, however, be placed so as not to distract the faithful from the actual celebration. They should not be too numerous, there should not be more than one image of the same saint, and the correct order of saints should be observed. In general, the piety of the entire community should be considered in the decoration and arrangement of the church.
>
> —*"General Instruction,"*
> *Roman Missal,* #278

Thus, in churches built after the Second Vatican Council, you are likely to see far fewer statues, pictures, and artistic representations of saints and martyrs.

In addition to these changes, the interiors of today's churches contain a less obvious change. As you have learned, altars in the past had to contain the sealed relics of two martyrs. As the *Roman Missal* now states, "It is fitting to maintain the practice of enclosing relics in the altar or of placing them under the altar. These relics need not be those of martyrs, but there must be proof that they are authentic" ("General Instruction," *Roman Missal,* #266). The reason for this change is explained in another Church document:

> The entire dignity of an altar consists in this: the altar is the table of the Lord. It is not, then, the bodies of martyrs that render the altar glorious; it is the altar that renders the burial place of the martyrs glorious. However, as a mark of respect for the bodies of the martyrs and other saints, and as a sign that the sacrifice of the members has its source in the sacrifice of the Head, it is fitting that altars should be constructed over their tombs, or their relics placed beneath altars.
>
> —*Dedication of a Church and an Altar,* #60

As Canon 1239.2 of the *Code of Canon Law* makes clear, "No corpse may be buried beneath the altar; otherwise Mass may not be celebrated on it." Only the relics of known saints and martyrs may be placed beneath an altar. The bodies of popes, cardinals, and bishops may be buried inside their churches but not under the altar.

Activity

1. Visit your parish church. Make a list of the ways the dead are remembered in visible, tangible ways. What is your favorite memento in the church?

2. Find out how your parish venerates Mary, the Mother of Jesus. Report your findings to the class.

Discussion

1. How is praying to the saints different from praying to God?

2. Do you think Catholics today need visual images in church to remind them of the saints and martyrs? Why or why not?

What about You?

People today remember the dead by keeping photographs of them, articles of clothing, or certain items that once belonged to them. Sometimes people also remember the dead by contributing money to the parish, to the arts, to a charitable organization, or to a building fund, or they make a Mass offering. This **memorial** allows the dead to "live on" in a way that benefits the community. ▪

What about you? When you die, how do you want others to remember you? Think about the ways you want certain people to remember you. Concentrate on intangible memories (a smile, friendship, a shared experience, a value, your personality, and so forth). Then write a eulogy for yourself—the way someone would remember you if you died (a) today or (b) fifty years from now.

memorial *A contribution that is made to a charitable organization or public cause in memory of someone who has died.*

How I Want to be Remembered

By my parents:

By my brothers and sisters:

By my friends:

By my classmates:

By my parish:

By my civic community:

Eulogy:

Journal

If you had to summarize your life by five mementos, what would these be? What would each memento symbolize about you?

Words to Know

canonization
casket
catacombs
crypt
disinterment
eulogy
mausoleum

memorial
pallbearer
relic
reliquary
shroud
wake

Review Questions

1. How were Jewish burial customs and laws reflected in the burial of Jesus?
2. How did Christians of the first two centuries remember the dead?
3. What were the original purposes of the catacombs?
4. How does the artwork in the catacombs help us understand the faith of the early Christians?
5. Explain the reason for the cult of relics in the history of the Church.
6. What are two tangible ways the dead are remembered in Saint Peter's Basilica?
7. What is the difference between worship and veneration? How is this difference reflected in church interiors today?

C•H•A•P•T•E•R

11

Americans
and
Death

IN THIS CHAPTER, YOU WILL

- appreciate the cemetery as a sacred place;
- learn about the death and burial customs of early America;
- consider gravestones as works of art;
- study the burial customs of black slaves;
- examine America's civil customs surrounding death;
- understand the meaning behind holidays such as Memorial Day and Decoration Day;
- explore Christian gravestone symbols and Catholic prayers for visiting a cemetery;
- write your own epitaph and design your own tombstone.

A Grave Problem

Kathleen Phillips thought her family had moved to the greatest town in America—until she saw the city's cemetery. Weeds had grown everywhere. In the oldest section of the graveyard, where citizens of the early nineteenth century had buried their dead, tombstone after tombstone had been toppled.

The newer section of the cemetery looked no better. Cracked markers looked as if they had been whacked by baseball bats. Other markers were covered with spray-can graffiti. Indeed, everything Kathleen saw made her sick.

On her next trip to the cemetery, Kathleen brought a number of her high school friends. They were as upset as she was. "But what can we do?" one of them asked.

They decided to meet again the following day, this time armed with ideas. They intended to present their ideas at the next city council meeting.

The students followed through on their plan. At the council meeting, Kathleen explained the problem with the cemetery and then outlined the students' ideas. "We'd like you to hire a landscape architect to design a 'new look' for the cemetery—perhaps turn it into a memorial park with benches and cobblestone paths. The fence needs fixing, and there should be a full-time caretaker to maintain the place. To prevent future vandalism, a security company needs to do regular patrolling at night, and someone needs to educate students about the cemetery's sacredness—that it's not something to destroy."

"And how do you propose that we pay for all this?" a council member asked.

Kathleen proceeded to outline five ideas for raising money, including an "adopt-a-grave" program where businesses could make tax-deductible contributions.

The council members were impressed. By the end of the meeting, they agreed to form a cemetery committee to pursue the students' suggestions.

"We've known about this problem for a long time," conceded one council member later. "But we didn't know what to do and, in frustration, we turned our backs on it. Now that we've got people concerned, I think we can turn the situation around." ▪

Discussion

1. Have you ever visited a cemetery in your city or town? What condition was it in? How did this make you feel?

2. Has your family ever visited or taken care of the graves of relatives?

3. Who should be responsible for the upkeep of graves—especially when there are no relatives of the deceased in the area to care for the grave?

4. Do you think paying for perpetual care should be mandated by state law?

5. Is a cemetery a sacred place? Why or why not?

Places of Culture

In some countries, such as Japan and Mexico, cemeteries are places of culture; they are festive places where people gather on certain holidays. In American culture, cemeteries run the gamut—from commercialized **burial parks** (Forest Lawn Cemetery in southern California), to acres of quiet simplicity (Arlington National Cemetery, Arlington, Virginia), to shunned places of neglect and vandalism.

Americans will continue to tolerate such diversity in the condition of their cemeteries until they are educated to the contrary. Part of such education includes learning about our own culture's approach to death. In this chapter, you will see how the citizens and slaves of colonial America handled death. You will learn the reasons behind certain customs—the tolling of bells, coffins, hearses, tombstones, and the funeral reception. And you will see how Americans traditionally celebrated civic holidays, such as Memorial Day and Decoration Day, that were associated with death.

Customs surrounding death are an important part of our American culture. Knowing about these customs can give you a sense of continuity with the past as well as a sense of responsibility toward the upkeep of present-day cemeteries. Before beginning this chapter, record in your notebook your answers to the above survey. ▪

Attitude Survey	I agree	I disagree	I'm not sure
I like visiting cemeteries; they teach me about the past.			
Families have a responsibility to care for the graves of relatives, even those they don't know.			
Death was much more a part of life in colonial times than it is today.			
Memorial Day, which marks the beginning of summer, is a good time for a barbecue.			
Tombstone art is more a message for the living than a memorial to the dead.			

burial park *A tract of land intended for ground burial of human remains.*

Arlington National Cemetery, a national burial ground in Arlington County, Virginia, became a military cemetery in 1864 by order of the secretary of war. A Confederate prisoner was the first soldier buried in Arlington National Cemetery, on May 13, 1864.

Activity

Find out the name of one city founder or famous person who is interred in your city's or town's cemetery. Write a biography of this person, using newspaper stories, town records, and death certificates. If time permits, present a dramatic scene from the person's life.

Of Interest

Of Interest

Death in Colonial America

Death was visible more frequently in colonial America than it is today. Thus the pilgrims and early colonists tended to be matter-of-fact in the way they prepared for death. Often when a child was born, for example, he or she was not named until after the first birthday—due to the high infant mortality rate. At birth, a cask of wine was set aside for the child's future wedding and, later, for his or her funeral reception. The Pennsylvania Dutch even built a *doedkammer*, or dead room, in their houses. This room would be used for visitation during funeral wakes, for viewing the body. Doors were wider than usual, so that a casket could easily be carried through.

Funerals were social occasions in early America, but they differed from funerals today in that people had to receive an invitation to attend one. At first, such invitations were relayed orally. In Dutch New Amsterdam and up the Hudson to Albany, the *aanspreecker*, or funeral inviter, rushed to the homes of relatives and friends of the deceased. He dressed in black and wore long crepe ribbons around his hat. By 1691, these inviters became public servants appointed by the mayor. The grieving families paid their salaries, according to the distance traveled and the length of time spent.

By the mid-1800s, funeral invitations were printed on white notepaper with a heavy black border. They were sent through the mail. Sometimes called a *ticket,* a *card,* or a *death notice,* the invitation was usually straightforward: "Yourself and family are respectfully invited to attend the funeral of Miss Abigail Jaspers from her family's residence, 37 Center Street, Boston, on Monday, September 9, at 2 o'clock and then to proceed to Bunker Hill Cemetery." If a person received such an invitation, he or she was expected to attend. Personal enemies who met at a funeral were expected to be polite.

At the funeral itself, the bereaved family was expected to wear black. Proper funeral flowers (if present) were always white or shades of purple. After the funeral service and burial, guests were treated to a feast. During the nineteenth century, a person could expect stewed chicken, ham, cold meats, cheese, mashed potatoes, applesauce, red beets, pie, and coffee at a Dutch funeral meal. ▪

Embalming

The first Americans did not embalm their dead. The family washed the body, clothed it, and laid it out for a home wake. Burial—the most common method of disposing of the dead—usually took place soon after death. If a person died during the winter and the ground was too frozen to dig a grave, he or she was buried under the snow in a coffin. After the spring thaw, a proper grave would be dug and the coffin buried. If a person died while on a sea voyage, he or she was buried at sea because there was no way to preserve the body.

Embalming did not become popular until the Civil War, when many families wanted the bodies of their dead soldiers returned home. Thomas Holmes, the father of modern embalming, practiced his art during the Civil War, especially upon officers killed in battle.

Coffins

The first colonists were buried without coffins. The corpse was wrapped in a shroud made from cerecloth (linen dipped in wax) or wool soaked in alum or pitch. A rich person might be buried in a fine shroud of cashmere. All shrouds were rectangular cloth bags, with drawstrings at the top.

The first coffins were crude, fashioned from wood by the colony's cabinetmaker. Because the coffins had to be made in a day, the woodworker usually had some planks dried and ready. The first rectangular burial boxes with perpendicular sides were made by William Smith of Meriden, Connecticut, in the second half of the nineteenth century.

Discussion
1. In what ways are funerals social occasions today?
2. Do you think people should wear black to a funeral today? Explain your reasons.

After that, the term *casket* came into use. Each box was "custom designed," according to the person's measurements. Ready-made coffins were not manufactured until the War of 1812. Some of them were lined with lead. ▪

Hearses

The first colonists used a wooden frame to carry a corpse to the grave site. The first **hearses** were open wagons or sleighs provided by the livery stable-keeper and pulled by a single horse. In the country, open wagons were filled with straw to cushion the coffin. During inclement weather, waterproof covers were used.

In the cities, the first hearses had only one compartment, with open windows and a door at the back. A roller on the rear floor helped ease the coffin in and out. Some hearses were decorated with woolen draperies or fringed curtains with tassels. Hearses for adults were painted black; those for children were white. The driver sat on a box attached to the front; he managed the horses (always black), which were draped in heavy veils of net.

As innovations in transportation took place, so did innovations in hearses. Abraham Lincoln's hearse was actually a funeral train that traveled nearly two thousand miles in twelve days. Later, funeral trolley cars came to be used in the cities. They carried the coffin, flowers, and mourners to the cemetery. In more modern times, elongated station wagons have served as hearses. Limousines transport the family of the deceased, while special **flower cars** carry the flowers to the grave site.

Bells

In early America, the sexton tolled the bell and dug the grave. The custom of tolling church bells originated in Europe. (At first, this practice was intended to frighten away evil spirits waiting to capture the soul.) The tolling bell was stationary. When struck by a

The casket of Dr. Martin Luther King Jr. is transported from Ebenezer Church to Morehouse College in Atlanta, Georgia, after his assassination on April 4, 1968.

heavy clapper, it produced a stately, solemn sound. In some places, the bell was rung once for a child, twice for a woman, and three times for a man. In other parishes, the bell would toll the age of the person.

Burial Places and Markers

In the earliest times, colonists camouflaged burial places so that the Native Americans would not be able to count the dead and realize how weak the colony was. In Puritan times (sixteenth and seventeenth centuries), many churches had adjacent cemeteries. These cemeteries became places to wander in or to have picnics in between church services. Most people were buried in the ground. Some families, however, built mausoleums, or walk-in tombs, above or below ground. Some parishes allowed members to be buried under the church building. In colonial times, it was even possible to be buried under one's own pew, for an extra fee.

hearse A vehicle for transporting the casket and remains.

flower car A convertible or other specially designed car that transports funeral flowers to and from the church and to the cemetery.

Discussion

How does the history of coffins show denial of death in our culture?

Of Interest

A grave marker in Washington Village, New Hampshire, reads: "Here lies the leg of Captain Samuel Jones which was amputated July, 1807." In a cemetery in Newport, Rhode Island, a tombstone commemorates Wait and William Tripp and "His Wife's Arm, Amputated February 20th, 1786."

---

grave marker A plank, a heap of stones, or a boulder used to mark the site of a grave.

tombstone A grave marker containing the name of the deceased, dates of birth and death, and perhaps an epitaph. A grave marker that is placed over a person's head is called a headstone; a grave marker that is placed over the feet is called a footstone.

epitaph The inscription on a tombstone or grave marker.

From the first colonial days, **grave markers** were used to identify the deceased. Usually these markers identified one person or a married couple. Sometimes the markers identified a body part that had been buried separately.

The first markers consisted of a board or a heap of stones. Later **tombstones** consisted of a single boulder, a slab of slate, schist, marble, limestone, greenstone, granite, mica stone, or red or brown sandstone. Markers placed over the deceased's head were called *headstones*; those placed over the feet were called *footstones. Wolf stones* were large flat stones that covered more than one grave and were intended to discourage marauding animals. *Table stones* were markers that outlined the grave and stood on four legs.

When churches were first built in America and graveyards started filling with their founders, it was not the material or the shape of the marker that was important but the **epitaph** written on it. These words not only memorialized the deceased but were meant to be words of warning to the living. Because many people could not read these epitaphs, tombstones were decorated with artistic symbols. These symbols were a kind of code whose message was meant to be studied and taken seriously. Today American tombstones are gaining new respect as art forms. The stones themselves, as well as rubbings of the stones, have been exhibited at museums and art galleries. ▪

Black Slaves and Death

Because of the country's segregation policies, black slaves were buried in separate cemeteries from whites. When a slave died, his or her body was laid out by other slaves on a "cooling board." A plate of salt and ashes, intended to absorb disease, was placed beneath the board and later interred with the body.

Slaves made a coffin, placed the corpse inside, and took it via ox cart to the graveyard. The slaves walked along behind the cart, singing spirituals.

One of these spirituals that has come down to us today is "Swing Low, Sweet Chariot." Based on 2 Kings 2:11, it is a song sung by a dying slave who is filled with happy expectation of being relieved of suffering, sorrow, sickness, and hard labor. For many slaves in early America, heaven was seen as the promised land, and death was seen as the chariot that took one home. Like many spirituals, the song can also be interpreted as looking forward to being transported to freedom by the underground railroad.

Activity

Visit a cemetery and study the tombstones.

- What is the oldest date on the stones found?
- What symbols are used? What do these symbols tell you about attitudes toward death and belief in the afterlife?
- What do the epitaphs tell about the dead—their nationality, religion, age, family relationships, cause of death?
- What Bible passages are included on the tombstones?
- Did you find any stones bearing your last name? Where could you look to find out if you are related to this person?

Slaves needed their master's permission to attend funeral services, even those of family members. And sometimes the permission was not given. Thus slave funerals were frequently held at night, when work stoppage was no problem. According to witnesses, these night funerals were impressive, solemn, and eerie ceremonies. The slaves processed with pine-knot torches and sang hymns. At the cemetery, there were prayers by a slave preacher, ritual ring dancing, and drumming (at least in the Georgia Sea Islands). As Rachel Anderson, an elderly Georgia coast resident, recalled:

> Use tuh alluz beat duh drums at fewnuls. Right attul duh pusson die, dey beat um tuh tell duh uddahs bout duh fewnul. . . . On duh way tuh duh grabe dey beat duh drum as dey is mahchin long. Wen duh body is put in duh grabe, ebrybody shout roun duh grabe in a succle, singin an prayin.

> —The Georgia Writers' Project, Works Projects Administration, *Drums and Shadows*

Following the African custom of decorating a grave with the personal belongings of the deceased, the slaves placed cups, saucers, bottles, pipes, medicine bottles, wash basins, crockery, and other effects on the graves. Frequently the items were broken or cracked in order to free "their spirits" and thereby enable them to follow the deceased.

Another reason for placing the personal belongings of the deceased on the grave was fear of the dead. As Sarah Washington speculated: "I dohn guess yuh be bodduh much by duh spirits ef yub gib em a good fewnul an put duh tings wut belong tuh em on top uh duh grave" (Frances Butler Leigh, *Ten Years on a Georgia Plantation Since the War*). ▪

After her former master had died, one of the ex-slaves on Frances Butler Leigh's plantation placed a basin, water, and several towels on his grave. She gave this explanation: "If massa's spirit come, I want him see dat old Nanny not forget how he call every morning for water for wash his hands." Leigh records this incident as a mark of respect and affection shown by the slave for her old master. The remark also might be interpreted as an attempt to allay the ghost of the former master once and for all, so that Nanny need not be bothered with him ever again.

While a fully developed cult of the ancestors did not persist in the United States, certain African funerary customs did remain. In Mississippi, for example, it was believed that the spirits of the dead roamed on Halloween. Thus the living cooked dinner for them at home or took food to their graves. Similarly, in the Sea Islands, there were those who "put a dish uh food out on the poach fuh the spirit, but some of em take cooked food tuh the grave an leave it theah fuh the spirit" (from *Drums and Shadows*).

Today in Hilton Head, South Carolina, it is possible to see ancient slave graves with crude headstones fashioned from cement. Throughout America it is almost impossible to find tombstones commemorating slaves. If the graves were marked at all, the markers were made of wood that has since rotted.

Because slaves frequently were unable to attend the funeral services of family members and friends, it was not unusual for the funeral sermon to be separated from the burial by several days, weeks, or even months. Such sermons—sometimes several at once—were usually preached on Sunday. The time lag did not bother the slaves nearly as much as if no sermon were preached at all. Regardless of whether the deceased was a sinner or saint, the funeral sermon gave the mourners peace of mind.

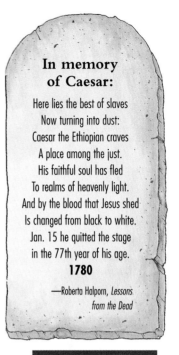

**In memory
of Caesar:**

Here lies the best of slaves
Now turning into dust:
Caesar the Ethiopian craves
A place among the just.
His faithful soul has fled
To realms of heavenly light.
And by the blood that Jesus shed
Is changed from black to white.
Jan. 15 he quitted the stage
in the 77th year of his age.
1780

—Roberta Halporn, *Lessons
from the Dead*

Of Interest

One slave tombstone may be seen in Attleboro, Massachusetts. The epitaph, while praising the slave whose name was Caesar, sadly reflects the racial prejudice of the times.

Journal
Imagine that you live in a culture that considers it customary to place personal items on the grave. What personal belongings would you want placed on your grave?

Activity
Research the funerals of blacks in more recent history, especially Pierre Toussaint (1853), Dr. Martin Luther King Jr. (1968), and Sister Thea Bowman (1990). How did these funerals reflect beliefs regarding death and resurrection?

American Civil Customs

As a nation, America is a melting pot of cultures and religions. For that reason, it has developed a nonsectarian approach to the funerals of its military and public officials. Various customs have become tradition—the flag at half-mast, the casket covered with a flag, presenting the folded flag to the next of kin, the playing of "taps," a gun salute, and so forth.

catafalque *An immovable platform upon which a casket is placed. A catafalque is usually used for the public visitation of a deceased government official.*

At no time in our history were American's civil funeral rites displayed more powerfully and experienced more deeply than in the televised ceremonies for President John F. Kennedy in 1963. Elected in November 1960, John Kennedy was the country's youngest, as well as its first Catholic, president. Three years later, this well-liked leader was assassinated in Dallas. Not only did the people of the United States mourn for him, the entire world grieved. Telegrams of sympathy were sent to the White House from all corners of the world.

President Kennedy's closed coffin was placed on a **catafalque**, draped with an American flag, and situated in a place of honor in the Capitol rotunda. A quarter of a million people walked past to pay their final respects to the slain president.

The next day, the funeral procession set out from the Capitol to Saint Matthew's Cathedral. Four army drummers led the horse-drawn wagon that carried the president's casket. Behind the wagon came a riderless horse with a pair of gleaming boots reversed in the stirrups—a tribute to the fallen leader. Jacqueline Kennedy, the president's widow, wore a black dress and a black veil as she walked behind the casket.

President John F. Kennedy's coffin, draped in the American flag, arrives on a gun-carriage at the capitol.

After the funeral Mass, the procession continued to Arlington National Cemetery. People lined the streets to get one last glimpse of their president. Fifty fighter planes flew overhead as the casket was lowered into the ground. Air Force One, the presidential plane, dipped its wings as it passed overhead. Representatives of the Armed Forces gave a twenty-one-gun salute. A single bugler played taps. Later, an eternal flame was installed at the grave site. This flame continues to burn today. ▪

 Activity

1. Explain what the symbols and rituals used in President Kennedy's funeral represent or mean to us as a nation today.
2. Compare the funerals of Presidents John F. Kennedy, Franklin D. Roosevelt, and Abraham Lincoln. How were they similar? How were they different? What beliefs were expressed by the actions?
3. Research the funeral of one of the Challenger shuttle astronauts, a soldier who died in the line of duty, or a public official who died recently. What were the civic symbols and rituals that were used? What did these symbols and actions mean?

American Holidays

It is customary for a business in America to close when its owner or manager dies. It is also customary for people to wear a white carnation on Mother's Day to recall and honor a deceased mother. In addition to these customs, the United States has developed several national and local holidays that honor the dead.

In celebration of All Saints' Day, children in some parts of the world take part in Mass dressed as their patron saint.

Memorial Day (last Monday in May)

This secular, patriotic holiday honors the military dead. At least twenty-five places throughout the country have claimed to originate this holiday. One of the oldest claims is that of Jackson, Mississippi, where Sue Landon Vaughn, a descendant of President John Adams, decorated Confederate graves on April 26, 1865.

On Memorial Day, it is customary for people to visit the graves of their loved ones. They leave some fresh-cut flowers or a plant and tidy up around the grave. In addition, people enjoy family reunions, backyard picnics, and barbecues. Many communities have parades and church services honoring the dead.

Decoration Day

In the South, Decoration Day (a local memorial holiday) is held anytime from late May until early September. Its purpose is to honor the dead and to maintain the cemeteries. Decoration Day is a significant social, religious, and patriotic occasion featuring picnics, preaching, speeches, and the homecoming of former neighbors and family members who have moved away.

All Saints' Day

Funerals in the French Quarter of New Orleans are often accompanied by a jazz band and parade. Cemeteries in New Orleans are all made of vaults above the ground because of the swampy condition of the land. On All Saints' Day, the vaults are whitewashed and profusely decorated with chrysanthemums. The downtown cemeteries are particularly festive. Street vendors do a lively business selling gumbo, snowballs, pralines, peanuts, balloons, mechanical birds, and toy skeletons. Traditionally, schools and many businesses are closed on this local holiday. ■

Catholic Cemeteries

It is natural to want to be buried near family members. Likewise, it makes sense to want to be buried near other members of the same community—people who share the same values and vision of life. That is why the major religions have their own cemeteries. Protestants of all denominations normally go to a local Protestant cemetery, and Jews are usually buried in their own burial ground. Catholics, too, have their own cemeteries. As you know, these cemeteries date back to the catacombs of the second century, when early Christians sought to be buried near the saints and martyrs.

Of Interest

The ancient Roman version of Decoration Day was *Parentalia*, the Festival of Parents, held in February. On this day people honored their ancestors by leaving food for the dead and decorating family tombs with flowers.

Discussion

1. How does your family celebrate Mother's Day, Memorial Day, Decoration Day, and All Saints' Day? How are the dead remembered on these days?

2. What is the origin and meaning of Veteran's Day? How does the nation remember its dead on this day?

Of Interest

Canon Law #1205 defines sacred places as "those which have been designated for divine worship or for the burial of the faithful through a dedication or blessing . . ."

Of Interest

The Catholic Cemetery Association was formed in 1949. It is an international organization, with members from Canada, Australia, and the United States. The nearly one thousand members come from about one half of the dioceses in these countries.

When Constantine legalized Christianity in the fourth century, Christians were permitted to build cemeteries above ground. Many of these cemeteries were adjacent to church buildings. They were seen as extensions of the Church itself and, hence, as holy. When the cemeteries moved to other locations, they continued to act as an extension of the Church.

Today, many parishes and dioceses own and operate Catholic cemeteries. These cemeteries are nonprofit corporations that offer economical burial and columbarium services. Catholic cemeteries are a business; but they provide an important spiritual dimension as well. They are vital parts of the Church's mission. They differ from secular cemeteries in two ways: their sacredness and their witness.

Only churches and cemeteries are consecrated as sacred ground. In fact, a Catholic cemetery is considered to be holy as is a parish church building in which the Blessed Sacrament is reserved in the tabernacle. Like a church, a cemetery is a place where people can come to pray and meditate. It is holy because it contains the bodies of Christians who have been sanctified by their participation in the sacraments and by their life in the Christian community. ▪

All Catholic cemeteries must have a cross that serves as a sign of their Christian identity and the Paschal mystery—the passing from death to life. All Catholic cemeteries must also be blessed, either by the bishop or his appointed representative. The words of blessing summarize the Church's beliefs about death and resurrection:

> Grant that this cemetery,
> placed under the sign of the cross,
> may, by the power of your blessing,
> be a place of rest and hope.
> May the bodies buried here sleep in
> your peace,
> to rise immortal at the coming of
> your Son.
> May this place be a comfort to the
> living,
> a sign of their hope in unending life.
> May prayers be offered here continually
> in supplication for those who sleep in
> Christ
> and in constant praise of your mercy.
> We ask this through Christ our Lord.
> Amen.
>
> —"Order for the Blessing of a Cemetery,"
> *Book of Blessings*

The Catholic cemetery witnesses to three realities. First, it witnesses to the membership of both living and dead in the community of the faithful, the communion of saints, the Body of Christ. Catholic cemeteries exist as extensions of the living community of the faithful. They are a model of the Church's own community that is awaiting resurrection.

Many parishes and dioceses own and operate Catholic cemeteries. These cemeteries exist as extensions of the living community of the faithful.

Journal

Find out how many of your ancestors are buried in a Catholic cemetery. Would you want to be buried in a Catholic cemetery? Why or why not?

Second, the Catholic cemetery witnesses to social justice. Just as the Church serves the needs of people by sponsoring schools, hospitals, and social service agencies, so the Church sponsors cemeteries as a way to carry out one of the Corporal Works of Mercy—burying the dead. The Church provides a Christian burial for all its members, the very poor as well as those who can pay for it.

Third, the Catholic cemetery witnesses to our belief in the resurrection. The cemetery itself, with its art, architecture, and design, is a collective symbol of hope. Instead of only testifying to the past, the Catholic cemetery looks forward to the future when all the faithful will rise from the dead and enjoy life everlasting.

Following a tradition that predates the entombment of Christ by Joseph of Arimathea, Catholic cemeteries have traditionally buried people. While the Church continues to prefer burial over cremation, most Catholic cemeteries today do contain columbaria for cremains. Catholics are encouraged, but not required, to be buried in a Catholic cemetery. As canon 1240 states, Catholics may be buried in a non-Catholic cemetery, provided the grave is properly blessed. Likewise, non-Catholic members of Catholic families may be buried in the Catholic cemetery. ▪

Cemetery Art

When you visit a cemetery, you will notice different types of styles represented in the cemetery art. Such art may take the form of statues, monuments, mausoleum designs, and tombstones. When you inspect such artwork more closely, you will notice that different times in history used different artistic symbols.

Symbols frequently chosen by the Pilgrims included skulls and crossbones, skeletons, and hourglasses. Eighteenth-century art favored winged cherubs, angels, and

Of Interest

The Catholic Church encourages its members to visit the graves of deceased family members and friends, especially on All Souls' Day (November 2), Memorial Day, and on the anniversary of death or burial.

realistic portraits. Nineteenth-century art included wreaths, swags, urns, weeping willows, birches, elms, doves, lambs, hands with pointing fingers, symbolic triangles, the eye of God, hearts, crosses, and crowns. Twentieth-century grave markers tend to be much more simple but sometimes have a photograph of the dead person on them.

As you have learned, such symbols not only praised the virtues of the deceased but were also meant to be a message to the living. The artwork was included for people who could not read; hence an elaborate "code" developed. Each symbol meant something specific.

Activity

1. Each year the Church sets aside a Sunday as National Catholic Cemetery Sunday. Find out when this Sunday is this year. Discuss ways to educate Catholics on this day about the value of Catholic cemeteries. Then put your plan into action.

2. Find out the names and locations of the nearest Catholic cemeteries. Visit one of these with your family or classmates. Prepare a prayer service for you to pray during the visit. Write a song or poem to include in your prayer service.

Here is the picture code of the artistic symbols you will find most frequently in graveyards throughout America: ■ ■

angels	heavenly hosts leading souls to heaven
arch	death as the passageway through which the soul travels
arrows	the dart of death
Bible	the word through which salvation is won
compass with letter "v"	a member of the Society of Freemasons
cross	boneslife's brevity
crowing cock	the soul awakening to repentance
crown	righteousness
cypress	hope
door	death as the door to heaven
dove	Christian devotion
evergreen	eternal life
gate	death as the gateway to heaven
grapes and vines	Christ
heart	heavenly bliss
hour glass	swift passage of time
lamb on top of a stone	a child, a "lamb" of God
lamb as part of a design	the soul as lamb of God
mermaids	Jesus as divine and human
rising sun	resurrection
rosette	the soul
torch	resurrection
tree	Tree of Life (only on Jewish stones)
trumpet	eventual resurrection
urn	container from which the soul rises to heaven
winged skull	certainty of death
willow	mourning and sorrow
winged cherub	the eternal soul, resurrection
scallop shell	our journey through life
sheaf of wheat	the elderly
shattered urn	the elderly

 Discussion

1. Which of these symbols did you find on tombstones during your visit to the cemetery?
2. If you made a list of new symbols, what would you include? Why?

 Activity

Design your own tombstone, choosing from the artwork symbols mentioned here. Then write your own epitaph to be read by those who will someday visit your grave.

Common inscriptions found on tombstones include the following:

R.I.P.	*Requiescat in pace* (may he/she rest in peace)
Beatae Memoriae	Of happy or blessed memory
Obiit	He/she died
Hic iacet	Here lies . . .

Catholics Believe

The bodies of the dead must be treated with respect and charity, in faith and hope of the Resurrection. The burial of the dead is a corporal work of mercy (Cf. Tob 1:16–18); it honors the children of God, who are temples of the Holy Spirit. (Catechism, #2300)

Words to Know

burial park

catafalque

epitaph

flower car

grave marker

hearse

tombstone

Review Questions

1. What was the function of the funeral inviter in early America? Why was this job necessary?
2. When and why did Americans begin to embalm their dead?
3. Give a brief history of coffins in America.
4. What different types of hearses were used in America's history?
5. What was the purpose of the epitaph on tombstones and grave markers?
6. What was the purpose of the artistic symbols on tombstones and grave markers?
7. How did the funerals of black slaves differ from those of white citizens?
8. What nonsectarian customs do we as a nation have regarding death?
9. What are the three purposes of Catholic cemeteries?

C•H•A•P•T•E•R

12

When Someone Dies

IN THIS CHAPTER, YOU WILL

- appreciate the social rituals that accompany death in our society;

- learn how a funeral director and funeral home can help the deceased's family through the social rituals of death;

- distinguish the difference between death notices and obituaries as well as their purpose;

- consider ways people can express sympathy to the bereaved family;

- see what is expected of people at the visitation;

- look briefly at the wake (vigil service), funeral, and committal service at the cemetery;

- examine some of the post-funeral memorial customs in our society;

- reflect on the Catholic tradition of praying for the dead as one of the works of mercy.

An Open or Shut Case

Funerals are social occasions in most cultures. Unfortunately, they may also be the source of contention. Consider, for example, the following letters to "Dear Abby."

DEAR ABBY: When my father died of cancer ten years ago, he had requested a closed-coffin funeral. What an uproar that created! Relatives and so-called friends who had not seen Dad in years were appalled. They said, "This is not customary! We wanted one last look at him." My response was, "Dad wanted you to remember him as robust and healthy, as he was before he became ill." We found a picture of Dad taken when

he was hale and hearty and placed it on his closed coffin, surrounded by flowers.

His daughter in California

DEAR DAUGHTER: Many other readers wrote about closed-casket funerals. Read on:

DEAR ABBY: Recently I drove 60 miles one way to pay my respects to a friend who had died of a heart attack, only to find a closed coffin. I was not very well acquainted with the widow, so I could have just as well paid my respects by sending her a sympathy card. My point in writing is to suggest to families that the words "Coffin will be closed" be added to the obituary in the newspaper. It may not be considered proper etiquette, but it will save a lot of hard feelings.

Finished Business in Bryan, Ohio

DEAR ABBY: I recall one funeral I attended a few years ago. It was for a loyal, longtime employee who had lingered with a terminal illness for a very long time. When his widow was asked why she wanted a closed-coffin funeral, she replied, "Nobody came to see him when he was alive, so why would anyone want to see him when he is dead?"

Pine Bluff, Arkansas ▪

—Taken from the *Dear Abby* column by Abigail Van Buren. © UNIVERSAL PRESS SYNDICATE. Reprinted with permission. All rights reserved.

Discussion
1. How would you respond to each letter?
2. Have you ever seen a dead person in a casket? How did you feel when you saw him or her?
3. Do you prefer open-coffin or closed-coffin funerals? Why?

Knowing What to Say and Do

As social events, funerals bring together diverse people. They can sometimes be occasions of reconciliation between enemies. At other times, they are scenes of bitter fighting and hurtful dissension. Family members, who are already stressed because of the death, may be overly sensitive to what others say and do. Well-meaning friends—either because they are nervous or not sure what to say—may unintentionally say or do the wrong thing.

For all these reasons, each society establishes an accepted "ritual" that begins when someone dies. In the United States, this ritual includes meeting with the funeral director, notifying family members and friends, writing an obituary, planning and then attending the wake, funeral or memorial service, and final committal service, eating a meal together, and choosing an appropriate tombstone or memorial. Knowing what to say and do at these times is not only a matter of social etiquette; it can help everyone involved get through this particularly difficult time.

In this chapter, you will be looking at what is expected of family members and friends when someone dies. Before beginning, respond in your notebook to the Attitude Survey. ▪

Where to Start

After someone dies, one of the first decisions family members must make is the choice of a **funeral home**. Once the phone call is made to the **funeral director**, the social rituals surrounding death begin. The funeral director will make sure that all legal requirements are met (see Appendix A) and will meet with the family to discuss the type of interment preferred—cremation, aboveground interment in a mausoleum, or ground burial.

Attitude Survey	I agree	I disagree	I'm not sure
Open-coffin funerals are morbid.			
An open coffin allows mourners to say their final good-byes to the deceased.			
When someone in my family dies, I want an open-coffin funeral.			
A wake or vigil service in the presence of the body should be held at the funeral home rather than at home.			
I would never want to be or marry a funeral director (mortician).			

funeral home *A building designed for preparation of the dead, the observance of wakes, visitations, and funerals. Another name for a funeral home is a mortuary.*

funeral director *Person who is licensed in the state in which he or she practices to arrange and conduct funeral ceremonies, rites, and rituals. Other terms for a funeral director are mortician and undertaker (obsolete).*

One of the first decisions family members must make after someone dies is the choice of a funeral home.

Journal

Write about a funeral you have attended.

- Did the ritual bring out the best in people or did it bring out the worst?
- How did you feel at the wake, funeral service, committal, and/or meal? Why did you feel this way?

Of Interest

niche A space in a columbarium used for inurnment or cremated human remains.

crematory or crematorium A building or structure containing a furnace to incinerate the bodies of deceased persons.

interment plot A space in a cemetery, intended for interment of human remains. A single plot may contain more than one grave, crypt, or vault.

death notice A paid notice in a newspaper announcing the death and funeral arrangements of a person.

obituary A newspaper column containing a biographical sketch of someone who has recently died.

Regardless of the interment chosen, numerous details still need to be handled. For example, if the dead person is to be cremated, the family needs to decide whether to have the cremation after a wake and funeral (in which case the deceased is embalmed and placed in a casket) or to have the cremation first and a Mass or memorial service later. Another decision involves disposing of the ashes. Depending upon state law, the family may have several options: to purchase an urn and a **niche** in the columbarium or a **crematorium**, to bury the urn in a family plot or in an urn garden especially designed for the interment of ashes, or to keep the cremains at home. If mausoleum interment or ground burial is chosen instead, the family needs to select a casket, vault, and a mausoleum space or **interment plot**. ▪

The funeral director, who has completed specialized training in mortuary science and grief counseling, guides the family through the decision-making process. He or she acts as an informed friend during this time of need and can be of great help to people who are unacquainted with the "business" of death and the rituals surrounding it. He or she can help the family select with the priest the time and place for the wake (or vigil service), the funeral or memorial service, and the committal service. The actual planning of these services (Scripture readings, music, readers, and so forth) is usually done by the family in consultation with a priest or parish minister. ▪

Notifying Others

Once the decisions about type of service, time, and place have been made, the family should notify other relatives, friends, employers, and business associates about the death. Many such people can be contacted by phone, E-mail, or telegram. In addition, the family can choose to write a **death notice** or an **obituary** for the local paper.

Death notices may be phoned to the classified ads department of one or more newspapers but should always be checked carefully by the family for correct information. Age is not usually included in the death notice unless the deceased is a child. The family's address is also not given, since thieves have been known to read a death notice in the newspaper and then break in when the house is unattended during the funeral. Here is an example of a typical death notice:

> SMITH, Lloyd A.—May 22, 1998; beloved husband of Millie Shepherd Smith; devoted father of Daniel Smith and Patricia Trudell; proud grandfather of Patrick, Scott, Melissa, Nicole, and the late Brian; retired lieutenant in the San Francisco Fire Department.
>
> Visitation at Reilly Funeral Home, 29th and Dolores Sts., today after 2 P.M.; vigil service 8 P.M.; funeral Mass Friday, May 24, 9:30 A.M. at St. Catherine's Church, 1310 Baywater Ave., Burlingame. Interment, Holy Cross Cemetery. Donations to Immaculate Conception Academy Memorial Scholarship Fund or spiritual bouquets preferred.

An obituary contains the same information as a death notice, with the addition of a biography of the deceased, date and place of

Journal

1. When you die, do you want a big funeral, a small (just family) funeral, or a memorial service? Explain.
2. When you die, do you want to be buried in the ground, buried in a mausoleum, or cremated? Why?

Activity

1. Interview a funeral director. Find out
   • why he or she decided to pursue this career;
   • what preparation, education, and training are involved;
   • what licensing is required;
   • what the annual salary range is;
   • how he or she helps families immediately following the death of their loved one and after the actual funeral.
2. Prepare and record a radio commercial for a funeral home.

death (name of hospital or "at home"), the cause of death (this is optional; sometimes "after a long illness" is used), age, important education details, contributions made to society, military service record, awards and publications, and membership in social clubs and professional organizations. ▪

Expressions of Sympathy

When friends and acquaintances learn of a death, social etiquette requires some type of expression of sympathy. The expression may be as simple as calling the family on the telephone or sending a sympathy card that has a printed consoling verse, along with a hand-written letter of condolence. People often choose to send flowers to the funeral home or to the church to be used during the vigil service, funeral, and **committal** service. The spray, wreath, or bouquet should have a plain white card attached with the name and address of the sender.

It should be noted that flowers are never appropriate at an Orthodox Jewish funeral; often they are not desired at Conservative or Reform Jewish funerals, either. In the past, the Catholic Church did not encourage the use of flowers at funeral services; now the *Order of Christian Funerals* allows for fresh flowers, used in moderation, in order to enhance the setting of the funeral rites.

Before sending flowers to any funeral, people should first check the death notice or obituary. If either says "Please omit flowers," this request should be respected. The family members may prefer to have only one floral bouquet that they purchase. Or the family may wish that the money be spent in another, more lasting, manner.

Often the family will request that donations be made in the deceased's name to

a specific charitable cause, such as the hospice where the person died, a heart research foundation, or a cancer foundation. Mourners make a check out to the charity, along with a note stating that this amount is contributed "in memory of" the deceased. The charity will then send the donor an acknowledgment, which may be used for tax purposes. The charity also notifies the family of the contribution.

Some Catholic families prefer Mass cards or "spiritual bouquets" to flowers. In this case, friends and relatives arrange for a Mass to be said for the deceased. The priest accepts a **Mass stipend** and fills in a card stating that the Mass is to be said for the repose of the deceased. Sometimes the date and time of the Mass are included so that the family can attend. The donor then gives or mails the card to the family of the deceased, usually before the funeral. Masses may also be arranged for the anniversary of death. ▪

committal The act of disposing of human remains by earth burial, mausoleum entombment, or columbarium inurnment.

Mass stipend A monetary offering given to a priest in connection with celebrating Mass for a certain intention. People frequently request that Masses be celebrated for deceased family members.

Of Interest

Major newspapers maintain a file of readily accessible information about famous people. Television stations keep on hand a similar video file. When someone famous dies, the newspaper may run feature articles about the person. The television station may air a special program in memory of the person.

 Activity
1. Imagine that one of your relatives has just died. Write a death notice, based on real choices from your community of funeral home, church, and cemetery.
2. Search through newspapers for feature articles about a famous person who died recently. Who was the person? What did the articles tell you about him or her? Compare the feature articles to a regular obituary. How do the two differ? How are they the same?

 Activity
Find out from your parish what a Mass card looks like and how parishioners can go about obtaining one. Check your parish bulletin to find out if the Masses this week are being offered for the repose of anyone. Report your findings to the class.

Visitation at the Funeral Home

If you reread the death notice found in this chapter, you will see a time and place for **visitation**. This optional ritual is a time when friends and family can pay their last respects by viewing the deceased person laying in a casket in a room at the funeral home. Family members may also make themselves available at the funeral home during these "calling hours." ■

visitation *Specified hours when friends and acquaintances pay their respects to the deceased and his or her family.*

The coffin is usually open during the visitation. The embalmed corpse is usually dressed in his or her "Sunday best." Oftentimes cosmetics have been applied to give the deceased the appearance of sleeping. The corpse may also be wearing eyeglasses and a wedding ring, as worn when alive. Deceased bishops and priests are dressed in their liturgical vestments. Religious men and women are usually dressed in their habits. A lay person may hold a Bible, crucifix, or rosary.

When a person arrives at the funeral home for the visitation, he or she should sign the guest register. The full name should be written legibly, in case the family later wishes to make an acknowledgment of the call. The visitor should express a few words of sympathy to the family. It is not appropriate to ask details about the illness or death unless family members discuss it first. According to custom, the visitor is expected to pass by the open coffin and pay his or her respect to the deceased by standing or kneeling for a moment with bowed head, while saying an appropriate silent prayer. If passing by the coffin is too difficult, the visitor does not have to do it. The entire length of the visit need not be longer than ten or fifteen minutes.

Before leaving, visitors should take a memorial card if one is available. A memorial card may have a picture of the deceased or a picture of a biblical scene on one side. On the back is the name of the deceased, the dates of birth and death, and a prayer or poem. The card is a way to help mourners work through their grief and serves as a reminder to them to continue to pray for the dead person. Visitors frequently place the memorial cards they have been given in their family Bible at home.

The Wake or Vigil Service

This ritual calls for a gathering of the family with friends and acquaintances in the presence of the deceased, either at the funeral home, the family's home, or in church. In some cases, the wake replaces the visitation. The coffin may be open or closed. ■

The wake ritual dates from the medieval custom of "rousing or waking the ghost," which was an attempt to bring the dead person back to life. These wakes were characterized by much drinking, dancing, calling out the dead person's name, and other types of raucous behavior. In early America,

---

Discussion

1. Have you ever been to a visitation at a funeral home? If so, describe your experience. Did you view the deceased? Why or why not?

2. When you die, do you want to have visitation hours? Why or why not?

Journal

When you die, do you want your casket to be opened or closed during the vigil service? Why?

the purpose of the wake was threefold: to console relatives, to make sure the person was really dead and not just in a coma, and to prevent someone (oftentimes medical students who needed a cadaver on which to practice) from stealing the body.

Wakes are found in numerous cultures. The Moluccans of Indonesia wake the body for the purpose of aiding the soul in its adjustment to the new way of life. Prayers, devotional acts, talking, and gossip are found at Basque wakes. Among the Merina people of Madagascar, the wake is a festive occasion with jokes, songs, dances, and games of dominoes. In Ireland, the wake may last for three days. The body is "laid out" in the person's best clothes as friends come to comfort the family. The wake is a major social occasion, with eating, drinking, dancing, singing, storytelling, and card-playing.

Traditionally at Catholic wakes, the priest led people in the Rosary. The words of each Hail Mary, "pray for us now and at the hour of our death," were particularly meaningful to those who were mourning the loss of their loved one. While some Catholics continue to prefer a wake and Rosary, the *Order of Christian Funerals* encourages Catholics to have a vigil service instead. This prayer service usually includes Scripture readings, psalms, and singing. Variations may include poetry, the recitation of words that were written or spoken by the deceased, and "testimonies" from family members and friends. ▪

The vigil service, with its theme of passing from death to new life, can provide a rich form of religious expression for all participants and can be an event of faith for them. It can also help family members deepen their own religious faith in the resurrection. ▪

The Funeral Service

The funeral service may be held either in a chapel at the funeral home or in a church. For Catholics, the funeral is almost always in church as part of a Mass.

Anyone may attend the funeral, unless the death notice says that it is private. While the wearing of black is no longer considered necessary at funerals, people should wear conservative, somber-colored clothes. Women may wear a hat. Men usually wear dark suits with conservative ties, white shirts, black shoes and socks.

At Protestant funerals, the casket may either be open or closed. It is always closed for Jewish, Episcopalian, and Catholic funerals. In the United States, cremated remains can now be brought to the Catholic funeral Mass, depending upon the bishop's approval. ▪

Ushers may be provided by the funeral home, the church, or by the family. Ushers should distribute programs or missalettes and escort people to their seats, walking on the left of those being seated. It is not proper for ushers to offer their arms, except to the old or infirm. Ushers should seat relatives and close friends toward the front of the church, keeping the front left pews free for the pallbearers.

The funeral service of Princess Diana was watched by millions of people worldwide.

 Discussion
1. Have you ever been to a wake? What was it like? Where was it held?
2. Have you ever been to a vigil service? What was it like? What readings and songs were used? Where was it held?

 Activity
Compare the rituals in this chapter to those in chapters 9 and 10. How are our present-day funeral customs connected to those of the past?

 Activity
Find out if your bishop allows cremains to be present at a funeral Mass.

Of Interest

Of Interest

---

pall *A large white cloth that is placed over a casket as a reminder of the white garment the person received at Baptism.*

cortege *A funeral procession with the casket.*

In today's society, both men and women may serve as pallbearers. Pallbearers do not volunteer their services; they wait to be asked. Etiquette requires that a person accept the honor of being a pallbearer unless there is some very valid reason (illness) for refusing. The family itself is often represented among the pallbearers. In many cases, the pallbearers do not actually carry the casket. They merely escort it into and out of the church. During the funeral, the pallbearers usually sit in the front pew to the left of the center aisle.

At Catholic funerals, unless it first gathers at the funeral home, the family gathers in the vestibule of the church before the funeral to meet the casket when it arrives from the funeral home. A large white cloth, or **pall**, is placed over the casket as a reminder of the deceased's Baptism and membership in God's family. At the start of the funeral, the altar servers and priest lead the procession into church. Pallbearers follow with the casket. Family members walk behind the casket. ▪

During the funeral Mass, the priest gives a brief homily based on the Scripture readings. The *Order of Christian Funerals* says that there is never to be a eulogy at the time designated for the homily. However, the rite does allow for a member or friend of the family to speak in remembrance of the deceased following the prayer after communion and before the final commendation begins. The eulogy, which contains details or anecdotes from the person's life, should be short and should also refer to the mourners.

After the final commendation, the altar servers, priest, pallbearers and casket, and family members process out in the same order in which they entered. Outside the church the casket is put into the hearse. If the funeral has taken place in the evening, the casket is taken to the funeral home overnight and then to the cemetery for burial the next day. If the funeral has taken place during the day, burial usually follows immediately.

Members of the family may follow the hearse to the cemetery in their own cars or in limousines provided by the funeral home. Flowers may be taken to the cemetery in a separate car. Police usually lead the procession to the cemetery. Cars in the procession turn their lights on. Other drivers are not supposed to break into this **cortege**.

At the cemetery, people park their cars and assemble at the grave site. Often, the ground near the grave will be covered with artificial turf. In inclement weather there may also be an outdoor tent to shelter the mourners. After a brief religious ceremony and blessing of the place of committal, the mourners are often invited to place a flower on the coffin. Mourners stay long enough to comfort family members. According to present-day custom, everyone leaves before the cemetery workers lower the casket into the ground.

The funeral rituals usually continue after the committal at the cemetery with the sharing of a meal in the home of a family member or in the parish hall. Quite

A brief religious ceremony and blessing of the place of committal occurs at the grave site.

Discussion

1. Some people think that children should not attend a funeral. What do you think?
2. Have you ever been to a funeral Mass? What do you remember about it?

often, friends or volunteers from the parish funeral committee will band together to prepare this meal. Many post-funeral meals are accompanied by singing and storytelling.

Memorial Services

Sometimes a memorial service (without the deceased's body or cremains) takes the place of a funeral service. Ordinarily, the Church encourages Catholics to have a funeral service rather than a memorial service. But sometimes the family has no choice. For example, in January 1991, two navy planes collided at sea off the coast of San Diego. Twenty-seven crew members died; their bodies were never recovered. Later, a common memorial service was held at Moffett Field. Individual memorial services were also held by the churches of the families.

A memorial service is sometimes held in addition to the funeral—especially when a person dies in another part of the country or in a foreign land and most of the family cannot attend the funeral. Memorial services may also be celebrated on the anniversary of death, for example, a month or a year later. Memorial services usually take place in a church but might be held in a home, garden, club, or organization to which the deceased belonged. The service itself consists of readings and prayers, a brief eulogy, and music. People speak briefly to the family and then leave.

Memorials

By law, all graves must have a grave marker. Most families also prefer to purchase a tombstone. The size of the tombstone is often regulated by the cemetery. Epitaphs no longer are popular. Most tombstones today contain only the name of the person, birth date, and date of death.

In addition to tombstones, Americans remember their dead in a great variety of tangible ways. Libraries, college buildings, and hospital wings may be named after the wealthy philanthropist who financed them. The memorabilia of a famous person, such as Elvis Presley or Princess Diana, may be collected together in a museum or park-like setting. Federal and state governments, too, will sometimes erect memorials to important leaders, heroes, and soldiers. ▪

Prayers for the Dead

As you have learned, most Jews in the Old Testament did not believe in life after death. Late in Old Testament history, however, there is evidence that at least some Jews embraced a different belief—that the dead lived on and that the prayers of the living could affect their welfare. An example of this belief is found in 2 Maccabees 12:39–45. After a certain battle, Judas Maccabee, the Jewish leader, directed that the bodies of slain Jews be gathered from the battlefield for burial. When his soldiers did this, they found under the tunic of each fallen man a valuable amulet taken from a Gentile temple at Jamnia. This religious violation was serious (cf. Deuteronomy 7:25). Judas immediately prayed to God to forgive the sin of these men. He also took up money to send to Jerusalem so that a sacrifice could be offered for them.

The custom of praying for the dead was strong among Christians. From the inscriptions on second-century tombs, it is clear that the Christians prayed for the dead. The first mention of public prayers for the dead in worship was recorded by Tertullian in A.D. 211. These prayers were anniversary-day observances for the dead. In the third century, prayers for the dead were added to regular Eucharistic celebrations.

Of Interest

During the second half of the nineteenth century, memorial photographs were popular. Family members assembled around the corpse to have their picture taken. One soldier in the Civil War who hurried home to have his photograph taken with his dead infant in his arms was James Garfield, who later became the twentieth president of the United States.

Of Interest

When Constantine died in A.D. 337, his body was placed before the altar, and the people together with the priests prayed for his soul.

Activity

Research one of the following memorials. Find out who is being honored, what the memorial looks like, and, if possible, approximately how many people visit the memorial each year.

- Tomb of the Unknowns, Arlington National Cemetery, Washington, D.C.
- Vietnam Wall Memorial, Washington, D.C.
- Pearl Harbor, Hawaii
- Space Mirror Memorial, Kennedy Space Center, Cape Canaveral, Florida
- Lincoln Memorial, Washington, D.C.
- Graceland, Memphis, Tennessee

indulgence *The remission before God of temporal punishment due for sins, remission that a person (with the right attitude and actions) acquires through the intervention of the Church.*

Of Interest

Some means of gaining a partial indulgence for the dead include the following:

- praying the Magnificat or Hail Holy Queen
- praying the Acts of Faith, Hope, and Love, as well as the Apostles' Creed
- making the Sign of the Cross
- visiting the Blessed Sacrament
- visiting a cemetery

Of Interest

Some means of gaining a plenary indulgence for the dead include the following:

- adoration of the Blessed Sacrament for at least one-half hour
- devout reading of Scripture for at least one-half hour
- making the Way of the Cross
- praying the Rosary in a church, public oratory, or private chapel, or in a family group, a religious community, or pious association

In 1274, the Council of Lyons declared—in connection with the doctrine on purgatory—that the dead could be assisted by intercessory prayers at Mass, almsgiving, prayers in general, and other devout practices according to the custom of the Church. In 1476, Pope Sixtus IV granted the first plenary **indulgence** applicable to the souls in purgatory. Unfortunately, some Catholics came to think that they could buy their way into heaven, regardless of how they lived. They paid stipends to priests to celebrate numerous Masses for the dead; wealthy Christians endowed monasteries so that Masses could be said regularly for the repose of their own souls and those of relatives; there was an overemphasis on indulgences and the money sometimes connected with them.

In 1840, the Sacred Congregation of Indulgences clarified the meaning of indulgences. It said that what is offered to God in the case of a plenary indulgence is fully sufficient to free the soul from purgatory, but what is actually affected will depend on the acceptance and the good pleasure of God. In other words, our good actions and prayers can

influence God but cannot control God. And the degree of faith and devotion plays a role in the effectiveness of our prayers, since our prayers are not magical.

In his 1967 apostolic letter "The Doctrine and Practice of Indulgences," Pope Paul VI defended the custom of praying for the dead as one of the Spiritual Works of Mercy. "The faithful who apply indulgences as suffrages for the dead are practicing charity in a superior way." This work of mercy stems from two theological principles: membership of both the living and the dead in the communion of saints and the Body of Christ and the role of human efforts in the building of God's kingdom. ▪

The *Code of Canon Law* states that in order to be capable of gaining indulgences, one must be baptized and in the state of grace. Proper disposition includes sorrow for sin, freedom from serious sin, performance of the required work, and the intention to gain the indulgence. A Catholic can gain a partial indulgence for the dead by praying customary prayers, by performing certain good works, by prayerfully carrying out duties and bearing the difficulties of everyday life, by giving of one's time or money to serve others in need, and by abstaining from pleasures, according to a spirit of penance.

To gain a plenary indulgence, it is necessary for a person to be free of all attachment to sin, to perform certain good works, and to fulfill each of the following:

- celebration of the Sacrament of Reconciliation
- reception of Holy Communion at Mass
- prayer for the intention of the pope (This is fulfilled by praying one Lord's Prayer and one Hail Mary, and sometimes the Apostles' Creed, but other prayers may also be said.)

Discussion

1. Do you think it is possible to buy your way into heaven? Does God discriminate between rich and poor?
2. Why are prayers for the dead an act of charity?

When You Die

The material in this section contains exercises involving the social aspects of death. Imagine that you will die in three months. Using the following outline, write an obituary you think would best describe you. Also write a poem or prayer that you would like included on your memorial card. Include a picture of yourself, if you so wish.

Your Obituary Outline

Full name: _____

Date of birth: _____

Date of death: _____

Cause of death (optional): _____

Your biography—including major achievements, affiliations, and honors received:

_____

_____

Names of survivors and their relationship to you: _____

_____

Date and hours of visitation: _____

Name of funeral home: _____

Time and place of vigil service: _____

Time and place of funeral ceremony: _____

Name of cemetery for burial: _____

OR cremation preferred: _____

Send flowers? _____

Send memorial donations to: _____

Your Memorial Card

Picture or photograph: Prayer or poem: _____

_____

_____

_____

_____

_____

Catholics Believe

. . . From the beginning the Church has honored the memory of the dead and offered prayers in suffrage for them, above all the Eucharistic sacrifice, so that, thus purified, they may attain the beatific vision of God. (Cf. Council of Lyons II [1274]: DS 856) The Church also commends almsgiving, indulgences, and works of penance undertaken on behalf of the dead. (Catechism, #1032)

Words to Know

committal

cortege

crematory or crematorium

death notice

funeral director

funeral home

indulgence

interment plot

Mass stipend

niche

obituary

pall

visitation

Review Questions

1. How can a funeral director assist the family after a death has occurred?
2. What is the difference between a death notice and an obituary?
3. What are ways that friends can show sympathy to the survivors?
4. What happens during a visitation?
5. What is the purpose of a wake or vigil service?
6. What is the difference between a funeral and a memorial service?
7. What are some post-burial rituals found in our society?
8. Why and how do Catholics pray for the dead?

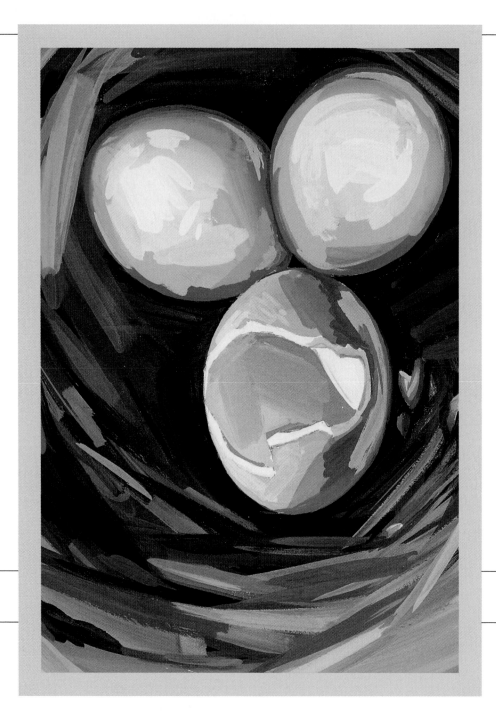

The Challenge *of* Hope

IN THIS UNIT, YOU WILL

Cast yourselves into the arms of God and be very sure that if he wants anything of you, he will fit you for the work and give you strength.

• *Saint Philip Neri*

I call heaven and earth to witness against you today that I have set before you life and death, blessing and curses. Choose life so that you and your descendants may live . . .

• *Deuteronomy 30:1*

- explore what the Church teaches about the four last things;

- study some of our Catholic rituals related to death and resurrection;

- consider ways you can refrain from inflicting suffering on others;

- grow in the virtue of hope and realize that your own suffering can be an opportunity to meet God face-to-face.

C•H•A•P•T•E•R

13

Life Everlasting

IN THIS CHAPTER, YOU WILL

- consider what déjà vu and near-death experiences tell us about life after death;

- study the meaning of the resurrection of the dead in Christian eschatology;

- explore Catholic belief about particular judgment and what happens at the moment of death;

- reflect on various concepts of heaven;

- examine the presence of evil in today's world and how our own free will makes hell possible;

- learn what the Bible tells us about the last judgment;

- appreciate the Church's belief in eternal life through the feasts of the Ascension and the Assumption;

- consider your own motivations for living a moral life.

Close Encounters

Here are some stories about teenagers who have had close encounters with death or a premonition of some type of afterlife. After reading each story, tell whether or not you have had any similar experiences.

- Daniel was preparing a report on English knights for history class. He had chosen the topic himself, because he had always been fascinated by that period of time. After getting several books from the library, Daniel settled down to study. Before long, he realized that what he was reading seemed very familiar. It wasn't that he had read about the same thing before; it was more like he had actually been there as a knight himself.

The more Daniel read, the more he felt that he had stumbled onto a former identity, someone he might have been in a past life.

- Emma, who had just gotten her driver's license, was thrilled when her parents said she could take the family car "to celebrate." Naturally, she took along a couple of friends. They laughed and talked so much that Emma lost her concentration. All of a sudden she found her car in the path of an oncoming semi truck. In the panic that engulfed her, Emma felt that she entered a parallel time. Every second was an hour; every action was in slow motion. As the semi rushed closer, Emma saw her whole life flash before her. Then, at the last minute, the truck swerved and missed the car. Emma and her friends were safe, but Emma never forgot her experience.

- José accidentally hit his head on a rock after diving into the lake. The next thing he knew, he was out of his body, watching his friends try to rescue him. José continued to watch as the paramedics arrived. Then he saw his dead grandfather, beckoning him toward a brightly lit tunnel. José, filled with warm and loving feelings, was just about to enter the tunnel when he was jerked back into his body. José opened his eyes and found himself staring up at the face of a paramedic. He felt glad to be alive but angry, too. The world of his grandfather seemed so appealing that he hadn't wanted to come back. ■

 Discussion

1. Have you ever had a déjà vu experience? Describe the feeling.
2. Have you ever had an out-of-body experience? Do you know someone who has had such an experience? Explain.
3. Do you know anyone who was clinically dead and was then revived? What did the person tell you about his or her experience?

Life after Life

Almost everyone has had some type of déjà vu experience, the sensation of being in a place or a situation before. Some people, such as the Hindus and Buddhists, believe that such experiences are "proof" that life continues on after death and are evidence of reincarnation. Some people say déjà vu can be explained as being caused by the time gap between the moment we first "see" an event and the moment it is fully processed by the mind or brain. (We have seen it "before"!) Other people are not quite sure what to think of these experiences.

In the early 1970s, Dr. Raymond Moody interviewed over one hundred people who had had near-death experiences, who were "clinically dead" but then revived. His findings, which were recorded in his book *Life after Life*, included factors such as out-of-body experiences, encounters with deceased loved ones, a light at the end of a tunnel, and overwhelming feelings of love and warmth. Most people said they didn't want to come back. All said they were no longer afraid of death.

Although Dr. Moody's findings do not prove the existence of life after death, they can be interpreted as pointing to it. Indeed, as you have seen throughout this book, belief in some type of **afterlife** is widespread among almost all cultures throughout the world. ▪ ▪

In this chapter, you will be studying a branch of theology known as *eschatology*. Eschatology deals with the "last things," which the Catholic Church defines as death, judgment, heaven, and hell. Not only will you learn what the Church believes about each of these, but you will also see how the Church celebrates its

Attitude Survey	I agree	I disagree	I'm not sure
When we die, God judges us according to how we have lived.			
Those who believe in Jesus and try to live the gospel will go to heaven.			
In heaven we will be united with God and those we loved during life.			
Hell doesn't really exist.			
Someday the world will come to an end.			

belief in an afterlife in the solemnities of the Ascension and the Assumption. First, though, answer in your notebook the following survey.

Resurrection of the Dead

Resurrection of the dead is one of the fundamental teachings of the Catholic Church (cf. Hebrews 6:2). This teaching is expressed in the Apostles' Creed, with the words "I believe in . . . the resurrection of the body and life everlasting," and in the Nicene Creed, with the words "We look for the resurrection of the dead, and the life of the world to come."

From the time of the Babylonian exile onward, the Jewish people used the phrase "resurrection of the dead" as a metaphor for the future restoration of Israel as a people. Isaiah's prophecy that "your dead shall live, their corpses shall rise" reflected a belief in Israel's corporate survival rather than individual life after death (cf. Isaiah 26:19). So, too, Ezekiel's vision of God bringing dry bones to life reflected Israel's hope for new life after the exile (cf. Ezekiel 37:1–14). At least that is the primary meaning of these passages.

afterlife *Continued life or the fullness of new life after death.*

eschatology *The branch of theology that deals with the four last things: death, judgment, heaven, and hell, as well as the final state of perfection of the people and of the kingdom of God at the end of time.*

Activity
View one of the following videos. Then report what type of afterlife is portrayed in the movie.
- *Always*
- *Heaven Can Wait*
- *Field of Dreams*

Do you agree or disagree with the film's portrayal of the afterlife?

Activity
Read the ancient Greek myth of Demeter (earth goddess of corn and harvest) and Persephone, her daughter. How does Demeter save her daughter from eternal death? What "proof" does the myth offer that life does exist after death?

As you learned earlier in this book, Jewish belief in individual resurrection of the dead came late in Old Testament history. During the time of Jesus, the Pharisees believed in the resurrection, but the Sadducees did not. The Pharisees, however, were not united in their belief. Some believed that everyone would be raised after death. Others limited resurrection to Israelites; still others limited it to the just.

All three synoptic Gospels record Jesus' views on the resurrection (cf. Matthew 22:23–33; Mark 12:18–27; Luke 20:27–40). Here is the account from Matthew:

> The same day some Sadducees . . . asked [Jesus] a question, saying, "Now there were seven brothers among us; the first married, and died childless, leaving the widow to his brother. The second did the same, so also the third, down to the seventh. Last of all, the woman herself

died. In the resurrection, then, whose wife of the seven will she be? For all of them had married her." Jesus answered them, ". . . in the resurrection they neither marry nor are given in marriage, but are like angels in heaven. . . . [God] is God not of the dead, but of the living."

The passage makes two important points: (1) the whole person (body and soul) rises from the dead and is somehow recognizable as that same unique person, and (2) the resurrected person is somehow changed. He or she is a new being, a new creation, "like angels in heaven."

These two beliefs about the resurrection are also found in the New Testament accounts of the post-resurrection appearances of Jesus. The risen Jesus is recognizable by his disciples, and yet he is changed. He still eats and drinks but can appear or disappear instantly. ▪

The risen Jesus is recognizable by his disciples, and yet he is changed. (The Incredulity of Saint Thomas, Guercino)

Discussion

1. Do you think a person who lost a parent at a young age and then lived a full life will be younger, older, or the same age as the parent in the afterlife?
2. Do you think the resurrected body of the psychologically disabled or the paraplegic will be made whole in heaven?

Like Christ, all believers will be raised up (cf. John 6:55). As Paul tells the Corinthians, how this will happen is not entirely clear. In answer to the questions, "How are the dead raised? With what kind of body will they come back?", Paul writes:

> Listen, I will tell you a mystery! We will not all die, but we will all be changed, in a moment, in the twinkling of an eye, at the last trumpet. For the trumpet will sound, and the dead will be raised imperishable, and we will be changed. For this perishable body must put on imperishability, and this mortal body must put on immortality.
>
> —1 Corinthians 15:51–53

When we are raised up, we will not merely survive death, but we will be changed radically.

In the early days of the Church, when the Apostles' Creed was being formulated, the Gnostics taught that only the soul lived on after death. The body, which was physical matter, was evil and therefore irredeemable. To counteract this belief, the wording of the Apostles' Creed clearly affirms belief in the resurrection of the body as well as the soul. The entire person lives on after death. All of God's creation—material and spiritual—is good. Likewise, all people—both believers and nonbelievers, the good and the bad—pass through death to an afterlife. ■ ■

Particular Judgment

According to Catholic thought, passing through death to an afterlife requires an intermediate step—that of **particular judgment**. In this step, the person who has died is judged by God and then is rewarded or punished accordingly.

The concept of particular judgment originated in the Old Testament. In numerous instances, the judgment of God is presented as merciful, righteous, and faithful to the covenant with Israel. God will not treat the innocent and the guilty alike (cf. Genesis 18:25), because God is a God of justice and uprightness (cf. Jeremiah 9:23).

Unfortunately, the Israelites' conception of the justice of God became tangled up with feelings of wrath and vindication against their enemies. As the psalmist writes,

> But those who seek to destroy my life
> shall go down into the depths of the
> earth;
> they shall be given over to the power of
> the sword,
> they shall be prey for jackals.
>
> —Psalm 63:9–10

If God could destroy Israel's enemies, then it followed logically that God's anger could also turn against Israel. Instead of loving God, many of the Israelites lived in fear and dread that they would be judged unfavorably by God.

particular judgment
Judgment that occurs at the moment of death, when each person goes either to heaven, hell, or purgatory.

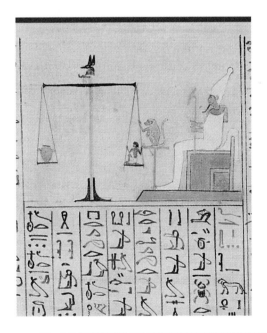

Of Interest

Particular judgment after death is found outside the Christian tradition as well. The *Egyptian Book of the Dead* shows an illustration in which a man is weighed against a feather. The feather is a symbol of truth and freedom from the burden of sin. Muslims believe that immediately after death, a person is judged by two angels named Munkar and Nakir.

Activity
Read each of the following Scripture passages. Then tell, in your own words, what the passage says about life after death.
- John 6:35–69
- John 11:17–27
- John 14:14
- Revelation 21:14, 22:15

Discussion
Discuss the similarities and differences between the following concepts:
- immortality of the soul
- resurrection of the body
- resurrection of the just
- resurrection of all people

It is interesting to note how the Gospels present Jesus' views of God's judgment. On the one hand, Jesus upholds the image of God as a just Judge who will separate the wheat from the chaff (cf. Matthew 13:24–30), the goats from the sheep (cf. Matthew 25:31–46), the just from the unjust (cf. Matthew 18:23–35), those who use their talents wisely from those who waste their talents (cf. Matthew 25:14–30). And as Jesus tells us in the parable of Lazarus and the rich man, God's judgment of us at death is permanent (cf. Luke 16:19–31). It cannot be changed. ▪

On the other hand, Jesus adds two very important dimensions to the concept of personal judgment. First of all, Jesus tells us

The punishment or reward we choose after death reflects a lifetime of other choices.

that God does not really judge us; instead, we judge ourselves. The punishment or reward we choose after death reflects a lifetime of other choices:

- how well we have loved others (cf. Matthew 25:31–46)
- our sincerity in following God's word (cf. Matthew 23:1–36)
- how we applied ourselves in advancing God's kingdom (cf. Luke 19:11–27)
- the strength of our belief in Jesus (cf. John 11:25)
- our willingness to forgive others (cf. Matthew 6:14–15) ▪

The way God will judge us at death holds no surprises. In essence, what happens to us then is chosen by us long before we die.

Second, Jesus stresses the mercy of God rather than human justice. This concept of God's mercy is seen clearly in the parable of the laborers in the vineyard (cf. Matthew 20:1–16) and in the parable of the prodigal son (cf. Luke 15:11–32). Jesus himself expresses the mercy of God in his forgiveness of Peter (cf. John 21:15–19), his crucifiers (cf. Luke 23:34), the good thief (cf. Luke 23:39–43), and the woman caught in adultery (cf. John 8:1–11). ▪ ▪

These two teachings of Jesus are seen in the Catholic belief about particular judgment after death. If we have lived according to the gospel and to the promptings of the Holy Spirit, then we will experience heaven, an afterlife of eternal bliss and happiness with God. If we have fallen short of our Christian commitment but are still basically oriented toward the gospel message, then we will experience purgatory, a stage of further

---

 Activity

1. Look up the gospel passages found in this section. Then write an essay on what they say to you about God's sense of justice.
2. View the video *Defending Your Life.* Then discuss whether or not you agree with the "theology" of judgment presented in it.

 Activity

Look up the gospel passages on how we judge ourselves. Then write a poem, song, or short story with a similar theme.

 Activity

1. Read the parables of the laborers in the vineyard (Matthew 20:1–16) and the prodigal son (Luke 15:11–32). Then write a modern version of one of the parables, with a teenager as the main character.
2. Look up the gospel passages about some of the times Jesus forgave others. Then discuss what you find easy or difficult about forgiving others in your own life.

 Discussion

1. Which do people judge more harshly: themselves or others? Explain.
2. Do you think it's harder or easier to forgive yourself than to forgive others? Explain.

purification before we enter heaven. If we have lived in sin and have chosen to reject the gospel, then we will experience hell, an afterlife of eternal suffering and separation from God. ■

Heaven

When the word *heaven* was first used by biblical writers, it referred to the skies above the earth. It was imagined as a definite place in the universe created by God (cf. Genesis 1:1). More important, it was the place where God lived (cf. Deuteronomy 26:15; Psalm 2:4).

Because the number "7" was important in Jewish numerology, some early Jewish writers referred to the "seven heavens." Being in "seventh heaven" was the highest possible degree of bliss. Later writers spoke of only three heavens; the last of these was God's dwelling (cf. 2 Corinthians 12:2).

According to the biblical view of the universe, God rules all things from heaven, where he is surrounded by his heavenly court. The heavenly hosts are nine choirs of **angels**, each with different ranks and duties. These heavenly hosts are referred to in each Mass in the preface to the Eucharistic Prayer. ■

Of Interest

The Church celebrates the feast of the Archangels Michael, Gabriel, and Raphael on September 29.

---

angels *Pure spirits with intelligence and free will who act as messengers of God.*

Nine Choirs of Angels (from highest to lowest)	
Seraphim	the closest angels to God
Cherubim	wise guardians and protectors
Thrones	who kneel in adoration before God's throne
Dominations	who move the stars and planets
Virtues	who are responsible for working miracles
Powers	angels who fight against evil
Principalities	who watch over whole countries
Archangels Angels	messengers from God in significant matters

The Three Archangels with Tobias, *Francesco Botticini*

 Journal

1. What are your feelings about being judged after death? Do you find judgment to be scary, or is it comforting?
2. If you were to die one minute from now, how do you think you would be judged?

 Activity

1. Look up the following Scripture passages, and discuss what each one says about angels. Then discuss what you believe about angels and their function in today's world.
   • Tobit 5
   • Matthew 1:18–25
   • Matthew 28:18
   • Luke 1:26–38
   • Luke 2:8–14
2. Find one TV program, movie, or popular song that deals with heaven or with angels. Report to the class the concept of heaven or angels that you found, and then explain whether you agree or disagree with the concept.

Of Interest

Throughout history, the devil has had many names: Satan, Beelzebub, the Anti-Christ, Lucifer, Belial, Old Gendy, Old Harry, Old Nick, Old Scratch, Serpent, Old Gooseberry, Apollyon, and Prince of Darkness.

beatific vision The intuitive, immediate, and direct experience of God enjoyed by the blessed in heaven.

Heaven is described as the place from which Christ came and to which he returned (cf. Matthew 3:16; Acts 2:2). It is also the ultimate home of the blessed who die in the Lord. Christians, after all, are citizens of heaven (cf. Philippians 3:20). We look forward to this home (cf. 2 Corinthians 5:1–5), inheritance (cf. 1 Peter 1:4), reward (cf. Matthew 5:12), and treasure (cf. Matthew 6:20; Colossians 1:5).

While heaven is not necessarily a geographic place, it is a state of complete and permanent happiness in which we will enjoy the **beatific vision**. In heaven we will know God firsthand as Father, Son, and Holy Spirit. Because of this union with God, we will know unending joy. A second reason for our joy will be our continuing knowledge and love of others with whom we had relationships during life. We join them, as well as the company of all the elect (Mary, the angels, and the saints), in a communion of one Spirit. ■ ■

Hell

Traditionally, hell has been described as the kingdom of evil, which is ruled by the devil. Even a cursory look at today's world strongly suggests the existence of such a kingdom. Daily, in some part of the globe, people are the victims of moral evils, such as war, death squads, and crime. We are also aware that within us there sometimes wages a personal battle between good (virtue) and evil (vice). ■ ■

Although belief in hell is not specifically included in either the Apostles' Creed or the Nicene Creed, the creedal statement that Christ will return to judge the living and the dead implies the existence of hell. What is *hell*? It is the state of eternal separation from God. The Bible calls it *Gehenna*. The name comes from an actual place southwest of Jerusalem that was formerly the site of a non-Jewish cult that offered human sacrifice.

Jewish writings refer to Gehenna as a place of punishment and suffering after death. It is a place of fire (cf. Matthew 5:22, 18:9; James 3:6) that is unquenchable (cf. Mark 9:43). It is a pit (cf. Matthew 5:29f; Mark 9:45, 47; Luke 12:5) in which the wicked are annihilated (cf. Matthew 10:28). It is a place of eternal torment (cf. Matthew 18:8, 3:10, 12, 7:19; Luke 3:9, 17), where the worms of decay never die (cf. Mark 9:48). Hell is a place of darkness (cf. Matthew 22:13, 25:30), where there will be continual weeping and gnashing of teeth (cf. Matthew 13:50, 24:51).

Such descriptions of hell, figurative though they may be, seem hard to reconcile

---

Journal

1. When have you been the happiest? Describe what prompted the happiness and what being happy felt like. How long did your feelings of happiness last?
2. In your own words, try to describe what you think it would be like to be completely and permanently happy.

Activity

Report to the class on the concept of heaven found in one of the following:
- *The Egyptian Book of the Dead*
- *Valhalla of the Vikings*
- Dante's *Paradiso*

Discussion

1. What are some of the examples of evil in the world today?
2. Do you think there is more or less evil now than there was five years ago?
3. Do you think there is more or less evil now than there was five centuries ago?

Journal

Have you ever felt the struggle between good and evil within yourself? Describe a specific example of this struggle and which side "won."

with Jesus' teaching about a God of love and mercy. That is why some Christians question whether hell exists. But the Church teaches that hell is a real possibility because of human free will. During life, we can choose not to believe the gospel or accept God's love or follow Jesus' example. Likewise in death, we can choose to reject God and communion with God's people. Hell, then, is not God's choice but our own. ■

The Last Judgment

Catholic teaching has always held to a belief in two separate judgments—the particular judgment that takes place at the moment of death and the **last judgment** that will take place at the end of the world. Belief in this second judgment is found both in the Apostles' Creed, which states "He ascended into heaven and sits at the right hand of God, the Father Almighty. From thence he shall come to judge the living and the dead," and in the Nicene Creed, which states "He ascended into heaven and is seated at the right hand of the Father. He will come again in glory to judge the living and the dead, and his kingdom will have no end."

The last judgment is a general judgment at the end of the world. It embraces all humans—living and dead, good and bad, baptized and unbaptized. Sometimes this event is called the *judgment of God* because the Trinity passes judgment and achieves the completion of God's plan for creation. At other times this event is called the *judgment of Christ*, the **parousia**, or the *Second Coming*. This judgment is Jesus' last and greatest act as Savior. In it, he completes the work assigned to him in the moment of his Incarnation. Finally, the last judgment is sometimes referred to as the **apocalypse**. At this event, God's entire plan of salvation will be revealed to us; God's kingdom will become a full reality.

At the last judgment, two major tasks will be accomplished. The dead shall rise again to be reunited with their bodies, and God's kingdom will be established in its entirety and fullness. Although both of these events are considered mysteries—beyond human understanding—we can get a sense of what they will be like by looking at Scripture.

Resurrection of the Body. Those who are physically alive when the last judgment takes place will somehow be changed in accordance with their relationship to God. For them, particular judgment and final judgment are the same. But for all those who have died, the final judgment will mark a never-ending reunion of body and soul. "[Christ] will transform the body of our humiliation that it may be conformed to the body of his glory, by the power that also enables him to make all things subject to himself" (Philippians 3:21).

Our bodies, Paul tells us, will be like the glorified body of Jesus. They will have splendor and will appear beautiful to behold (supernatural radiance or lucidity). They will have agility (the ability to move through space with the speed of thought), subtlety (the ability to pass through matter, just as Christ passed through the closed doors of the upper room), and impassability (they will not suffer or age).

The Kingdom of God. At the last judgment, Christ will usher in his everlasting kingdom (cf. Matthew 16:28; Luke 1:33, 9:27). As a future reality that Christians are supposed to make their highest priority during life (cf. Matthew 6:33; Luke 12:31), the reign of God will become a full, present reality at the end of the world. Jesus describes this kingdom in many of his parables. Essentially, it is a kingdom of love, joy, peace, and justice. ■

Of Interest

An older translation of the Apostles' Creed says that Jesus "descended into hell." These words mean that Jesus truly died and remained dead for a short time. The new translation says that Jesus "descended to the dead"; thus it renders more accurately the meaning of the original language, where Jesus is said to have gone to Sheol when he died. *Sheol* is the underworld, the realm of the dead; in contrast, hell is the place of fire and eternal separation from God.

---

last judgment Final judgment by Christ at the end of the world and the general resurrection from the dead.

parousia The Second Coming of Christ, which will mark the final judgment and the perfection of God's kingdom at the end of the world.

apocalypse Word that refers to the end of the world, with a general resurrection and final judgment, as well as to the events leading up to it. Christians refer to this event as the last judgment or the Second Coming of Christ.

Activity

Read one of the sections from Dante's *Inferno* to find out how Dante described hell. What type of sinners were in hell? What punishments did Dante ascribe to certain sins? Report your findings to the entire class.

Activity

Look up the following parables in the Bible. What does each one tell you about God's kingdom?

- Matthew 13:1–15
- Matthew 13:24–30
- Matthew 13:31–32
- Matthew 13:33
- Matthew 13:44
- Matthew 13:45–46
- Matthew 13:47–50
- Matthew 18:23–25
- Matthew 20:1–16
- Matthew 22:1–10

The early Christians in the community of Thessalonica believed that the last judgment would happen in their own lifetimes. They based their belief on prophecies saying that the disciples would not finish their preaching before the Second Coming (cf. Matthew 10:23) and that the present generation would not die before the last judgment (cf. Matthew 24:34; Mark 13:30; Luke 21:32; 1 Thessalonians 4:13ff; 1 Peter 4:7; Revelation 3:11, 22:20).

Biblical scholars have argued that such passages at least primarily predict the fall of Jerusalem rather than the last judgment. They point instead to other Scripture passages in which Jesus warns that the last judgment will come like a thief in the night without warning. As the parables of the wise and foolish virgins (cf. Matthew 25:1–13) and the talents (cf. Matthew 25:14–30) tell us, we should be prepared to face judgment at all times. ■

Ascension *Christian belief that Jesus returned to heaven in his glorified body after the resurrection.*

Of Interest

The Church celebrated the Ascension before the fifth century but it was observed in connection with Easter and Pentecost.

Celebrating Belief in Eternal Life

The Church celebrates its belief in eternal life in many different ways. Among them are the solemnities of the Ascension of the Lord and the Assumption of Mary. Here is a closer look at each.

The Ascension

The **Ascension**, which is observed the fortieth day after Easter, commemorates the departure of Christ into heaven with a glorified human nature (cf. Mark 16:19; Luke 23:51; Acts 1:1–11). Since the fifth century, the Church has celebrated the solemnity of the Ascension as a pledge that we, too, will be glorified at the last judgment. This hope in our own resurrection is expressed in the opening prayer for the Mass of the day:

> God our Father,
> make us joyful in the ascension of your
>   Son Jesus Christ.
> May we follow him into the new
>   creation,
> for his ascension is our glory and our
>   hope.
> We ask this through our Lord Jesus
>   Christ, your Son,
> who lives and reigns with you and the
>   Holy Spirit,
> one God, for ever and ever.
>
> —*Sacramentary*

The Scripture readings for the day are filled with allusions to the last judgment. Psalm 47 tells us that God will mount his throne amid shouts of joy and reign over all nations (cf. Psalm 47:6, 9). Jesus will sit at God's right hand, above every "principality, power, virtue, and domination" (cf. Ephesians 1:21). In the first reading, from the Acts of the Apostles, the disciples ask Jesus when they could expect God's kingdom to come. Jesus

Activity

1. Look up the following passages describing the signs that the last judgment is imminent. Then discuss when you think the last judgment will happen.
   • Thessalonians 2:1–12
   • Peter 3:10–12

2. Look at a copy of *The Last Judgment,* a fresco painted by Michelangelo on the altar wall of the Sistine Chapel. Describe the fresco in your own words. How does it reflect the Church's teaching about the Second Coming of Christ?

tells them that the time is not for them to know. Meanwhile, they are to be his "witnesses in Jerusalem, in all Judea and Samaria, and to the ends of the earth" (Acts 1:8) and to know that he is with them "to the end of the age" (Matthew 28:20).

The Easter candle is lit at the Ascension liturgy, as it is at every liturgy during the Easter Season, both as a reminder of Christ's resurrection and of the hope we have for our own resurrection from the dead. The Rite of Christian Initiation of Adults suggests that a celebration be held on this day for the neophytes (the newly baptized) and their godparents. In union with these new members, the Church prays that all may receive the gift of the beatific vision (cf. Ephesians 1:17–19). ■

The Assumption

The **Assumption**, which is observed on August 15, celebrates the taking into heaven of Mary—body and soul—at the end of her life on earth. The solemnity was first celebrated in the sixth century in the East; Christians in the West began celebrating it in the seventh century. It was popularly known as the *Natale* (the falling asleep) or the *Dormition of Mary*. The Assumption was not actually proclaimed a dogma of the Church, however, until 1950.

The Assumption honors Mary for her role in salvation history. "And she gave birth to a son, a male child, who is to rule all the nations with a rod of iron" (Revelation 12:5). The solemnity also honors Mary as the first disciple of Jesus, as someone who "believed that there would be a fulfillment of what was spoken to her by the Lord" (Luke 1:45). She is the first of Christ's followers to experience reunion of body and soul after death (cf. 1 Corinthians 15:22–23). The Assumption also gives witness to the hope of all Christians in the glory that

awaits us at the last judgment. Thus the opening prayer of the Mass states:

> All-powerful and ever-
> living God,
> you raised the sinless
> Virgin Mary,
> mother of your Son,
> body and soul to the
> glory of heaven.
> May we see heaven as
> our final goal
> and come to share her
> glory.
> We ask this through our
> Lord Jesus Christ, your Son,
> who lives and reigns with you and the
> Holy Spirit,
> one God, for ever and ever.
> Amen.
>
> —*Sacramentary*

Since ancient times it has been a custom in the Church to bless the produce of the fields, gardens, and orchards on the solemnity of the Assumption. Just as the harvest is a time of reaping the seeds sown by human hands, so the last judgment is seen as a time when God reaps the fullness of Christ's kingdom. "Then your people, enriched by the gifts of your goodness, will praise you unceasingly now and for ages unending" (*Order of Blessings*). ■

Of Interest

Our Lady of the Assumption is the patron saint of France, India, Malta, Paraguay, and South Africa. (Painting by Philippe de Champaigne, *Assumption of the Virgin*.)

Assumption *Catholic belief that Mary was taken body and soul into heaven after her death.*

Catholics Believe

Christ's ascension marks the definitive entrance of Jesus' humanity into God's heavenly domain, whence he will come again (cf. Acts 1:11); this humanity in the meantime hides him from the eyes of men (cf. Col 3:3). Jesus Christ, the head of the Church, precedes us into the Father's glorious kingdom so that we, the members of his Body, may live in the hope of one day being with him for ever. (Catechism, #665–666)

Activity

1. Find out when the solemnity of the Ascension is this year. Select songs that would be appropriate for the Mass on this day.
2. Find out the names of the neophytes and catechumens in your parish. Prepare a celebration or activity with them in which you share what you have learned about the resurrection.

Discussion

1. How can Mary be a role model for today's teenagers?
2. What songs do you think would be appropriate for Mass on the solemnity of the Assumption?

Catholics Believe

"Finally the Immaculate Virgin, preserved free from all stain of original sin, when the course of her earthly life was finished, was taken up body and soul into heavenly glory, and exalted by the Lord as Queen over all things, so that they might be the more fully conformed to her Son, the Lord of lords and conqueror of sin and death" (LG 59; cf. Pius XII, Munificentissimus Deus (1950): DS 3903; cf. Rev 19:16). The Assumption of the Blessed Virgin is a singular participation in her Son's Resurrection and an anticipation of the resurrection of other Christians. . . . (Catechism, #966)

Of Interest

Another custom on the solemnity of the Assumption has been the blessing of harbors and fishing boats. This custom is still observed today by Portuguese Catholics in New England.

A Life of Virtue

In almost every time in history, some preachers have used the afterlife to motivate people to live good Christian lives. These preachers quote Bible verses describing the excruciating torments of hell in what are referred to as "fire and brimstone" sermons. Such sermons are intended to put the "fear of God" into people so that they persevere in virtue rather than vice. Fear of eternal punishment is thought to deter people from sin. There is a big problem, however, with overusing hell in this way. Such motivation, even if it works, keeps people at an infantile stage of spiritual development. They never really "grow up" as Christians.

Think about your own life and your motives for doing good. When you were a small child, you most likely kept a family rule or obeyed your parents because you knew you would get spanked or be sent to your room if you didn't. You were motivated by something outside yourself—the pain of punishment. You didn't do the good action because you valued it as good. You simply did it because you wanted to avoid punishment.

If, during your childhood, your parents were always consistent in punishing you when you did something bad, then you probably stopped doing the bad action. But if your parents were like most parents, they probably slipped up now and then or didn't always catch you "in the act." You learned that sometimes you could get away with acting bad. So what did you do? If punishment was the only thing motivating you, you probably kept right on doing bad. You saw your parents mostly as disciplinarians, as the dispensers of punishment. Your probably feared them; you may even have hated them at times. ▪

As you grew older, you probably were motivated to do good in order to get a reward. You may have done your chores to get an allowance. Or you may have worked hard in school because you wanted your parents to praise you when they saw your report card. ▪

This second motivation is definitely more mature than acting out of fear of punishment. That is why some religious educators and homilists have stopped talking about hell and, instead, have focused on the wonders of heaven. They try to make future union with God and eternal life the motivating force for living a virtuous life now. The problem with this approach by itself alone is that it still leaves people at a less-than-fully mature stage of spiritual development. The motivation for following the gospel remains on the outside, and only in the future. Heaven could become something we "earn" and God a distant Boss. We may still not have grown up spiritually.

The change from childhood to adulthood occurs in most people during the teenage years. This change is not just physical; it is a moral change as well. What this means is that we are no longer motivated to do good solely because we fear punishment or desire a reward. We have somehow internalized what it means to be virtuous, and we choose to do good regardless of whether others know about it or not.

This internalization of Christian virtues is what following Jesus is all about. Mature Christians choose to keep the Ten Commandments and live the Beatitudes because such actions are good in themselves. Furthermore, they are part of an ongoing and dynamic relationship with God. Such actions express personal identity, friendship with Jesus, and membership in the people of God.

Journal

1. What are some examples from your childhood of decisions you made that were based on fear of punishment?
2. How consistent were your parents in carrying out their threats of punishment?

Discussion

1. How were you punished as a child when you did something bad? Was the punishment effective in stopping your behavior? How did the punishment affect your attitude toward your parents?
2. How were you rewarded as a child when you did something good?

So what does this all mean in practical terms? When we live in the Spirit, we act with "love, joy, peace, patience, kindness, generosity, faithfulness, gentleness, and self-control" (Galatians 5:22–23). These virtues make up the kingdom of God—not just the kingdom of God that will come in completeness at the end of time, but the kingdom of God that is already taking shape within us (cf. Luke 17:20). For this reason, Paul urges us to put aside the motivation of childhood morality and to mature spiritually (cf. 1 Corinthians 13:1–11). ■ ■

Discussion

1. "Virtue is its own reward." What do you think this phrase means? Give examples if possible.
2. You have learned in this course that we die as we have lived. Debate whether we can find happiness in the afterlife if we have not been happy in this life.

Journal

1. On a scale of 1 to 10, how much of the gospel message do you think you have internalized? How much of your moral behavior is still motivated by external influences (fear of punishment or desire for approval)?
2. Suppose there were no heaven or hell. Would that make a difference in the way you choose to live? Why or why not?

Words to Know

afterlife	beatific vision
angels	eschatology
apocalypse	last judgment
Ascension	particular judgment
Assumption	parousia

Review Questions

1. How do people who have had near-death experiences describe what happened to them?
2. According to Catholic teaching, what are the four last things?
3. What did the Jews around the time of the Babylonian exile primarily mean by the phrase "resurrection of the dead"?
4. What are two points that Jesus makes about the resurrection of the dead?
5. What heresy does the statement "resurrection of the body" counteract?
6. What two things does Jesus tell us about particular judgment after death?
7. What is one description of heaven that is found in the Bible?
8. Why does the Church teach that hell exists?
9. What two things will happen at the last judgment?
10. Why is hope of reward (heaven) or fear of punishment (hell) not a fully mature motivation for living a moral life?

C•H•A•P•T•E•R

14

Catholic Rituals

IN THIS CHAPTER, YOU WILL

- reflect on various symbols of passing from death to new life;

- explore the meaning of the Holy Thursday liturgy;

- see how belief in the resurrection is part of the Good Friday liturgy;

- look at different parts of the Easter Vigil service;

- study the suggested liturgy for a funeral vigil service or wake;

- examine the Catholic funeral liturgy and rite of committal;

- appreciate how Baptism connects us to the death and resurrection of Jesus;

- plan the readings and songs you would like at your own funeral.

Symbols of New Life

Each of the symbols found on this page is used by Christians to celebrate the passing from death to new life. Take a moment to think about all that you have learned about death and new life in this book. Then write your own reflections on each symbol and how it embodies belief in the resurrection. ▪

Symbol	Meaning
cross	
water	
sacrificed lamb	
poured-out wine	
broken bread	
lit candle	
white garment	
spring flowers	
eggs	

Discussion

Which symbol speaks most clearly to you? Why?

Celebrating New Life

You have seen how belief in life after death has permeated almost all cultures. You have also seen how no definitive proof can be offered for the existence of such an afterlife. Belief in the resurrection remains a matter of faith.

And yet it is this belief—both in the resurrection of Christ and in our own resurrection at the end of time—that remains the cornerstone of Christianity. "Christ has died, Christ is risen, Christ will come again" is proclaimed by millions of Catholics throughout the world at each Eucharist. Our belief is so strong that it must be celebrated. ▪

Attitude Survey	I agree	I disagree	I'm not sure
As the Messiah, Jesus conquered death once and for all.			
Easter is a one-day celebration of the resurrection.			
Baptism celebrates our own passage from death to life.			
A Catholic funeral should be a somber event.			
It is important to me to select the Scripture readings and music for my own funeral.			

In this chapter, you will explore some of the Catholic rituals that celebrate the passing from death to life. You will look first at the liturgies of the **Easter Triduum** and then at the *Order of Christian Funerals*. Finally, you will look at the Church's Rite of Baptism and spend time planning your own funeral liturgy.

Before beginning, take some time to complete in your notebook the above survey.

Easter Triduum *The Christian celebration of Christ's passing from death to life; the Easter Triduum begins on Holy Thursday with the evening Mass of the Lord's Supper, includes the Good Friday service, the Easter Vigil service, and Masses on Easter Sunday, and ends with evening prayer on Easter Sunday.*

The Easter Triduum begins at evening Mass on Holy Thursday and ends with evening prayer on Easter Sunday. It celebrates the Passover of Christ from death to new life.

Activity

Select one of the symbols of new life at the beginning of this chapter. Use it in some creative way (poem, song, sculpture, painting, dance, video, or slide production) to celebrate your beliefs about death and new life. Your creative project should refer to what you have learned in this course and reflect how your values, ideas, or attitudes have changed.

Passover (1) A Jewish feast
held each spring to celebrate
the Exodus event. (2) A term
used to describe the Paschal
mystery, Jesus' passing from
death to new life.

Holy Thursday The
Thursday before Easter Sunday,
on which the Church begins its
celebration of the Easter
Triduum, focusing particularly
on the institution of the
Eucharist.

Good Friday The Friday
before Easter Sunday.
Christians remember on this
day the Paschal mystery,
especially the passion and
death of Jesus.

Easter The first Sunday after
the first full moon following
the spring equinox. On this
day, Catholic and Protestant
Christians celebrate in a special
way the resurrection of Christ.

Of Interest

During the singing of the "Gloria"
on Holy Thursday, the church
bells are rung. Then they remain
silent until the "Gloria" at the
Easter Vigil. This ancient custom
marks the solemnity of the
passion and death of Jesus and
looks forward to the joy of the
resurrection.

The Easter Triduum

The Church's main celebration of the Paschal
mystery is three days, not one. The Easter
Triduum, which begins at evening Mass on
Holy Thursday and ends with evening prayer
on Easter Sunday, celebrates the **Passover** of
Christ from death to new life. It is simplistic to
say that **Holy Thursday** celebrates the Last
Supper of Jesus and the institution of the
Eucharist or that **Good Friday** commemorates
Jesus' dying on a cross or that **Easter** Sunday
celebrates his rising from the tomb. Each liturgy
of the Triduum celebrates the entire Passover
event—Christ's dying and rising, as well as the
promise of our own dying and rising. It is
within this context of the whole that the
Church focuses during the Easter Triduum on
particular moments.

Holy Thursday

The first moment of the Easter Triduum is the
Mass of the Lord's Supper, which is celebrated
in the evening on Holy Thursday. We
remember Jesus' self-sacrifice of himself so that
we could have new life, and we give thanks in
the Eucharistic meal of love.

Both of these sentiments are found in the
opening prayer:

> God our Father,
> we are gathered here to share in
>   the supper
> which your only Son left to his Church
>   to reveal his love.
> He gave it to us when he was about
>   to die
> and commanded us to celebrate it as the
>   new and eternal sacrifice.
> We pray that in this eucharist
> we may find the fullness of love and life.
> Grant this through our Lord Jesus
>   Christ, your Son,
> who lives and reigns with you and the
>   Holy Spirit,
> one God, for ever and ever.
>
> *—Sacramentary*

The Scripture readings remind us that the
Eucharist is rooted in the Exodus experience
of the Israelites, who were set free from slavery
in Egypt and given a new life in the promised
land. The readings recount how the angel of
death passed over the houses of the Israelites as
they were preparing to leave Egypt and how
the angel struck instead the
houses of the Egyptians.

After the homily, people
representing a cross section of
the community have their
feet washed. In this symbolic
action we remember that we
are to give our lives in selfless service of others, just as
Jesus did. As the prayer after
communion expresses it, the
sacred Bread and Wine we
share are a foretaste of the
heavenly banquet. ▪

Discussion

At every Mass, we say or sing an antiphon called "The Lamb of God." Discuss the
Passover imagery in ascribing this title to Jesus.

Almighty God,
we receive new life
from the supper your Son gave us
in this world.
May we find full contentment
in the meal we hope to share
in your eternal kingdom.
We ask this through Christ our Lord.

—*Sacramentary*

Following this prayer, the Holy Eucharist is transferred to another location, to an altar of repose. The **ciborium** of consecrated hosts is carried through the church in procession, while the people sing the "Pange Lingua" and/or other hymns. Adoration of the Blessed Sacrament can continue at the altar of repose up until midnight. Meanwhile, the main altar is stripped. All crosses in the church are removed or covered. ■

Good Friday

The liturgy of Good Friday is not a Mass but rather a communion service that consists of three parts: the Liturgy of the Word, the Veneration of the Cross, and Holy Communion.

• *Liturgy of the Word.* The Scripture readings present Jesus as Isaiah's Suffering Servant, as one who "learned obedience from what he suffered" and thus became "the source of eternal salvation for all who obey him" (Hebrews 4:9). The Passion account presents Jesus as the king of a heavenly kingdom that is greater than any earthly one. The Liturgy of the Word concludes with prayers of intercession for the Church, the pope, the clergy, the laity, those preparing for Baptism, the unity of all Christians, the Jewish people, non-Christians, atheists, all in public office, and those in need. ■

• *Veneration of the Cross.* During this time, people are asked to show reverence to a cross that is unveiled. All are given a chance to venerate the cross—either individually or collectively—by kissing it, genuflecting, or bowing.

ciborium *Container used for the consecrated Hosts at Mass. Often the ciborium is made of gold or silver.*

Of Interest

The Church asks Catholics to fast and abstain from meat on Good Friday to honor the suffering and death of Jesus and to enter more deeply into the experience of his dying and rising.

At the liturgy of Good Friday, the assembly is given a chance to venerate the cross by kissing it, genuflecting, or bowing.

Activity

1. Review the events of the first Passover in Exodus 12–14. Then discuss how Jesus enacted this Passover in his own dying and rising.
2. Read the following Scripture readings for Holy Thursday. What images of death and new life are found in them?
   - Exodus 12:1–8, 11–14
   - Psalm 116:12–13, 15–18
   - 1 Corinthians 11:23–26
   - John 13:1–15
3. Obtain a copy of the song "Pange Lingua." What images of death and new life are found in the lyrics?

Discussion

Why do you think the Church prays for the following groups of people on Good Friday?
- the Jewish people
- those of other religious beliefs
- atheists

The liturgy of Easter Sunday begins with the Service of Light, during which the assembly lights small candles from the Easter candle and process into church.

symbols and actions of the Easter Vigil attest to the Church's belief in the resurrection and serve as a centerpoint to the Triduum and as the center of the entire Church year.

• *Service of Light.* The liturgy begins in darkness, reminiscent of the darkness of the tomb. Outside the church, the priest and ministers light the new fire, saying:

Dear friends in Christ,
on this most holy night,
when our Lord Jesus Christ passed from
    death to life,
the Church invites her children
    throughout the world
to come together in vigil and prayer.
This is the passover of the Lord:
if we honor the memory of his death
    and resurrection
by hearing his word and celebrating his
    mysteries,
then we may be confident
that we shall share his victory over death
and live with him for ever in God.

—Sacramentary

The Easter candle is then lit from this fire and taken in procession into the church. All the people light their smaller candles from the Easter candle (if local fire regulations allow it). The Proclamation that is sung calls on the choirs of angels and all creation to praise the Risen Christ.

• *Liturgy of the Word.* Nine readings may be read—seven from the Old Testament and two from the New Testament. These readings recall how God saved people throughout history and then finally sent a redeemer. Each reading is accompanied by a responsorial psalm and prayer. For pastoral reasons, the number of Old Testament readings may be (and usually is) reduced; however, the reading from

• *Communion Service.* The communion service begins with the Lord's Prayer. The sacred Bread that is used for Communion was consecrated on Holy Thursday. The prayer after communion recalls not only Christ's death but also his resurrection and our own future restoration to life.

At the conclusion of the service, all depart in silence. The altar is stripped; only the cross remains with four candles. ■

Holy Saturday

To commemorate the time Jesus spent in the tomb, the Church spends this day in prayer and meditation. No Mass is celebrated. Aside from the main liturgy, Communion is given only as viaticum. The altar is left bare throughout the day.

Easter

The liturgy of Easter Sunday begins after dark on Saturday with the celebration of the Easter Vigil. This service has four parts: the Service of Light, the Liturgy of the Word, the Liturgy of Baptism, and the Liturgy of the Eucharist. The

Of Interest

On Holy Saturday, Mexican Americans have a custom of blessing animals—dogs, pigeons, parakeets, turtles, cats, roosters, and so forth. It may be an adaptation of the Roman custom of blessing animals to encourage their fertility, a rite that took place in early April, when homage was paid to Venus, the goddess of love.

Activity

Read the following Scripture passages for Good Friday. Then discuss how Jesus' passion and death can give meaning to someone who is suffering from serious sickness or a terminal condition.
• Isaiah 52:13–53:12
• Psalm 31:2, 6, 12–13, 15–17, 25
• Hebrews 4:14–16, 5:7–9
• John 18:1–19:42

Exodus must always be used. After the last reading from the Old Testament, the Gloria is sung while the church bells are rung. The Liturgy of the Word then proceeds as usual, with the second reading, alleluia, Gospel, and homily ■

• *Liturgy of Baptism.* Throughout Lent, the **catechumens** who have been "elected" to Church membership prepare for Baptism. This Baptism ideally takes place at the Easter Vigil. The rite begins with the singing of the Litany of the Saints, which asks all the saints of heaven to pray for the Church and for these new members. The priest then blesses the water by lowering the Easter candle into it and saying:

May all who are buried with Christ
in the death of baptism
rise also with him to newness of life.
We ask this through Christ our Lord.
Amen.

—Sacramentary

The priest then baptizes all the candidates. Adult **neophytes** are confirmed immediately if a bishop or a priest with the faculty to confirm is present. The Rite of Baptism concludes with a renewal of baptismal promises by the entire community. All baptized Catholics once again promise to reject Satan and his works and to believe all that the Church teaches, including the resurrection of the body and life everlasting. This renewal takes the place of the Creed. ■

• *Liturgy of the Eucharist.* After the Rite of Baptism, the liturgy continues in the same way as all Masses. The prayer over the gifts alludes to the coming of God's kingdom at the end of time.

Lord,
accept the prayers and offerings of
    your people.
With your help
may this Easter mystery of our
    redemption
bring to perfection the saving work you
    have begun in us.
We ask this through Christ our Lord.

—Sacramentary

catechumens *The unbaptized who are taking part in the process that leads to Baptism in the Catholic Church.*

neophytes *The newly baptized.*

The Baptism of catechumens who have been "elected" to Church membership ideally takes place at the Easter Vigil.

Activity

Divide your class into nine groups, one group for each set of readings and psalm responses listed here. Read your assigned reading and then prepare to report to the class about what the readings say about passing from death to life.

• Genesis 1:1–2:2
    Psalm 104:1–2, 5–6, 10,
        12–14, 24, 35
• Genesis 22:1–18
    Psalm 16:5, 8–11
• Exodus 14:15–15:1
    Exodus 15:1–6, 17–18
• Isaiah 54:5–14
    Psalm 30:2, 4–6, 11–13

• Isaiah 55:1–11
    Isaiah 12:2–6
• Baruch 3:9–15, 32–4:4
    Psalm 19:8–11
• Ezekiel 36:16–28
    Psalm 42:3, 5; 43:3, 4
• Romans 6:3–11
    Psalm 118:1–2, 16, 17, 22–23
• Matthew 28:1–10

Activity

Look up one of the following Scripture passages to find out how water is a symbol of passing from death to life. Write a short essay about what you discovered.

• Genesis 1
• Genesis 7:1–9:17
• Exodus 14:10–31
• Joshua 3
• Matthew 3:13–17

According to custom, food may be blessed either before or after the Easter Vigil service or on Easter Sunday morning for consumption at the family's Easter meal. This custom arose because of the traditional Lenten fast. Easter was the first day when meat, eggs, and other foods could be eaten again. The prayer of blessing, which may be given by a priest, deacon, or lay person, is as follows:

God of glory,
the eyes of all turn to you
as we celebrate Christ's victory over sin
    and death.
Bless us and this food of our first
    Easter meal.
May we who gather at the Lord's table
continue to celebrate the joy of his
    resurrection
and be admitted finally to his heavenly
    banquet. . . . Amen.

—*Book of Blessings*

Order of Christian Funerals

Since All Souls' Day 1989, the *Order of Christian Funerals* has been mandatory in the United States. This order contains the liturgies approved by the Church for celebrating the deaths of Catholics. As directed by Vatican II, these revised funeral rites clearly express the paschal character of a Christian's death. All three of the rites—the vigil service, the funeral liturgy, and the rite of committal—confidently proclaim "that God has created each person for eternal life and that Jesus, the Son of God, by his death and resurrection, has broken the chains of sin and death that bound humanity" (*Order of Christian Funerals*, #1).

The Vigil Service

The vigil service is celebrated by the family and Christian community sometime after death and before the funeral liturgy. A priest, deacon, or lay person (in the absence of a priest or deacon) presides. The Order includes

two types of services: the vigil for the deceased (to be used when the vigil is celebrated at the home of the deceased, in a funeral home, or in some other suitable place) and the vigil for the deceased with reception at the church (to be used when the vigil is celebrated in church). Both types of vigil services consist of introductory rites, the Liturgy of the Word, intercessory prayers, and a concluding rite.

- *Introductory Rites.* The purpose of these rites is to gather the community and prepare all to listen to God's word. In the vigil for the deceased, the introductory rites include a greeting by the presider, an opening song that expresses belief in eternal life, an invitation to prayer, and an opening prayer. In the vigil with reception at the church, the presider greets the family at the entrance of the church, sprinkles the casket with holy water, and spreads the pall over the casket. An opening song is sung as family members process with the casket into church. An invitation to prayer and an opening prayer then follow.

- *Liturgy of the Word.* This part of the service consists of Scripture readings from the Old or New Testament, a responsorial psalm (preferably sung), a gospel reading, and a homily. The purpose of the Liturgy of the Word is "to proclaim the paschal mystery, teach remembrance of the dead, convey the hope of being gathered together in God's kingdom, and encourage the witness of Christian life" (*Order of Christian Funerals*, #60).

- *Prayers of Intercession.* The community prays to God to have mercy on the deceased person. It does this first in a litany, to which people respond "Lord, have mercy." After everyone prays the Lord's Prayer, the presider prays a concluding prayer. At this time, a member or friend of the family may speak in remembrance of the deceased.

- *Concluding Rite.* The vigil ends with a blessing and may be followed by a closing song.

The Church encourages mourners to have a vigil service rather than a simple wake. Members of the local parish are encouraged to attend the vigil to show concern and support for the mourners and, thus, take part in the Church's ministry of consolation. In addition, parishioners are encouraged to participate fully in the prayers and songs of the vigil service. ▪

The Funeral Liturgy

For hundreds of years, the priest wore black vestments at funeral liturgies. The color black emphasized mourning for death but did little to symbolize the joy of resurrection. In 1970, the United States Bishops' Committee on the Liturgy allowed white vestments to be worn for funeral liturgies, besides purple or black vestments.

The *Order of Christian Funerals* provides two forms of liturgies: the funeral Mass (which is preferred) and the funeral liturgy outside Mass. The main parts of the funeral Mass are the reception of the body, the Liturgy of the Word, the Liturgy of the Eucharist, and the final commendation and farewell. The funeral liturgy outside Mass has the same structure, omitting the Liturgy of the Eucharist. ▪

- *Reception at the Church.* The funeral Mass begins at the entrance of the church, where the priest and family members welcome the casket. The reason for gathering at church is given as follows:

  Since the church is the place where the community of faith assembles for worship, the rite of reception of the body at the church has great significance. The church is the place where the Christian life is begotten in baptism, nourished in the eucharist, and where the community gathers to commend one of its deceased members to the Father. The church is at once a symbol of the community and of the heavenly liturgy that the celebration of the liturgy anticipates. . . .

  —*Order of Christian Funerals*, #131

The priest begins by greeting the family members. He sprinkles the casket with holy water in remembrance of the deceased person's Baptism. Family members then help place the funeral pall over the coffin. This white cloth is a reminder of Baptism and the garment given at Baptism. After the pall is in place, the priest and altar servers lead the entrance procession. The casket, together with pallbearers and family members, follows. During the procession, a song is sung by the assembly.

The casket is positioned in the center aisle near the lit Easter candle, another symbol of the Risen Christ and the deceased person's Baptism. Family members may choose to put another symbol of the Christian life (a Bible, a cross, or a Book of the Gospels) on the casket. After this has been completed, the priest prays an opening prayer.

- *Liturgy of the Word.* This essential ingredient in the funeral celebration has the same structure as that found in other Masses. The first reading, either from the Old or New Testament, is followed by a sung responsorial psalm. The second reading is optional. A sung gospel acclamation precedes the gospel reading and homily. The *Order of Christian Funerals* clearly states that the homily should "dwell on God's compassionate love and on the paschal mystery of the Lord, as proclaimed in the Scripture readings" rather than be an eulogy. In the general intercessions, the community prays for the deceased and his or her family members as well as for the needs of the entire community.

Of Interest

For centuries, the funeral Mass was called a *requiem Mass* because of the first Latin word of the Introit, which translated as "Eternal rest grant unto them, O Lord." Despite the new emphasis on the resurrection, the *Mass of Resurrection* is an incorrect title for a funeral Mass and is reserved only for the Easter liturgy itself.

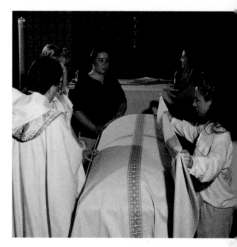

The funeral pall, placed over the coffin, is a reminder of Baptism and the garment given at Baptism.

Activity
Make a list of songs you would consider appropriate to use as the opening and closing songs at a vigil service. Be prepared to discuss the dying/rising themes you find present in the lyrics.

Activity
Listen to a recording of a requiem composed by Bach, Handel, or another classical composer. Write your thoughts as you listen to the music. Which section particularly affected you?

- *Liturgy of the Eucharist.* Members of the family are encouraged to bring the gifts to the altar while a presentation song is sung. The structure of this part of the Mass remains unchanged, with the exception that the priest may incense the gifts and altar and family members may speak in remembrance of the deceased after communion.

- *Final Commendation and Farewell.* This part of the liturgy is both an acknowledgment of separation from the deceased and an affirmation that all will be reunited at the resurrection on the last day. The priest invites everyone to pray in silence. Then he incenses the casket and sprinkles it with holy water (if this was not done at the beginning of Mass). After a song of farewell is sung, the priest prays a prayer of commendation.

Into your hands, Father of mercies,
we commend our brother/sister N.
in the sure and certain hope
that, together with all who have died in
    Christ,
he/she will rise with him on the last
    day.

[We give you thanks for the blessings
which you bestowed upon N. in this
    life:
they are signs to us of your goodness
and of our fellowship with the saints in
    Christ.]

Merciful Lord,
turn toward us and listen to our prayers:
open the gates of paradise to your
    servant
and help us who remain
to comfort one another with assurances
    of faith,
until we all meet in Christ

and are with you and with your
    brother/sister for ever.
We ask this through Christ our Lord.
Amen.

—"Prayer of Commendation A," *Order of
Christian Funerals* (#404)

The priest and servers, pallbearers with the casket, and family members then process out of church in the same order as before. At this time, the assembly sings a closing song. ■

Rite of Committal

This part of the funeral liturgy may be celebrated at the grave, mausoleum, crematorium, or at sea (in the case of water burial). The *Order of Christian Funerals* provides two forms for this rite. The rite of committal is used when the final commendation was already included in the funeral liturgy. The rite of committal with final commendation is used when there was no funeral liturgy or no commendation during the funeral liturgy.

The structure of both forms is simple. Both begin with an invitation to prayer, a Scripture verse, and a prayer over the place of committal. The prayer has several options, depending on whether the body will be entombed, cremated, or buried at sea.

The words of committal express the community's beliefs regarding death. "Through this act the community of faith proclaims that the grave or place of interment, once a sign of futility and despair, has been transformed by means of Christ's own death and resurrection into a sign of hope and promise" (*Order of Christian Funerals,* #209).

After the committal, the people are invited to join in the intercessory prayers and the Lord's Prayer. Following the concluding prayer, the priest says a prayer over the people and blesses them. During the closing song, people may place flowers or soil on the casket. ■

Discussion
1. What are the similarities between the symbols found in the funeral liturgy and those found in the Easter Vigil service?
2. What do you think incense symbolizes?
3. What are some songs that would be appropriate for a funeral Mass?

Discussion
1. Do you think it is important for friends of the family to attend the vigil service, the funeral, and the rite of committal? Why or why not?
2. What are some appropriate songs to sing at the place of interment?

The Rite of Baptism

The Church's liturgies of Easter and Christian funerals reflect an earlier celebration—that of Baptism. Paul explains the importance of Baptism and its connection to death and resurrection:

> Do you not know that all of us who have been baptized into Christ Jesus were baptized into his death? Therefore we have been buried with him by baptism into death, so that, just as Christ was raised from the dead by the glory of the Father, so we too might walk in newness of life.
>
> —Romans 6:3–4

Presently the Church has two concurrent practices regarding the reception of new members: the Baptism of Infants and Children and the Order of Christian Initiation of Adults (OCIA). Both rites celebrate dying and rising to new life—dying to sin and rising to new life with Christ.

Regardless of which rite is followed, the following parts are included at some point: Liturgy of the Word, prayers of intercession, prayer of **exorcism**, blessing of water, renunciation of sin and profession of faith, receiving the lighted candle, prayer over ears and mouth, and a conclusion. Here is a brief look at what happens in each part, as well as its meaning.

- *Liturgy of the Word.* Because God's word gives us life and is essential to Christian living, the Church recommends that Baptisms take place during Mass. If not, a Liturgy of the Word should be part of the baptismal rite. This liturgy includes one or two Scripture readings, especially a reading from the Gospels. The gospel reading is followed by a short homily, prayers of intercession, and the Litany of the Saints.

- *Exorcism.* In this prayer the community prays that the person be delivered from original sin and all personal sins. (In the OCIA, rites of exorcism take place during Lent.) Next there is an anointing with the oil of catechumens, either on the breast or the hands. The oil is a symbol of the wisdom, strength, and protection that Christ brings to the baptismal candidate by the anointing.

*B*aptism **unites** *us to the* **passion, death,** *and* **resurrection** *of Christ. It* **joins** *our* **suffering** *to his.*

Pope John Paul II, *The Christian Meaning of Human Suffering*

- *Profession of Faith.* After blessing the water, the priest invites the candidate (or in the case of infants, the godparents and parents) to reject Satan and evil and to make a profession of faith. This profession, which is based on the Apostles' Creed, states belief in the resurrection, ascension, and Second Coming of Jesus, as well as the resurrection of the body and life everlasting.

- *Baptism.* The actual Baptism may be performed in one of two ways: (a) immersion of the whole body or of the head only or (b) infusion, the pouring of water over the head of the candidate. As this action is taking place, the priest says "N., I baptize you in the name of the Father, and of the Son, and of the Holy Spirit."

- *Post-Baptismal Rites.* Immediately after Baptism, the neophyte is anointed with **chrism**. This holy oil, forms of which are also used at Confirmation and Holy Orders, is an effective sign that the newly baptized shares in the priesthood of Christ and is a member of the people of God. The neophyte is then given a white robe (a symbol of new life in Christ) and a candle that has been lit from the Easter candle (a symbol of the light of faith).

exorcism *A rite in which evil spirits are driven out of a person or place by the authority of God and with the prayer of the Church.*

chrism *holy oil (olive or vegetable oil mixed with balm), forms of which are used at Baptism, Confirmation, and Holy Orders.*

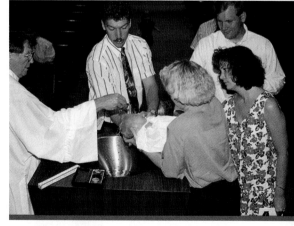

Of Interest

In order to be a baptismal sponsor, three requirements must be met:
- The person must be mature enough to undertake this responsibility.
- The person must have received Baptism, Confirmation, and Eucharist.
- The person must be a member in good standing of the Catholic Church.

Of Interest

In the early days of the Church, Baptisms took place in eight-sided pools with steps. The persons to be baptized walked down into the pool, thereby symbolizing death to sin. After being baptized, they walked up the steps on the other side, thereby symbolizing resurrection and new life. The eight sides symbolized the Christian belief that the resurrection was the eighth day of creation.

- *Opening of Ears and Mouth.* The priest touches the person's ears and mouth and prays that the person will receive the grace needed to hear the word of God and to work for salvation. (This rite occurs during Lent in the OCIA.)
- *Conclusion.* The rite concludes with the Lord's Prayer and a prayer of blessing for the new Christian.

In recent times, the Church has come to recognize a "baptism of desire" besides the realized celebration of the Sacrament of Baptism. For this reason the Church allows catechumens and infants who die before Baptism to have an ecclesiastical funeral and burial. ▪

Catholics Believe

Baptism, the original and full sign of which is immersion, efficaciously signifies the descent into the tomb by the Christian who dies to sin with Christ in order to live a new life. "We were buried therefore with him by baptism into death, so that as Christ was raised from the dead by the glory of the Father, we too might walk in newness of life" (Rom 6:4; cf. Col 2:12; Eph 5:26). (Catechism, #628)

Planning Your Funeral

Use the following list to choose readings for your funeral liturgy. Then fill in the outline on the next page.

First Reading

____ 2 Maccabees 12:43–46	____ Romans 5:5–11	____ 2 Corinthians 4:14–5:1
____ Job 19:1, 23–27	____ Romans 5:17–21	____ 2 Corinthians 5:1, 6–10
____ Wisdom 3:1–9	____ Romans 6:3–9	____ Philippians 3:20–21
____ Wisdom 3:1-6, 9	____ Romans 6:3–4, 8–9	____ 1 Thessalonians 4:13–18
____ Wisdom 4:7–15	____ Romans 8:14–23	____ 2 Timothy 2:8–13
____ Isaiah 25:6a, 7–9	____ Romans 8:31b–35, 37–39	____ 1 John 3:1–2
____ Lamentations 3:17–26	____ Romans 14:7–9, 10b–12	____ 1 John 3:14–16
____ Daniel 12:1–3	____ 1 Corinthians 15:20–23, 24b–28	____ Revelation 14:13
____ Acts 10:34–43	____ 1 Corinthians 15:20–23	____ Revelation 20:11–21:1
____ Acts 10:34–36, 42–43	____ 1 Corinthians 15:51–57	____ Revelation 21:1–5a, 6b–7

Responsorial Psalm

____ Psalm 23	____ Psalm 63	____ Psalm 130
____ Psalm 25	____ Psalm 103	____ Psalm 143
____ Psalm 27	____ Psalm 116	
____ Psalms 42 and 43	____ Psalm 122	

Activity

1. Ask a parish director of religious education to speak to your class about the OCIA. What is the process that catechumens go through? How long does this process take? What liturgical rites are involved?
2. If possible, attend a Baptism in your own parish. Then report on how the actions and symbols of the rite affected you and your faith.

Gospel Acclamation

____ Matthew 11:25	____ John 6:40	____ 2 Timothy 2:11b–12a
____ Matthew 25:34	____ John 6:51a	____ Revelation 1:5a, 6b
____ John 3:16	____ John 11:25–26	____ Revelation 14:13
____ John 6:39	____ Philippians 3:20	

Gospel Reading

____ Matthew 5:1–12a	____ Luke 23:33, 39–43	____ John 11:17–27
____ Matthew 11:25–30	____ Luke 23:44–46, 50,	____ John 11:21–27
____ Matthew 25:1–13	52–53, 24:1–6	____ John 11:32–45
____ Matthew 25:31–46	____ Luke 24:13–35	____ John 12:23–28
____ Mark 15:33–39	____ Luke 24:13–16, 28–35	____ John 12:23–26
____ Mark 15:33–39, 16:1–6	____ John 5:24–29	____ John 14:1–6
____ Luke 7:11–17	____ John 6:37–40	____ John 17:24–26
____ Luke 12:35–40	____ John 6:51–58	____ John 19:17–18, 25–30

My Choice of Readings and Songs

<u>Vigil Service</u>

Opening Song:
First Reading:
Responsorial Psalm:

Gospel Acclamation:
Gospel:
Closing Song:

<u>Funeral Liturgy</u>

Choice of Christian Symbol for
     Placing on the Casket:
Entrance Song:
First Reading:
Responsorial Psalm:
Second Reading (optional):
Gospel Acclamation:
Gospel:

Song during Presentation
     of Gifts:
Holy, Holy, Holy:
Memorial Acclamation:
Great Amen:
Lamb of God:
Communion Song:
Closing Song:

<u>Rite of Committal</u>

Scripture Verse (select one)
____ Matthew 25:34
____ Philippians 3:20
____ John 6:39
____ Revelation 1:5–6
Concluding Song:

Words to Know

catechumen

chrism

ciborium

Easter

Easter Triduum

exorcism

Good Friday

Holy Thursday

neophyte

Passover

Review Questions

1. What is one of the unique characteristics of the liturgy for Holy Thursday?
2. What is one of the unique characteristics of the liturgy for Good Friday?
3. What is one of the unique characteristics of the liturgy for the Easter Vigil?
4. How does each of these liturgies reflect belief in the passing of Jesus from death to life?
5. What are the main parts of the vigil service from the *Order of Christian Funerals*?
6. What are the main parts of the funeral Mass from the *Order of Christian Funerals*?
7. What are the main parts of the rite of committal from the *Order of Christian Funerals*?
8. What are the two Rites of Baptism celebrated in the Church today?
9. How do the actions and symbols of Baptism reflect Catholic beliefs about death and resurrection?

C•H•A•P•T•E•R

15

Gospel Living

IN THIS CHAPTER, YOU WILL

- focus on the rising presence of violence in modern society;

- see how domestic violence contradicts the nature of Christian family life;

- consider the role alcohol plays in fatal car accidents;

- see how abortion differs from contraception and why the Catholic Church regards all direct abortions as immoral;

- examine the potential of nuclear weapons to destroy life universally;

- understand the arguments for and against capital punishment;

- study some of the Church documents that relate to issues of violence and peace;

- reflect on ways you can be a peacemaker in your own life.

Senseless Violence

She was a bubbly state-champion cheerleader. He was a tough football player who fancied himself both a break-dancer and a balladeer. Saturday night, Renelyn Simmons and Andre Bradley, both high school honor students, were gunned down by a gang member who fired a shotgun at a crowd of teenagers walking toward a neighborhood pizza parlor. Three other people were injured.

"As far as senseless goes, this is about as senseless as you can get," said Jeannette Newman, Bradley's aunt. "The ones that are trying to head in a productive direction and lead by example are the ones that get shot down," said Herman Simmons, father of the slain cheerleader.

Police said the slaying took place about 11 P.M. A white car with tinted windows passed the crowd of friends. The two people inside the car flashed gang signs, and the group, not recognizing them, responded with waves. The teens thought it was one of their friends. The two men in the car shouted obscenities and parked about a block ahead. Then the passenger hoisted a shotgun and fired into the crowd. The pellets traveled about 50 yards, striking Simmons and Bradley. Two other people in the group suffered superficial injuries. And another 50 yards away, a pellet hit the leg of Lisa Cole, who is pregnant and was outside with her dog.

Detectives spent Sunday morning interviewing neighbors and taking notes on gang graffiti in the area. They had no suspect descriptions and no motives for the shooting.

"This wasn't a party; this wasn't a gang. They were just walking. That's what's so shocking," said Newman, Bradley's aunt.

"They were both A-B students, always happy, smiles on their faces," said a friend. "They had so much going for them."

Today was to be a milestone day for each of the two teens. Bradley was going to collect his first paycheck from his week-old job selling swimming pool products. Simmons was going to start advanced summer studies at a community college. ∎

—Adapted from "Honor students slain: Pair die in drive-by shotgun blast," © *The Arizona Republic* (June 8, 1998). Article by Richard Ruelas. Used with permission. Permission does not imply endorsement.

In Memory

Renelyn Simmons, 16, and Andre Bradley, 16, both honor students at Apollo High School in Phoenix, Arizona, were killed on June 6, 1998.

Discussion

1. Why do you think so many people in today's society own and carry guns?
2. Do you think people are naturally violent, or is violence something we learn?
3. Do you find the violence in TV shows and movies to be entertaining? Why or why not?

A Way of Life

Unfortunately, senseless violence seems to be an increasing fact of American life. No place—our schools, our public buildings, or our own neighborhoods—is safe from, or immune to, violence. As a 1991 national survey revealed, 14 percent of all Americans carry a pistol with them or in their car. More and more teenagers and elementary students are bringing guns, knives, and other weapons with them to school. Violent crimes, especially **homicides** committed by strangers, relatives, and gang members, are on the upswing.

Is violence inherent in human nature, or is it something we teach our children? Just watch cartoons on Saturday morning TV and decide for yourself. Everywhere you turn, violence seems to be an integral part of our social network. Such violence is a far cry from the gospel message of peace and turning the other cheek (cf. Matthew 5:39). No course on suffering and death would be complete if it did not examine our own way of living and our relationships. Do we foster peace in the situations in which we find ourselves, or are we, too, part of the problem? Do we inflict needless suffering on others?

The message of Jesus about how to live as Christians in the world is very clear. He condemned the Pharisees for causing others suffering (cf. Luke 11:42, 45). He taught nonviolence in the Sermon on the Mount (cf. Matthew 5–7). Jesus would not let the disciples call down fire on an inhospitable village (cf. Luke 9:51–56). He rebuked Peter for cutting off the ear of a soldier who came to arrest him (cf. Mark 14:47). In short, Jesus refused to cause suffering to others. He taught his followers to live in the same way.

In this chapter, you will explore five different expressions of violence—domestic violence, drunk driving, abortion, war, and capital punishment. You will read specific Church documents that call us, in contrast, to live as peacemakers. Finally, you will explore the existence of violence in your own life and discover ways you can promote life rather than suffering and death in your daily relationships.

Before proceeding, respond in your notebook to the above survey. ■

Attitude Survey	I agree	I disagree	I'm not sure
Most families experience some type of domestic violence.			
Drinking alcohol and driving recklessly are fun.			
All abortions are wrong.			
War is never justified.			
Capital punishment is a strong deterrent to crime.			

homicide *The intentional killing of a human being.*

Of Interest

The statistic on the number of people who carry a pistol with them or in their car came from a national survey published in *The Day America Told The Truth: What People Really Believe about Everything That Matters.* In the survey, 7 percent of the people said they would kill a stranger for ten million dollars.

Of Interest

According to the National Center for Injury Prevention and Control (NCIPC), over thirty-four thousand Americans died in 1996 from injuries resulting from firearms.

Jesus refused to cause suffering to others. He taught his followers to live in the same way.

Activity

1. Watch a cartoon program on Saturday morning. Record the number and types of violence that take place during the show. Analyze what such violence is teaching children, and report your findings to the class.

2. Write a report on gang violence. Why do teenagers join gangs? What are the reasons gang members seek to kill others? What can be done to educate children about the risks of joining a gang?

fratricide The killing of one's brother.

matricide The killing of one's mother.

parricide The killing of either or both parents.

patricide The killing of one's father.

sororicide The killing of one's sister.

uxoricide The killing of a wife by her husband.

Of Interest

In 1974, the first battered women's shelter was opened near London. During the next ten years, 500 battered women's shelters were established in the United States.

Domestic Violence

Domestic violence refers to the violence that takes place in a wide range of family and other intimate relations (siblings, parent-child, other relatives, married and unmarried partnerships, terminated partnerships, and the abuse of elderly parents by their adult children). The violence itself may involve physical contact between persons, use of a weapon, a threat with a weapon, explicit verbal threat of bodily harm, and other actions causing mental or psychological harm. All too often such violence ends in death. Among the fatal crimes associated with domestic violence are **fratricide**, **matricide**, **parricide**, **patricide**, **sororicide**, and **uxoricide**.

In 1990, the *Journal of American Medicine* reported that intimate violence was the leading cause of injuries to women. More women were battered that year than the total number of women involved in car crashes, rapes, and muggings. A 1984 Atlanta report on fatal domestic violence showed that 52 percent of the victims were women and 74 percent of the perpetrators were male. In 1998, the Family Violence Prevention Fund in San Francisco estimated that 3 to 10 million children had witnessed domestic violence that year.

Other studies in the United States have shown that marital violence occurs in one out of four marriages. One million children are physically abused by parents or caretakers every year. And one million elderly people are abused each year by their adult children. From these statistics, it is clear that domestic violence is commonplace and that the perpetrators and victims of such violence are ordinary people. ■

The Judeo-Christian ethic of peace contrasts strongly with such violence: "And I will grant peace in the land, and you shall lie down, and no one shall make you afraid" (Leviticus 26:6). The importance of loving and trusting family relationships is also clear: "Your wife will be like a fruitful vine within your house; your children will be like olive shoots around your table" (Psalm 128:3). "And let the peace of Christ rule in your hearts, to which indeed you were called in the one body" (Colossians 3:15).

The World Synod of Bishops emphasized in 1980 the love and caring that are to characterize Christian families. Such family love finds its roots in the Sacrament of Marriage and is strengthened by the Eucharist, by shared prayer, and by the support of the Christian community. For these reasons, the bishops deepened their commitment to family ministry. ■ ■

Drunk Driving

Problems at home or work often "spill over" onto the road. Across the United States in 1994, over 30,000 people died in alcohol-induced motor accidents. In 1995, drunk driving was to blame for 41.4 percent of all fatal car accidents. By 1998, road rage and aggressive driving were also added to the list of fatal road violence.

Despite the sobering statistics, there is a glimmer of hope. National designated driver campaigns and organizations such as MADD (Mothers Against Drunk Driving) and SADD (Students Against Drunk Driving) have begun to have a positive impact. During the past decade, the percentage of high school seniors who used alcohol at least once has fallen by 9 percent. Over the past fifteen years, drunk driving fatalities have dropped 35 percent and teenage drunk driving accidents are down 67 percent.

 Discussion

What do you think are some of the factors that might contribute to domestic violence?

 Discussion

Discuss how each of the following can help families grow in love:
- the Sacrament of Marriage
- Eucharist
- shared prayer
- the Christian community

 Activity

1. Find out what your diocese and civic community are doing to help victims of domestic violence. What services, shelters, and counseling are available?

2. The Sunday between Christmas and New Year's Day is the Feast of the Holy Family. Prepare a Mass or prayer service for this day, focusing on the importance of peace and love in family relationships. Celebrate this Mass or prayer service with the class in attendance. Invite family members to attend also.

In 1995, drunk driving was the cause of 41.4 percent of all fatal car accidents.

Still, DUI (driving under the influence of alcohol) continues to be a serious problem. In 1998, the National Institute on Alcohol and Drug Abuse reported that 50 percent of the alcohol sold in this country was consumed by just 10 percent of the drinkers. Of all adult Americans, 63 percent drank alcohol. That was up from 56 percent in the early 1990s. According to a 1998 study of the National Highway Traffic Safety Administration, a higher percentage of traffic deaths related to alcohol occurs on Saint Patrick's Day (March 17) than on any other day of the year. ▪

Abortion

The medical definition of **abortion** used here refers to the expulsion of the fetus from the womb, with resulting death. In some cases, an abortion is spontaneous; it is then referred to as a "miscarriage." In other cases, the abortion is deliberately induced. The reasons for inducing abortion vary greatly—financial distress, "bad timing," birth defects found in the fetus, rape, incest, endangerment of the mother's health, too many children already. According to the *Roe vs. Wade* decision of the Supreme Court (1973), a woman is not required to have a specific reason in order to end a pregnancy. Under the law, she may even seek a legal abortion simply because she doesn't want the child.

Percentage of Auto Accidents That Are Alcohol Related

- Saint Patrick's Day — 63
- New Year's Eve/Day — 52
- Memorial Day — 51
- Fourth of July — 47
- Thanksgiving — 46
- Ordinary weekday — 40

abortion *The spontaneous or induced (caused by human choice) expulsion of a fetus from the womb.*

Of Interest

In 1990, alcohol consumption per person in America was twenty-eight gallons per year. By 1995, the per-person consumption was twenty-five gallons per year.

Of Interest

In 1998, beer constituted 88 percent of all alcoholic beverages consumed by Americans.

Discussion

1. Among teens in your local area, do you think drinking and driving is more of a problem today than ten years ago? Explain your position.
2. Why do you think alcohol seems so appealing to some teens?
3. What are some actions teens themselves can take to reduce the problem of drunk driving?

In 1992, American women between the ages of fifteen and forty-four aborted 379 fetuses for every 1,000 live births. That amounted to approximately 1,529,000 abortions. The great majority of women who had abortions were unmarried and white. Most had no prior children or abortions. Sixty percent of the women were under twenty-five; almost half of this group were teenagers.

Since the Church teaches that life begins at conception, it considers induced abortion—for any reason—morally wrong. Thus Code 1398 of Canon Law states: "A person who procures a successful abortion incurs an automatic (*latae sententiae*) excommunication."

What the Church condemns is a "successful abortion"—a case where the abortion has taken place and the fetus has been killed as a result of a procedure whose primary purpose is to end the life of the fetus. The Church, however, does take into consideration a moral principle called the *double effect*. A certain action may have two effects, one that is intended and one that is not intended. For example, suppose a pregnant woman is found to have cancer. In order to save her life, she must have chemotherapy and radiation treatments. In such a case, the Church would allow the medical treatment, even though the secondary (unintended) result might be the killing of the fetus. However, every possible effort would have to be made to save and protect both lives. ∎

Abortion has become one of the most controversial and emotional moral issues of our time. Basically, it has divided people into two camps: pro-life, those who oppose abortion, and pro-abortion, those who favor abortion. The fundamental stance of each group is summarized in the following table:

Pro-Life	Pro-Abortion
1. Human beings are required to respect the nature of their bodies, including the reproductive process.	1. Human beings are free to do whatever they think is right with their bodies.
2. Life begins at the moment of conception.	2. It is unclear when life actually begins.
3. All life, especially that of the most vulnerable and the unborn, is sacred.	3. Quality of life determines whether life is sacred or not.
4. The unborn have a right to be born.	4. A woman has a right to determine what happens to her own body.
5. It is wrong to kill an innocent human being and wrong to legalize an action that is immoral.	5. It is wrong to put one's moral position (anti-abortion) into law.
6. If abortions were not legal, fewer women would seek them.	6. Women will always want abortions. It is safer to obtain an abortion legally rather than illegally.
7. There are not enough babies for all the people who want to adopt them.	7. Unwanted children are often abused, neglected, or grow up to be criminals.

Discussion

1. If abortion is a serious sin, why is it not all right to bomb abortion clinics and maim or kill women who seek abortions? Explain.
2. What can Catholic parishes and high schools do to support unmarried students who get pregnant?
3. Imagine this situation: a senior in high school is told by his girlfriend, a junior, that she is pregnant. What do you think they should do?

The controversy between the two groups has become so intense that some political campaigns are run on this one issue alone. Politicians may or may not be elected to public office depending on their abortion stance. Likewise, justices of the Supreme Court may or may not be voted for by members of the Senate depending on their abortion views.

Since the 1973 Supreme Court decision, numerous pro-life groups have sought to get the decision reversed. Their efforts seem to be having some success. In its 1989 *Webster vs. Reproductive Services* ruling, a more conservative Supreme Court upheld the legality of some new state restrictions on abortion. In 1991, the Supreme Court said it was not unconstitutional for the federal government to ban federally financed birth control clinics from providing abortion information.

Where the legal battle surrounding abortion will end is anyone's guess. But one thing is clear: the Catholic Church will always be on the side of life rather than on the side of death. ■

War

In May 1998, India set off five nuclear tests, surprising the world and serving as a grim reminder of the ever-present danger of nuclear weapons. Because of the nuclear "first strike" capacity of a growing number of nations, regional wars now have the deadly potential of escalating to world dimensions and destroying all life as we know it.

The killing force of nuclear weapons is derived either from fission (the breaking apart of atomic particles) or fusion (the combining of hydrogen atoms to form helium). One type of fusion weapon, the neutron bomb, can kill people while doing only limited damage to buildings. In addition to the destruction caused by the initial blast, nuclear explosions produce blinding light, searing heat, and lethal radiation that may persist in the air, ground, and water for hundreds or thousands of years, causing a long-term **nuclear winter**. Scientists theorize that conditions of semi-darkness, killing frosts, and subfreezing temperatures, combined with high radiation, would destroy most animal and plant life. Humans would die in large numbers due to starvation, exposure, and disease.

The devastating capacity of nuclear weapons was seen on August 6, 1945, when the United States dropped an atomic bomb on Hiroshima, Japan. Most of the city was destroyed, and seventy to eighty thousand people were killed. Thousands more died in subsequent years due to radiation poisoning. The United States dropped a second atomic bomb on Nagasaki, Japan, on August 9, 1945. It killed thirty-nine thousand people outright and injured about twenty-five thousand more. About 40 percent of the city's buildings were completely destroyed.

nuclear winter
Environmental devastation that (it is theorized) would probably result from a nuclear war.

Of Interest

Today Hiroshima, Japan, is a spiritual center of the peace movement for the banning of atomic weapons. Peace Memorial Park contains a museum and monument dedicated to those who died in the atomic explosion. Nagasaki is also a spiritual center for movements to ban nuclear weapons.

Activity

1. Find out about the Birthright program and how it provides alternatives to abortion for couples with troublesome pregnancies.
2. Research how your elected officials (senators, representatives, governor, mayor) stand on abortion. Report your findings to the class.
3. Find out who the current justices of the Supreme Court are as well as their views on abortion.
4. Interview your mother or another woman about the experience of pregnancy.
5. Find out what your diocese is doing to support (a) women who are pregnant and (b) women who have had abortions.

arms control An agreement between countries to limit the development, testing, deployment, or use of nuclear weapons.

disarmament The actual destruction or reduction of nuclear weapons.

arms limitation An agreement to limit the number of nuclear weapons.

pacifism Opposition to all war or violence as a means of settling disputes.

just war theory A moral position that states war may be justified if it meets certain criteria.

Fear of worldwide death caused by a nuclear war has prompted international **arms control**, **disarmament**, and **arms limitation** agreements. In 1963, the Soviet Union, United Kingdom, and United States signed a Nuclear Test-Ban Treaty that banned tests of nuclear weapons in the atmosphere, outer space, and underwater. This treaty was subsequently signed by 120 countries. In 1968, the Treaty on the Non-Proliferation of Nuclear Weapons, which was signed by 140 countries, sought to reduce chemical, biological, and nuclear weapons. The 1972 Strategic Arms Limitation Talks (SALT I) between the United States and the Soviet Union limited both the size of nuclear arsenals and the development of more advanced strategic weapons. In the 1987 Intermediate-Range Nuclear Forces Treaty, the United States and the Soviet Union agreed to eliminate medium-range land-based missiles. ▪

Two moral positions regarding war exist within the Church—pacifism and the just war theory.

Christian Ethics and Warfare

Two moral positions regarding war exist within the Church. The first position, known as **pacifism**, interprets the gospel as forbidding all use of violence. The second position, known as the **just war theory**, acknowledges some legitimate use of force.

Pacifism

A pacifist is someone who refuses to bear arms or to use force as a means of settling disputes. This refusal is usually based on religious beliefs.

During the Civil War, members of the Society of Friends absolutely refused to bear arms because they believed that God forbade warfare and military service. As a result, laws were passed that exempted Quakers, Mennonites, and others who were conscientious objectors from military service. Since the Civil War, there have been some pacifists who objected to each war that has occurred. Some gave alternative nonviolent service; some went to jail. Pacifists raised national consciousness during the Vietnam War in the 1960s. Many of them burned their draft cards and moved to Canada. ▪

Just War Theory

The just war theory states that war may be waged by Christians if it is a just war. In order to be considered just, the war must meet the following six criteria:

- It must be waged for a just cause. (To liberate an occupied country is a just cause. To invade a country for its resources is not a just cause.)
- It must be declared by the proper authority. (In the United States, Congress alone can declare war.)

 *Activity*

Your teacher will provide you with a list of countries that have nuclear weapons. Choose one country, and research the following: how many warheads are in its arsenal today, what the range of these warheads is, and whether or not the country has signed any test-ban treaty or has agreed to any form of disarmament. After presenting your country's nuclear capability, have a class discussion about the potential or non-potential for nuclear war some time in the next fifty years. What do you think today's teens can do to help prevent such a war?

 Activity

Look up the following Scripture passages. Then report to the class how the Bible may be used to justify a pacifist's position.
- Isaiah 2:4
- Isaiah 9:4
- Matthew 5:9
- Matthew 5:38–48
- Matthew 26:52

- It must be waged with a right intention. (For example, freedom rather than personal gain.)
- It must be a last resort. (All peaceful means to resolve the conflict must have been tried.)
- It must have a likely outcome of success. (It is not moral to risk the lives of soldiers if you can't possibly win.)
- Proportional means must be used. (No more force than is necessary may be used. According to Catholic teaching, the use of nuclear weapons is immoral and may not be permitted.)

Using this theory, some Christians become selective conscientious objectors (COs). They are not opposed to war in general, but they may oppose a specific war because it is not just. One example of a selective CO was Franz Jaegerstaetter, a Catholic peasant in Austria. On August 9, 1943, he was beheaded in Berlin because he refused to serve in what he was convinced was "an unjust war being waged by an immoral regime." The laws of the United States do not allow for Catholics to become selective conscientious objectors, a common Catholic position rooted in the just war theory. ▪

Capital Punishment

Another type of violence that ends in homicide is **capital punishment**. Capital punishment is based on a sense of justice that says "an eye for an eye, a life for a life." The criminal must pay for his or her crime. Formerly in history, a person could be put to death for committing a wide range of crimes. As John 8:1–11 tells us, women in the time of Jesus could be stoned to death according to Jewish law for committing adultery. (Roman law did not permit the Jews actually to carry this out.) According to Roman law, non-

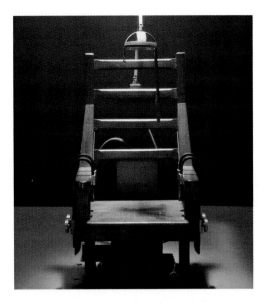

Capital punishment is based on a sense of justice that says "an eye for an eye, a life for a life."

Romans and slaves could be crucified for committing crimes such as murder, robbery, piracy, treason, and rebellion.

In colonial America, a person suspected (not necessarily convicted) of arson could be burned at the stake. Couples caught in adultery could be hanged. Men or women suspected of witchcraft could also be burned or hanged. In eighteenth-century England, several hundred different offenses could warrant the death penalty. Enlightenment writers of the eighteenth century brought about many reforms in the way criminals were punished. Limits also were placed on the number and type of crimes that might incur the death penalty.

In its 1972 *Furman vs. Georgia* decision, the United States Supreme Court ruled that capital punishment as it was then practiced in Georgia and other states violated the Eighth and Fourteenth Amendments because it was cruel and unusual punishment. In 1976, however, the Supreme Court upheld the constitutionality of revised state laws calling for capital punishment. Some states now have the death penalty; others do not. ▪

Of Interest

In 1948, an international group of Catholics known as *Pax Christi* was founded to work for disarmament, to educate people for peace, and to provide alternatives to violence. There are over nine thousand members of *Pax Christi* in the United States today.

---

capital punishment The killing of a criminal for particular crimes committed.

Activity

1. Read act 4, scene 3 of Shakespeare's play *Henry V* (Henry's speech just before the Battle of Agincourt). Then discuss what motivated the soldiers to go into battle. Do you think these same reasons motivate people today to go to war?

2. Find out how much the United States is spending this year on defense (nuclear and conventional weapons). Do you think this expense is justified? Why or why not?

Journal

What are your views on capital punishment? Why?

abolitionists *People who oppose the practice of capital punishment.*

retributionists *People who favor the use of the death penalty.*

Are there crimes so horrible that the death penalty is warranted? And if so, should television cameras be allowed to broadcast the death? These are heated questions being asked by more and more people. The debate over capital punishment deals with four important values: respect for the sanctity of human life, the protection of human life, the preservation of order in society, and the achievement of justice through law. The people who cite these values to argue against capital punishment are called **abolitionists**. People who use these same values to support capital punishment are called **retributionists**. A summary of both positions may be found in the following table. ▪

Arguments For and Against Capital Punishment	
For (Retributionists)	**Against (Abolitionists)**
1. Capital punishment acts as a deterrent to crime. If a person is sentenced to life in prison, he or she has nothing to lose by committing additional crimes. No further punishment can be given. But if the person knows that he or she could get the death penalty, the person may not commit the crime.	1. Capital punishment does prevent a criminal from committing any more crimes. But it does not necessarily deter a criminal from committing a capital crime, nor does it deter other criminals.
2. Most capital crime offenders are beyond reform or rehabilitation. If they should escape, be pardoned, or be paroled, the community would be at risk.	2. It is never too late for God's grace to touch and transform hearts. It is possible for even the worst criminal to reform and to be rehabilitated. Capital punishment deprives a criminal of further time in which to reform.
3. Justice calls for punishment or retribution in order to restore the order that has been violated by the criminal. Murder requires a like punishment.	3. Justice may not be served by capital punishment. An innocent person may be executed. (During the twentieth century, at least eight innocent men were executed in the United States.) An execution, once it has occurred, cannot be revoked. Furthermore, some argue that the death penalty is socially discriminating. There is some evidence to suggest that it is applied much more often to the poor and to minority groups, who cannot afford good lawyers and numerous appeals.
4. The prison system is already too crowded. The cost of maintaining a murderer runs into tens of thousands of dollars each year.	4. Every human life (even that of a criminal) has unique worth and dignity. Respect for life is more important than money. Indeed, executions may cost more money than imprisonment, but the fifth commandment tells us that it is wrong to kill another human being. People should not become killers in order to punish a murderer. Executions are cruel and unusual punishment. ▪

Discussion

In 1991, KQED television station in San Francisco applied to the United States District Court for permission to televise the execution of criminals in the gas chamber. At that time, it was refused. Debate whether or not such permission should be granted in the future. Also debate whether or not you think televised executions would change people's opinions about the death penalty.

Activity

1. Research the methods that have been used to impose the death penalty in the United States. In addition, make a list of all capital offenses (crimes that can be punished with the death penalty). Present your information to the class.

2. Find out if your state has a death penalty. If so, for what crimes can the death penalty be imposed? When did the last execution take place? How are the criminals executed? Then debate whether or not you think your state's law should be changed.

The Church's Stance

Here are some excerpts from official Church documents relating to the types of violence discussed in this chapter.

Domestic Violence

We must have a coherent *national* firearms policy responsive to the overall public interest and respectful of the rights and privileges of all Americans. The unlimited freedom to possess and use handguns must give way to the rights of all people to safety and protection against those who misuse these weapons.

—United States Catholic Conference, *Handgun Violence: A Threat to Life* (1975), #8

The love between husband and wife and, in a derivatory and broader way, the love between members of the same family . . . is given life and sustenance by an unceasing inner dynamism leading the family to ever deeper and more intense communion, which is the foundation and soul of the community of marriage and the family.

—Pope John Paul II, *Apostolic Exhortation on the Family* (1981), #18

Another task for the family is to form persons in love and also to practice love in all its relationships. ▪

—World Synod of Bishops, *A Message to Christian Families in the Modern World* (1980), #12

Drunk Driving

The virtue of temperance disposes us to avoid every kind of excess: the abuse of food, alcohol, tobacco, or medicine.

Those incur grave guilt who, by drunkenness or a love of speed, endanger their own and others' safety on the road, at sea, or in the air.

—*Catechism of the Catholic Church*, #2290

Abortion

The direct interruption of the generative process already begun, and above all, directly willed and procured abortion, even if for therapeutic reasons, are to be absolutely excluded as licit means of regulating birth.

—Pope Paul VI, *On the Regulation of Birth (Humanae Vitae)* (1968), #14

. . . followers of Christ are obliged not only to be personally opposed to abortion, but to seek to remove circumstances which influence some to turn to abortion as a solution to their problems, and also to work for the restoration of a climate of opinion and a legal order which respect the value of unborn human life. . . . ▪

—United States Catholic Conference, *National Catechetical Directory* (1979), #105b

War

Preventing nuclear war is a moral imperative.

—National Conference of Catholic Bishops, *The Challenge of Peace: God's Promise and Our Response* (1983), #234

Under no circumstances may nuclear weapons or other instruments of mass slaughter be used for the purpose of destroying population centers or other predominantly civilian targets.

—National Conference of Catholic Bishops, *The Challenge of Peace: God's Promise and Our Response* (1983), #147

Catholics Believe

Since the first century the Church has affirmed the moral evil of every procured abortion. . . . Direct abortion, that is to say, abortion willed either as an end or a means, is gravely contrary to the moral law. . . . (Catechism, #2271)

Discussion

1. Why do you think many victims of family violence never tell anyone?
2. Debate whether or not all people should have access to firearms.

Discussion

What are the reasons the Church gives for saying that abortion is wrong?

Catholics Believe
All citizens and all governments are obliged to work for the avoidance of war. (Catechism, #2308)

Catholics Believe
. . . the Church does not exclude recourse to the death penalty, if this is the only possible way of effectively defending human lives against the unjust aggressor. If, however, nonlethal means are sufficient to defend and protect people's safety from the aggressor, authority will limit itself to such means . . . (Catechism, #2267)

Peace cannot be limited to a mere absence of war, the result of an ever precarious balance of forces. No, peace is something built up day after day, in the pursuit of an order intended by God, which implies a more perfect form of justice among men and women.

—Pope Paul VI, *The Development of Peoples* (1976), #76

Capital Punishment

We believe that in the conditions of contemporary American society, the legitimate purposes of punishment do not justify the imposition of the death penalty. Furthermore, we believe that there are serious considerations which should prompt Christians and all Americans to support the abolition of capital punishment.

—United States Bishops, *Statement on Capital Punishment* (1980), #9

Abolition sends a message that we can break the cycle of violence, that we need not take life for life, that we can envisage more humane and more hopeful and effective responses to the growth of violent crime.

—United States Bishops, *Statement on Capital Punishment* (1980), #10

Abolition of capital punishment is also a manifestation of our belief in the unique worth and dignity of each person from the moment of conception, a creature made in the image and likeness of God. ■ ■

—United States Bishops, *Statement on Capital Punishment* (1980), #11

Being a Peacemaker

Christian peacemaking has three dimensions: the recognition of violence, the avoidance of violence, and the day-to-day working at peace. ■

To help you grow as a peacemaker, complete the two exercises on the next page. Use the questions to reflect (don't write down your responses) on the presence of and the potential for violence in your own life. Choose a quiet spot away from others while you do your reflecting. Then write down some specific ways you can build community and eliminate hostility in your relationships.

Discussion
Brainstorm about just punishments for crimes and effective ways to rehabilitate criminals.

Activity
Design a poster that promotes life and peace in some way.

Activity
1. Find out how peace and nonviolence were a part of the life of one of the following people:
   - Saint Ignatius of Antioch
   - Saint Francis of Assisi
   - Dorothy Day
   - Saint Martin of Tours
   - Saint Catherine of Sienna
2. Report on the peacemaking efforts of a recent Nobel Prize winner. How is this person a role model for teens today?
3. Find out more about *Pax Christi* USA. What is this organization doing in your diocese to promote peace?

Violence Questionnaire

1. What percentage of the TV programs you like to watch are violent?

2. On a scale of 1 to 10, how often do you get angry?

3. Do you act in nonviolent or violent ways when you get angry?

4. Have you ever felt so angry that you wanted to kill someone?

5. On a scale of 1 to 10, how peaceful is the relationship between your parents?

6. Has one or both of your parents ever abused you physically?

7. Has a parent or relative ever threatened to cause you physical harm?

8. Have you ever threatened to harm a brother or sister?

9. Have you ever hit a brother or sister?

10. Have you ever threatened to harm a boyfriend or girlfriend?

11. Have you ever hit a boyfriend or girlfriend?

12. Has a boyfriend or girlfriend ever hit you?

13. Have you ever tried to get revenge after a relationship has broken up?

14. Do you or does any member of your family belong to a gang?

15. Do you or other family members have access to guns or other weapons?

Working at Peace

Identify practical ways you can build community and decrease hostility in each of the following relationships:

- parents
- siblings
- other relatives
- boyfriend or girlfriend
- classmates
- teachers
- friends
- neighbors
- students of other schools

Words to Know

abolitionists	matricide
abortion	nuclear winter
arms control	pacifism
arms limitation	parricide
capital punishment	patricide
disarmament	retributionists
fratricide	sororicide
homicide	uxoricide
just war theory	

Review Questions

1. List and define four types of domestic violence.
2. What are the five worst days of the year for alcohol-related car accidents?
3. Why does the Catholic Church regard induced abortion as immoral?
4. What is the moral principle known as "double effect"?
5. Explain the pro-life position and the pro-abortion position.
6. Why does the Church consider nuclear war immoral?
7. What is the ethical stance of a pacifist or conscientious objector?
8. What the six criteria needed for a just war?
9. What are the arguments for and against capital punishment? What is the Church's stance?
10. What are the three dimensions of Christian peacemaking?

C•H•A•P•T•E•R

16

Hope *and* Healing

IN THIS CHAPTER, YOU WILL

- explore the kind of hope to which Christians are called;

- connect true happiness with growth in wholeness and holiness—union with God;

- understand that union with God requires single-heartedness, discernment, and integrity;

- distinguish between utilitarian prayer and contemplative prayer;

- see how our stage of faith affects how we respond to suffering and death;

- examine the characteristics of paradoxical faith and incarnational faith as they relate to suffering and death;

- view the Eucharist as a primary sacrament of hope and healing;

- reflect on the importance of prayer and Eucharist in your life, both in your own healing and in your ability to reach out in love to others.

The Miracle Girl

Kassie Arner didn't know how close she'd come to dying until Easter morning.

"The pastor said, 'Here's the girl that had a 5 percent chance of living,' and everyone was just floored," said her mom, Lorrie. "Kassie just looked up at her dad as if he had a lot of explaining to do."

Even now, six weeks after the 11-year-old girl was able to leave the hospital, her dad, David, is still not sure he can explain it. What he knows is that his little girl came down with the flu, took an afternoon nap, and didn't wake up. When they rushed Kassie to the hospital, her lips and fingers were blue, a lung had filled with fluid, and her organs had begun to shut down. The diagnosis: a severe lung infection called strep-pneumo. Doctors gave her a 5 percent chance of living through the night. They darted in and out of the critical care unit, hooking Kassie up to life-support machines. Kassie's parents held her hands and prayed.

Kassie doesn't remember what they said to her when she slept through the month of March. But they believe she heard them. Her parents were there when Kassie opened her eyes in late March. "I thought it was just a big dream, and it was time to wake up," Kassie said. "I saw everybody, but when I tried to talk to them, I couldn't."

It took almost two weeks until she could talk. But then Kassie rebounded quickly, leaving the hospital after five weeks.

When Kassie began physical rehabilitation last month, she couldn't lift a 2-pound weight. Now she can curl almost 60 pounds. Her teammates are back to calling her "Speedy." But her father has a new nickname—"Long Shot."

"I never have to worry ever again about whether there is a God or not," he said. "I've witnessed miracle after miracle." ▪

—Adapted from "Playing with heart: 'Miracle girl' beats odds of survival," ©*The Arizona Republic* (May 30, 1998). Article by Jennifer Barrett. Used with permission. Permission does not imply endorsement.

Discussion

1. Do you believe in miracles? Have you had any experiences of miracles in your own family?
2. If you were Kassie, how would you feel about (a) getting so seriously sick? (b) being in a coma for almost a month? (c) having to undergo extensive physical therapy? (d) being alive?
3. What effect do you think prayer has on medical healing? Did prayers heal Kassie, or was it the treatment her doctors provided?

The Power of Prayer

Kassie Arner is a very lucky girl. She lived, even though the odds were against her. Instead of being angry that she got so sick or that she had to undergo extensive rehabilitation, she is grateful for just being alive. Her story does not tell us if she is a person of faith or if she prays on a regular basis. All we know is that her family members prayed when she was in a coma, and their prayers were heard.

Indeed, prayer can be a very effective weapon against suffering and death. It can even bring about miracles. But what about the times in our lives when we are not in pain or in danger of death? Do we continue to pray when everything is okay? Or do we wait until the next serious crisis before we call out to God for help?

One of the purposes of this course is to help you deal better with suffering and death as you encounter them in your life. But this course will be wasted if you come away only with facts and knowledge. What is most important is how the facts and knowledge have led you to prayer and have strengthened your faith on an everyday basis. Do you believe, without doubt, in God's love and mercy? Is God real to you? Do you feel God's strength and presence with you at all times? Or do you need a miracle, like Kassie's, to believe that God exists? ▪

Throughout this course, you have discovered how the experience of suffering and death can lead us to gospel living—avoiding behavior that causes suffering to others and taking effective action to relieve suffering wherever it occurs. In this chapter, you will explore an even more essential truth: how a personal relationship with God can transform experiences of suffering and death into hope and healing. It's an important chapter—one that can teach you how to be happy, no matter what happens in your future. ▪

Attitude Survey	I agree	I disagree	I'm not sure
We can't find happiness without first suffering.			
We can't be happy while we are suffering.			
The only appropriate prayer in times of suffering is "Thy will be done."			
God sometimes relieves suffering in response to prayer.			
Our own suffering is an opportunity to meet God face-to-face.			

Before proceeding, respond in your notebook to the Attitude Survey.

Do you believe in God's love and mercy? Is God real to you? Do you feel God's strength and presence with you at all times?

Discussion
Father William Thomas Cummings, a World War II chaplain, once said "There are no atheists in foxholes." What do you think he meant by this statement? Do you agree or disagree with his statement?

Discussion
In his essay "Where I Lived and What I Lived For," Henry David Thoreau wrote "I went to the woods because I wished to live deliberately, face the essential facts of life, and see if I could not learn what it had to teach, and not, when I came to die, discover that I had not lived." What do you think he meant by the phrase "to live deliberately"? What is the difference between merely existing and being fully alive?

hope *The theological virtue that enables us to trust that God is always working for our good and will someday bring us eternal happiness.*

union with God *A state of eternal happiness, life, and oneness with God.*

holiness *The perfect state of goodness and righteousness. God alone is perfectly holy, but God calls all people to become holy.*

Catholics Believe

. . . Hope is the confident expectation of divine blessing and the beatific vision of God . . . (Catechism, #2090)

Catholics Believe

Desire for true happiness frees man from his immoderate attachment to the goods of this world so that he can find his fulfillment in the vision and beatitude of God. "The promise [of seeing God] surpasses all beatitude. . . . Whoever sees God has obtained all the goods of which he can conceive" (St. Gregory of Nyssa, De beatitudinibus 6: PG 44, 1265A). (Catechism, #2548)

The Nature of Christian Hope

It has been said that life would be unbearable if we didn't have dreams and hopes. It has also been said that Christians are people of **hope**. Our hope is not mere wishful thinking or unrealistic dreams of miracles. Nor is our hope focused on the attainment of perfect health or the accumulation of material goods. Instead, our hope is based on the person and teachings of Jesus. We hope to obtain all that God has promised to give us—true happiness and eternal life.

What exactly is true happiness and eternal life? According to the Bible, it is something that lasts rather than corrodes or rusts with time.

> "Do not store up for yourselves treasures on earth, where moth and rust consume and where thieves break in and steal; but store up for yourselves treasures in heaven, where neither moth nor rust consumes and where thieves do not break in and steal."
>
> —Matthew 6:19–20

We hope to possess the kingdom of God in its fullness. We hope for nothing less than beatific vision:

- to see God face-to-face (cf. Romans 8:24–25; Hebrews 11:1)
- to enter into God's rest (cf. Hebrews 4:1–11)

- to enjoy full and abundant life in the holies of heaven (cf. Hebrews 10:19–23)
- to find complete acceptance in the "home" Christ has prepared for us (cf. 2 Corinthians 5:1, 8; John 14:2; Philippians 3:20–21)

In short, what we hope for is **union with God**. *Union with God* is a term that describes the wholeness and **holiness** that all Christians seek. Because the experience of union with God is indescribable, the Bible uses various analogies to help us understand it. Union with God is the forgiveness of our sins and redemption from death (cf. Exodus 12:1–30); it is the buried treasure (cf. Matthew 13:44), the priceless pearl (cf. Matthew 13:45–46), the bread of life (cf. John 6:25–58). For people of true faith, hope in eternal life is unshakable. We know that no situation is hopeless. Nothing—not even the worst imaginable suffering and evil—can separate us from God's love. God is always present to us when we suffer. God always brings good out of evil. ▪

As you have learned throughout this course, every suffering can be redemptive. For this reason, the New Testament tells us:

> Beloved, do not be surprised at the fiery ordeal that is taking place among you to test you, as though something strange were happening to you. But rejoice insofar as you are sharing Christ's sufferings, so that you may also be glad and shout for joy when his glory is revealed. If you are reviled for the name of Christ, you are blessed, because the spirit of glory, which is the Spirit of God, is resting on you.
>
> —1 Peter 4:12–14

Activity

Look up the Scripture passages found on this page. Then, in your own words, describe what it is that you hope for. What do you think true happiness—full and eternal life in union with God— is like?

Seeing God's Face

To see God's face is what gives life its sense of fulfillment and vitality. Whenever we are in union with God, we have a sense of full and abundant life, because God alone is a "living" God. God not only gives us life; God is life. We believe that God the Father sent Jesus, his Son, to save us from death—not only from the bodily death that occurs at the end of our earthly lives, but also from the psychological and spiritual death that occurs from sin, suffering, and not being fully alive each day. Jesus came so that we might live life fully, embrace it, and savor its every moment (cf. John 10:10).

How do we reach union with God? How do we see God's face, both in good times and in bad? The Bible gives us several answers. First, we are to be **single-hearted** in our pursuit of union with the Holy Trinity. Single-heartedness is the virtue that enables us to envision a goal and keep our attention and energy focused on reaching it. Sometimes single-heartedness is described as **purity of heart** because we want one thing with all our hearts (cf. Matthew 6:21). Being one with God is our number one priority. We are not in any way divided in our thinking, motives, or desires. We are very clear about what our treasure is, and we do everything possible to obtain it.

Second, the Bible tells us that we are to have discernment between temporary happiness and eternal happiness. The good things of the world—wealth, fame, good health, physical beauty—are fleeting and do not last. God's goodness, however, lasts forever and alone brings true happiness. For this reason, the Bible tells us to "strive first for the kingdom of God and his righteousness, and all these things will be given to you as well" (Matthew 6:33). As Saint Augustine once said,

> *T*he **search** *for the* **God** *of life is* **never-ending** *and often* **painful**.
>
> Paula Ripple, *Growing Strong at Broken Places*

"Our hearts, O God, are always restless unless they rest in You."

Third, the Bible tells us that union with the Blessed Trinity implies **integrity**. People who are single-hearted are morally good people. Because they seek God first, they seek to become like God, like Jesus, in all relationships and situations. Indeed, to see the face of God is not only to be received favorably by him; it implies a transformation of our very identity. We become completely one with God to the point that there is no longer any important barrier between us and the three divine Persons. We are divinized; we receive eternal life (cf. Genesis 33:10; Job 33:26).

Seeing God's face is not easy. We are tempted to see God's face in good times but not in our pain and suffering. That is why Saint Thomas Aquinas reminds us that God is an eternal mystery. He says that in this life, we cannot know what God is but only what God is not. The Holy Trinity cannot be understood by us completely with logic; we continually come to know God through experience, through relationship. Indeed, the three Persons of the Trinity are relations. The mystery of suffering and death invites us to enter into the mystery of God. We are challenged to live fully in the midst of suffering; we are called to stand in silent awe and wonder before the Holy Trinity of everlasting life, light, and love. ▪

single-heartedness *The virtue that enables us to envision a goal and keep our attention and energy focused on reaching it. The ability to want just one thing with all our hearts.*

purity of heart *Single-minded focus on goodness and the things of God. Single-heartedness; having motives that are free from moral fault or guilt.*

integrity *Acting according to the values we hold true. Integrity means being faithful to our values and beliefs. Our actions match what we say.*

Journal

Describe a goal you had to work to achieve. How were single-heartedness, discernment, and integrity important to your success?

> *Nothing in our life has greater potential for uniting us with Jesus than suffering.*
>
> Father Richard Hauser

A Lifelong Process

Throughout the chapters of this book, you have learned that there are different stages in the process of grieving and in the process of dying. The same is true with seeing God's face. Union with God is a lifelong process. It is a radical transfiguration in which we surrender ourselves completely to the will of God. We no longer seek our own wishes; we see all things from God's perspective.

Indeed, the purpose of **religion** and **prayer** is to lead us to this type of conversion. We no longer talk *about* God and the spiritual life; we enter *into* a face-to-face relationship with the Creator, Redeemer, and Sustainer of life. The word *religion* comes from a Latin root that means "binding or bonding together." The purpose of true religion is to put us in touch with God and with other people who share the same faith. True religion redeems us from isolation. It strengthens us with the knowledge that we are not alone, that God never abandons us, that no suffering can make us appear ugly or repulsive to him. The word *prayer* means "heartfelt conversation with God." True prayer has more than a functional or utilitarian purpose. In utilitarian prayer, people reduce God to a vending machine. Just as we insert coins into a vending machine to produce the object of our choice, so we use prayer to manipulate God into giving us what we want. In true prayer, which is sometimes called *contemplative prayer*, people simply spend time in God's presence. We see and praise God's face; we discover God's features in our own suffering and in the faces of those who suffer around us.

Utilitarian vs. Contemplative Prayer

Utilitarian prayer is not bad. But it is imperfect. People "stuck" at this stage of faith seek to control God and turn God into their servant. They relate to God only when they want something in return. For example, such people ask God to cure them of illness or to take away their pain. Their focus is on themselves and what benefits them rather than on God's will. Such people make themselves the center of the universe; they idolatrously turn God into their slave.

Contemplative prayer, on the other hand, leads us to realize the truth about God.

> For now we see in a mirror, dimly, but then we will see face to face. Now I know only in part; then I will know fully, even as I have been fully known.
>
> —1 Corinthians 13:12

> I had heard of you by the hearing of the ear, but now my eye sees you . . .
>
> —Job 42:5

God is the master; we are his servants. We can't manipulate God by our good actions or our prayers. We can't force God to be "just" and send suffering only to those who "deserve" it. Instead, when we see God face-to-face, we realize the magnitude of God's love and goodness. We rightly attribute everything good that happens to God's mercy and grace rather than to our efforts or worthiness. Our relationship with God becomes authentic. We know the "truth," and the truth sets us free (cf. John 8:32). ▪

religion The praise and service of the Trinity as expressed in divine worship and in daily life. A person's total response to the demands of faith; religion is a living faith, a personal relationship with and a self-commitment to God.

prayer The raising of the mind and heart to the Blessed Trinity in praise, thanksgiving, contrition, and petition. Prayer may be vocal or silent, solitary or with others.

Discussion
1. What is the purpose of religion? Of prayer?
2. What is the difference between utilitarian prayer and contemplative prayer?

Stages of Faith

To understand the difference between utilitarian prayer and contemplative prayer, it is helpful to study the work of theologian James Fowler. In the early 1980s, Fowler described seven stages of faith in the process of becoming one with God. Here is a summary of these stages:

Stage	Type of Faith	How the Person Relates to God
1	Immature Faith	The person has a basic, naive trust in God, others, and self—mostly due to idealism and a lack of experience with suffering and death. A teenager in this stage would never question why suffering and death exist or why bad things sometimes happen to good people.
2	Imitation Faith	The person copies, or imitates, the faith he or she sees in the moods, actions, and lives of others. The specifics of a person's faith are strongly influenced by Bible stories and imagination. A teenager in this stage practices the externals of religion and approaches suffering and death as admired adults or peers do. Motivation to face suffering and death is external, based on winning the approval of God or other people.
3	Literal-Minded Faith	The person believes everything told to him or her about faith, word for word. The person has a fundamental approach to religion, prayer, and the Bible. A teenager in this stage emphasizes belief that prayer can cure illness and prevent death. If these results do not occur, then the person's prayer was somehow faulty.
4	Conventional Faith	The person believes in God's justice. The just will be rewarded and those who suffer must somehow deserve it. A teenager in this stage believes that our good actions will be rewarded. If the suffering seems unjust (those who suffer are truly innocent), this teenager may experience a crisis of faith, thinking that nothing the Church teaches is true.
5	Reflective Faith	The person takes responsibility for his or her own actions, attitudes, beliefs, and sense of meaning. A teenager in this stage chooses to believe in God's love—not because the Church says so, but because that is what he or she truly believes. The person is resigned to the fact of suffering and death and figures God must have a reason.
6	Paradoxical Faith	The person has experienced suffering and death firsthand as well as human imperfection and limitations. However, the person still chooses to believe in God's kingdom of love, peace, and perfection. A teenager in this stage is aware of the injustice present in the world but does not give in to discouragement. The teen continues to hope that God's kingdom will one day become a reality.
7	Incarnational Faith	The person believes because God is a real, felt experience. The person's will and God's will are closely aligned. The person is whole, holy, and completely happy, even in times of suffering. The person reaches out in love, striving to relieve the suffering of others.

Fowler's last two stages (paradoxical and incarnational faith) are most closely connected to the full Christian understanding of suffering and death. They are also most closely connected to the Church's sense of what gives true happiness and meaning in life. For these reasons, it is important to discuss these last two stages in more detail. ▪

Paradoxical Faith

A *paradox* is a reality or truth that seems to defy usual logic. In paradoxical faith, a person believes simultaneously in two things

We stand speechless before God.

that ordinarily do not go together. For example, a person of paradoxical faith recognizes the presence of unjust suffering and evil in the world. At the same time, the person truly believes in God's omnipotence, justice, and love. It's not that the person has "given up" trying to make sense of the mystery of suffering and death; the person is content to live with the unexplainable.

The cross of Jesus is a paradox. It is inconceivable to the human mind that Jesus, the Son of God, would embrace suffering and death. And yet his passion and death won for us salvation. His actions set us free from eternal suffering and death caused by sin.

Finding God in the midst of suffering and death is also a paradox. Suffering and death seem to be the ultimate evils, yet that is where many saints have found God most clearly. Paul, for example, said the following about the paradox of suffering:

> Three times I appealed to the Lord about this, that it would leave me, but he said to me, "My grace is sufficient for you, for power is made perfect in weakness." So, I will boast all the more gladly of my weaknesses, so that the power of Christ may dwell in me. Therefore I am content with weaknesses, insults, hardships, persecutions, and calamities for the sake of Christ; for whenever I am weak, then I am strong.
>
> —2 Corinthians 12:8–10

Through the crucible of suffering and death, we are ushered into God's presence. We stand speechless before God, accepting the fact that our questions remain unanswered in any clear, definitive way. ▪

Journal

1. How would you describe your faith at this time in your life?
2. How would you describe your present love for God?

Activity

Look up the following Scripture passages dealing with paradox. How do you make sense out of these passages?

- Happy are those who suffer (Matthew 5:3–10).
- If you want to find yourself, lose yourself (Matthew 10:39).
- The greatest in heaven is humble, like a child (Matthew 18:1–5).
- The last will be first (Matthew 20:1–16).

Incarnational Faith

Incarnational faith is not easy to describe completely. The word *incarnation* means "to take on human flesh." In the mystery of the incarnation, we believe that God took human form in Jesus; God's "Word became flesh and lived among us" (John 1:14). In incarnational faith, we believe that God makes us more fully human and that we become more and more Godlike. Despite the difficulty in explaining such a state of union with God, we can describe four characteristics of incarnational faith. These four characteristics are an immersion in grace, a complete surrender to and trust in God, a sense of inner strength, and an increased ability to reach out to others in love, patience, and joy.

Immersion in Grace

Some people mistakenly think that grace is a "thing," something we earn, like money. Incarnational faith teaches us that **grace** is an experience, a sharing in the Trinity's own life, love, and light. It is God's free gift to us, something that stems from love rather than justice or "earning."

In contemplative prayer, grace fills us with a sense of the presence of the Holy Trinity as well as a sense of the strength of the Trinity. We know that God is truly with us. His love is within us and surrounds us. We feel validated—not because God removes us from suffering and death, but because God walks with us in these times of adversity. We experience God's mercy, his ever-faithful covenant of love, life, and light.

God's grace helps us realize we are not in control. Our salvation is not about power or ability or worthiness. It is about God's freely given generosity and love. We come to see that God's grace is much bigger than our sense of

The gospel of **suffering** *is being* **written** *unceasingly, and it speaks* **unceasingly** *with the* **words** *of this strange* **paradox***: The springs of* **divine power** *gush forth* **precisely** *in the midst of human* **weakness.**

Pope John Paul II, *The Christian Meaning of Human Suffering*

justice. The love from the Trinity enfolds us and permeates us, even when we don't deserve it. We realize fully the truth of the following Scripture passage:

> By grace you have been saved.
>
> —Ephesians 2:5

Love is a free gift, or it is nothing. ▪

Complete Surrender to and Trust in God

In incarnational faith, we so believe in God's love for us that we trust God in every circumstance. With Job, we come to realize that the plan of God is beyond human knowledge (cf. Job 38–39). God indeed has a plan, even if we cannot grasp what it is. We don't just begrudgingly resign ourselves to accept the fact that God's ways are not our ways; we surrender our will to God's will. With Jesus, we say, "not what I want but what you want" (Matthew 26:39). We unite our suffering with that of Jesus, and together our trust in God as a loving Father gives his Son praise. ▪

grace *A sharing in God's own life, love, and light. Grace is God's free gift to us.*

Activity

Read the following Scripture parables. What do they teach us about the relationship between God's grace and justice?

• Matthew 20:1–16
• Luke 15:11–32

Discussion

What is the difference between resigning ourselves to something and surrendering ourselves to God's will? What attitudes are involved?

The greatest saints have had such trust in God. Consider, for example, the following prayers of Saint Teresa of Avila and Blessed Elizabeth of the Trinity:

> Let nothing trouble you
> Let nothing frighten you
> Everything passes
> God never changes
> Patience
> Obtains all
> Whoever has God
> Wants for nothing
> God alone is enough.
>
> —Saint Teresa of Avila

O my God, Trinity whom I adore, help me forget myself entirely so to establish myself in you, unmovable and peaceful as if my soul were already in eternity. May nothing be able to trouble my peace or make me leave you, O my unchanging God, but may each minute bring me more deeply into your mystery! Grant my soul peace. Make it your heaven, your beloved dwelling, and the place of your rest. May I never abandon you there, but may I be there, whole and entire, completely vigilant in my faith, entirely adoring, and wholly given over to your creative action.

—Blessed Elizabeth of the Trinity

Inner Strength and Healing

The transformation that takes place within us in contemplative prayer gives us strength and healing. Instead of being angry at God as the cause of our suffering, we see God as the source of our strength. We no longer pray for miracles because a miracle has already happened within us. We have seen God in our own suffering and in the suffering of others. United with God, we somehow find the necessary courage to bear the unbearable, to remember all that we have rather than all that we have lost. Because we are one with God, we discover we can cope with whatever problems or pains life sends us.

Pope John Paul II concurs:

> To the suffering brother or sister Christ discloses and gradually reveals the horizons of the Kingdom of God: the horizons of a world converted to the Creator, of a world free from sin, a world being built on the saving power of love. And slowly but effectively, Christ leads into this world, into this Kingdom of the Father, suffering man, in a certain sense through the very heart of his suffering. For suffering cannot be transformed and changed by a grace from outside, but from within. And Christ through his own salvific suffering is very much

O*nly when we have come to* **realize** *that God's* **love** *is freely* **bestowed** *do we* **enter** *fully and definitively into the* **presence** *of the God of* **faith**. **Grace** *is* **not opposed** *to the quest of* **justice** *nor does it play it down; on the contrary, it* **gives** *it its full* **meaning**. *God's* **love**, *like all true love,* **operates** *in a world not of cause and effect but of* **freedom** *and* **gratuitousness**.

Gustavo Gutierrez, Gustavo, *On Job: God-Talk and the Suffering of the Innocent*

present in every human suffering, and can act from within that suffering by the powers of his Spirit of truth, his consoling Spirit.

—Pope John Paul II, *The Christian Meaning of Human Suffering*

True healing only takes place when our pain is somehow internalized in a meaningful way, in union with God and the passion of Jesus. From failure, we rise like the mythical phoenix to a richer, more fulfilling life. Through suffering, we take God's hand and attain both peace and forgiveness. We are given new life; we are also enabled to offer that new life to others. Instead of being defeated by suffering and death, we become persons of genuine compassion, mercy, love, and forgiveness. ▪

Increased Ability to Love

Father Henri Nouwen, in his book *Wounded Healers*, tried to express the reality of the healing aspects of union with God. When we are truly one with God, we act as agents of hope and healing to others, even though our own lives are not yet free from suffering and death. Our faith and hope can be a strong witness of God's abiding presence and goodness. We can strengthen others in their quest to see God's face in the midst of their suffering. Our suffering, far from being in vain, has purpose and meaning. Instead of wallowing in our misfortune, we reach out in self-sacrificial **love** to others. We become Christ to them. We make Christ real in their lives. They see God's face in us, just as we see God's face in them.

We don't know precisely what happened to Paul on the road to Damascus, but in some way he saw the risen Son of God and experienced a radical conversion. From then on, he approached everything in life, including suffering and death, with new eyes. The New Testament tells us he was five times whipped with forty lashes, three times beaten with rods, once stoned with rocks, three times shipwrecked, and frequently endured hardship. And yet through these sufferings, he was still able to say with faith:

For we do not proclaim ourselves; we proclaim Jesus Christ as Lord and ourselves as your slaves for Jesus' sake. For it is the God who said, "Let light shine out of darkness," who has shone in our hearts to give the light of the knowledge of the glory of God in the face of Jesus Christ. But we have this treasure in clay jars, so that it may be made clear that this extraordinary power belongs to God and does not come from us. We are afflicted in every way, but not crushed; perplexed, but not driven to despair; persecuted, but not forsaken; struck down, but not destroyed; always carrying in the body the death of Jesus, so that the life of Jesus may also be made visible in our bodies.

—2 Corinthians 4:5–10

I am now rejoicing in my sufferings for your sake, and in my flesh I am completing what is lacking in Christ's afflictions for the sake of his body, that is, the church.

—Colossians 1:24

Hopefully, what you have learned and reflected upon throughout this course will lead you to a similar faith, hope, and selfless love. May your experiences of suffering and death, whatever they may be, lead you to a face-to-face encounter with the living God. May you experience, firsthand, our God who is the source of all salvation and healing. ▪

Through suffering, we take God's hand and attain both peace and forgiveness. We are given new life and enabled to offer that new life to others.

love (a) The theological virtue that enables us to worship, praise, and value God above anything or anyone else. (b) The moral virtue that enables us to relate unselfishly to others, with sincere concern, understanding, and forgiveness.

Activity
Express your understanding of the experience of healing in some creative way—poem, dance, sculpture, drawing, song. Be prepared to share your work with the class.

Activity
Go back and respond again to the Attitude Survey in each chapter of this book. Then compare your present answers with the previous ones you gave in your notebook. How have your attitudes changed as a result of this course?

The Eucharist is our Bread of Life. In it we find strength in times of suffering, healing in times of brokenness, and new life in times of death.

---

agape meal A memorial meal of love, sometimes celebrated with a funeral.

The Bread of Life

You have learned throughout this course that the Sacraments of Reconciliation and the Anointing of the Sick are called the Church's *Sacraments of Healing*. In Reconciliation, we obtain forgiveness of our sins and spiritual healing. In the Anointing of the Sick, we celebrate both spiritual and physical healing. There is another sacrament, however, that is also a healing agent in the lives of Christians. This healing sacrament is the Eucharist.

The word *Eucharist* means "thanksgiving." In every Eucharist, we thank God the Father for Jesus' triumph over sin and death. We join our sufferings with the passion of Jesus, with the hope that we may be brought to loving union with the Blessed Trinity and with others. As Jesus himself said, the Eucharist is our Bread of Life. In it we find strength in times of suffering, healing in times of brokenness, and new life in times of death. As the Church teaches, the Eucharist is both a meal and a memorial.

In many ways, the Eucharistic meal is similar to the meal eaten as part of Jewish funeral rites from the days of Jeremiah. The funeral meal had two purposes—to console mourners and to reestablish a oneness, or bond, with the dead. Frescoes in the catacombs tell us that the early Christians continued the practice of holding an **agape meal**, or funeral meal, near the tomb or mausoleum on the day of burial. In contrast to the funeral banquets (*refrigeria*) common at that time, the meal the Christians shared was the Eucharist.

You know that the Eucharist was established by Jesus at his Last Supper and was anticipated by the miracle of the multiplication of the loaves. The first Eucharist was a seder meal commemorating the Jewish Passover. Today the Church regards the Eucharist as a memorial that represents Christ's own passing from death to new life, the Bread of Life that nourishes us on our own journey toward eternal life, and a sacrament that both points to and makes possible our bonds of oneness with both the living and the dead. ▪

Our belief in the Eucharist as a source of hope and healing may be seen in the communion rite at Mass, in the wording of the Eucharistic Prayers, and in each of the memorial acclamations:

- Christ has died, Christ is risen, Christ will come again.
- Dying you destroyed our death, rising you restored our life, Lord Jesus, come in glory.
- When we eat this bread and drink this cup, we proclaim your death, Lord Jesus, until you come in glory.
- Lord, by your cross and resurrection, you have set us free. You are the Savior of the world.

Activity

1. Compare the gospel accounts of the miracle of the multiplication of loaves. Why are there discrepancies between the accounts? What do you think is the major reason for including the miracle in each gospel?
   - Matthew 14:13–21
   - Mark 6:30–44
   - Luke 9:10–17
   - John 6:1–13

2. Compare the accounts of the Last Supper. How do they show the Eucharist as a memorial meal of Jesus' death? How do they show the Eucharist as the source of hope and healing?
   - Matthew 26:26–29
   - Mark 14:22–25
   - Luke 22:14–20
   - 1 Corinthians 11:23–26

3. Read about the following appearances of the Risen Christ. Why do you think eating a meal was a part of each account?
   - Luke 24:30–35
   - Luke 24:36–43
   - John 21:1–14

Because of these beliefs, the Catholic Church has celebrated the Eucharist as an integral part of its death rituals—the funeral itself, Masses for the Dead that are celebrated on All Souls' Day and anniversary dates, and the practice of celebrating **viaticum** with those who are dying.

When the Eucharist is celebrated as the last sacrament of Christian life, it is called *viaticum*, which means "food for the journey." This last Eucharist is seen as nourishment that strengthens the dying person on his or her passage through death to eternal life. It is celebrated in anticipation of the heavenly banquet in God's kingdom. It unites the participants both with one another and with Christ's own death and resurrection.

The sacrament of viaticum may take place within or apart from Mass, although the former is preferred. (In this case, the priest follows the Mass of the Holy Eucharist or the ritual Mass for viaticum.) Depending on the condition of the dying person, the presider (or the deacon or Eucharistic minister in the case of viaticum outside Mass) should make every effort to involve the dying person, the family, friends, and other members of the local community in the planning and celebration. ▪

Both forms of the sacrament (within or apart from Mass) include Scripture readings, prayers, and songs. After the homily, the dying person is invited to make a profession of faith by the renewal of baptismal promises. If a priest is present, he may give an apostolic pardon for the dying at the conclusion of the penitential rite. One of the following forms may be used:

A. Through the holy mysteries of our redemption,
   may Almighty God release you from all punishments
   in this life and in the life to come.

May he open to you the gates of paradise
and welcome you to everlasting joy.
Amen.

B. By the authority which the Apostolic See has given me,
   I grant you a full pardon and the remission of all your sins
   in the name of the Father, and of the Son, and of the Holy Spirit.
   Amen.

—From the *Roman Ritual: Pastoral Care of the Sick*

During the sign of peace, all those present are encouraged to embrace the dying person. If possible, communion should be given under both species. Both of these actions are signs of God's strength and healing.

viaticum *A word that means "food for the journey." Viaticum refers to the Eucharist that is received by a dying person, in preparation for death and eternal life.*

Of Interest

White vestments are usually worn for the celebration of viaticum. The ritual Mass for viaticum is not permitted during the Easter Triduum, on Christmas, Epiphany, Ascension, Pentecost, the Feast of the Body and Blood of the Lord, or a holy day of obligation. On these days the Mass of the day is said instead. The Mass of the day must also be said on Sundays of Advent, Lent, and the Easter Season; however, one reading from the ritual Mass for viaticum may be chosen on these days.

Journal

Have you ever attended a celebration of viaticum? What are your memories of that event? How did the celebration express or affect your own belief in the resurrection?

Celebrating Life and Healing

Waiting until you are seriously sick and near death is not necessarily the best time to plan and prepare a Mass for viaticum. Take some time, right now, to think about how you would like to celebrate your last moments on earth. Decide on the people you would like to be present with you. Use the following outline. Perhaps use the songs and Scripture readings as a prayer service to celebrate life and healing with your family and friends now.

Mass for Viaticum

People I would like present:

Priest:

Opening Song:

First Reading: (circle one)
- 1 Kings 19:4–8
- Job 19:23–27

Responsorial Psalm: (circle one)
- Psalm 23
- Psalm 34
- Psalms 42 and 43
- Psalm 116
- Psalm 145

Second Reading: (circle one)
- 1 Corinthians 10:16–17
- 1 Corinthians 11:23–26
- Revelation 3:14b, 20–22
- Revelation 22:17, 20–2

Gospel Acclamation: (circle one)
- John 6:51
- John 6:54
- John 10:9
- John 11:25; 14:6

Gospel Reading: (circle one)
- John 6:41–51a
- John 6:51–58

Song after the Renewal of Baptismal Promises:

Eucharistic Prayer (circle one)
  I   II   III   V

Memorial Acclamation: (circle one)
  A   B   C   D

Communion Song:

Closing Song:

Being an Agent of Hope and Healing

You have learned that when we are one with God, we are empowered to act as agents of hope and healing to others. Brainstorm ways you can act as an agent of hope and healing in each of the following situations. Finally, write your reflections on how frequent participation in the Eucharist can help you reach out in these ways to others. ▪

> . . . *I*t is no longer *I who* **live,** *but it is* **Christ** *who lives* **in me.**
>
> Galatians 2:20

Situations

You have recently had an argument with parents or family members.

A friend or family member is diagnosed with a serious and possibly life-threatening illness.

A grandparent is dying.

A classmate no longer goes to church because of the way he or she was treated by a parish leader.

A friend is depressed about not meeting an important goal, such as qualifying for a certain college or making the final cut in a sports competition.

A classmate has just been killed in an automobile accident.

A friend is turning to drugs or alcohol as a way of "solving" problems.

How the Eucharist can strengthen me:

Journal

What is one improvement you can make to live life more fully?

Words to Know

agape meal	prayer
grace	purity of heart
holiness	religion
hope	single-heartedness
integrity	union with God
love	viaticum

Review Questions

1. What is the nature of Christian hope?
2. What are three metaphors found in the Bible to describe union with God?
3. According to the Bible, what are the three things necessary to reach union with God?
4. What is the purpose of religion?
5. What is the difference between utilitarian prayer and contemplative prayer?
6. What are the seven stages of faith, according to James Fowler?
7. Cite two paradoxes that are found in Scripture.
8. What are the four characteristics of incarnational faith?
9. What is *grace*?
10. What is *viaticum*?

death certificate A legal document certifying the time, place, and cause of death.

morgue A place to which human remains are removed pending proper identification and release to relatives; a morgue may be a special building in more populous areas or a special section in a hospital.

autopsy The examination and dissection of a dead body in order to determine the cause of death.

donor Individual who makes a gift of all or part of his or her body after death (organs, tissues, eyes, bones, arteries, blood, other body fluids, and any other parts of the human body).

Appendix A:
Legal Aspects of Death

The Death Certificate

A **death certificate** is a legal document stating the person's identity, the time of death, and the cause of death. In all states, a death certificate is required before a body can be buried or cremated. This requirement is to prevent the destruction of evidence, if it turns out that a crime was committed. If the deceased was under a doctor's care, that doctor or another licensed physician issues the death certificate. If the deceased was not under a doctor's care, or if there is a question of death by violence, a coroner or medical examiner is called in to examine the body and to issue the death certificate.

Identification. Under usual circumstances, family members or friends identify the deceased person. This may happen at the scene of death or in a **morgue**. In cases where an unknown person dies, the coroner must make every effort to identify him or her. Identification requires detective work—a search through fingerprint files, dental records, missing persons' photographs, blood and genetic matching. If the body is never identified, it is buried with a marker saying "John Doe" or "Jane Doe." If the body is identified but no one claims it, the coroner buries it "in the manner provided for interment of the indigent dead." According to the law, the unclaimed dead may be embalmed and used for scientific and educational purposes.

Time of Death. Despite advances in medical science, determining the time of death is not always easy. As you learned in chapter 2, a person is considered dead when there is permanent cessation of (1) total brain function, (2) spontaneous function of the respiratory system, and (3) spontaneous function of the circulatory system. But what about the person whose brain waves are flat yet continues breathing on his or her own? Or what about the person whose brain is alive, but whose other bodily functions must be sustained by machines? Are these people dead, or are they alive?

Knowing the exact time of death is important in forensic science, which deals with deaths where murder or violence has occurred. It is also important if any vital organs are to be donated to a transplant program. The organs must be taken as soon after death as possible in order to ensure healthy tissue for a successful transplant.

In December 1990, Pope John Paul II called on scientists to keep trying to "determine as precisely as possible the exact moment and the indisputable sign of death." He also cautioned them to be prudent in deciding when to remove organs for transplant. "Neither individuals nor society are permitted to endanger life, whatever benefits might possibly accrue as a result," he said. According to Christian moral principles, doctors cannot sacrifice one person, "even though it may be for the benefit of another human being who might be felt to be entitled to preference" (From Felician A. Foy, ed., 1991 *Catholic Almanac* [Huntington, IN: Our Sunday Visitor, 1990], p. 70).

Cause of Death. All states have laws that require an **autopsy** of the deceased in cases of sudden or unexplained death. When a coroner is required to investigate the cause of death, he or she is entitled to custody of the corpse until the conclusion of the autopsy or medical investigation. It is a misdemeanor to perform an autopsy without written authorization. This authorization must be obtained from the deceased (before death), the survivors, the public administrator of the deceased's estate, or the coroner.

Disposition of the Body

Believe it or not, you have no legal say in how your body will be disposed of after death, unless you **donate** your body or parts of it for anatomic research or organ donation. Even if you state in writing that you want to be buried in the ground or buried in a mausoleum or cremated, your family has no legal obligation to carry out your wishes. Once you die, your body is treated under the law as property or quasi-property that belongs to your surviving spouse, your surviving children, your surviving parents, your next of kin, or the executor of your **legal will**. These people, upon their written authorization, can decide how your remains will be interred.

Regardless of what your family or executor decides, your estate is financially liable. This means that you must pay for the funeral, burial, or cremation. If there is not enough money in your bank account to cover these costs, responsibility for payment falls to all family members.

Disposal by Cremation. Some states require a special permit or authorization for cremation. The crematorium requires before the actual cremation the signature of the next of kin or the executor of the will. This authorization usually includes instructions for disposition of the ashes or for shipping them to some other community. Some crematoriums are insured against lawsuits that might arise from performing a cremation without proper authorization. In some states, when it is impossible for a crematorium to secure all of the necessary signatures, an affidavit attesting to the desire of the deceased to be cremated acts as proper authorization.

In most states, a person can inurn, inter, or scatter cremains so long as they do not create an offense to anyone or violate another's property rights. The exception to this is California, Washington, and Nevada, which prohibit the scattering of ashes. The National Park Service also forbids the strewing of ashes in national parks because of the possible creation of a public nuisance. In 1965, California permitted scattering of ashes beyond the three-mile limit at sea and from an airplane flying more than five thousand feet over non-populous areas. In some states, it is necessary to secure a permit before shipping cremains to another state.

Disposition by Burial. Most states, for health reasons, limit burials to sites designated as cemeteries. In California, for example, it is against the law to bury someone within the city limits except in a cemetery. One exception to the cemetery rule is found in New York. There, a person may be buried in any family burying ground, provided it is no closer than 100 feet to a residence without the owner's permission. Many states require a grave liner or concrete **vault** if one is to be buried in the ground.

Other laws exist regarding the cemetery itself and disinterment. In most states, for example, it is a misdemeanor to vandalize a cemetery. California law states that it is a felony to remove unlawfully, to mutilate, or to disinter human remains. No remains can be legally removed from any cemetery except upon written order of the health department or superior court.

legal will *A legal document that states what a person wants done with his or her possessions after death.*

vault *A metal receptacle to receive the casketed remains, which provides protection against the elements of the earth and prevents the ground above a casket from sinking after deterioration has taken place.*

Of Interest

In several states, cremation may not take place for 48 hours following death, unless a health officer orders immediate cremation in the case of contagious disease. Only two states—Massachusetts and Michigan—have laws that require the corpse to be placed in a casket for cremation. In all other states, the corpse may be cremated in a cardboard container.

Of Interest

Embalming is neither prescribed nor prohibited by Canon Law. Church custom, however, prohibits the embalming of a pope. When a pope dies, his body is washed, clothed, and then made available for public viewing. This custom was problematic in the case of Pope Paul VI. The heat caused his skin to turn green.

Embalming

Each state has laws specifying the conditions under which a corpse may or may not be embalmed. For example, in most states it is against the law (except by permission of the coroner or justice of the peace) to embalm a corpse if the cause of death is unknown or if the death is related to a car accident or crime. On the other hand, embalming is not always a legal requirement. In New York, Ohio, South Dakota, Georgia, Kentucky, Maryland, Tennessee, Vermont, and Virginia, embalming is not mandatory under any circumstances. The decision to embalm a corpse is solely at the discretion of the executor or next of kin.

A summary of the embalming laws of the other states, as well as those of the District of Columbia and Puerto Rico, may be found on the next two pages. Use the legend below to interpret individual states' embalming laws, found on the next page.

Embalming Laws

Legend

Embalming or cremation is required in the following situations:

A. The body is transported across state lines.

B. Final disposition does not take place within 30 hours after death.

C. Death has occurred by unusual or communicable disease or suspected communicable disease (leprosy, plague, smallpox).

E. The body is transferred by common carrier (airline, railroad, truck).

I. Final destination is not reached within 24 hours.

K. The body is not buried within 24 hours after death.

L. Final destination is not reached within 48 hours.

M. The body is not buried or cremated within 72 hours.

R. The body is to be exposed to the public for more than 24 hours.

Embalming or refrigeration is required in the following situations:

D. If a body is to be stored or transported longer than 24 hours.

N. If a body is not buried or cremated within 48 hours after death.

O. Final destination will not be reached within 36 hours after death.

P. If a body is to be transported longer than 8 hours.

Embalming or a hermetically sealed coffin is required in the following situations:

G. Body is transferred by common carrier (airline, railroad, truck) across state lines.

H. Body is stored for more than 24 hours.

J. Death is a result of a contagious disease (leprosy, plague, smallpox).

Embalming may be required in the following situations:

F. Death is a result of a contagious disease (leprosy, plague, smallpox).

Embalming is NOT required in the following situations:

Q. If body is buried or cremated within 18 hours after death.

Embalming Laws

Alabama—A, B

Alaska—C

Arizona—A (unless transportation is to be provided by a family member or by a licensed undertaker within 24 hours after death), C, D

Arkansas—D

California—E, F

Colorado—D, G

Connecticut—A, E

Delaware—H

District of Columbia—C

Florida—A, C, D

Georgia—C, I

Hawaii—G, J

Idaho—E

Illinois—C, E

Indiana—C

Iowa—C, E

Kansas—K

Louisiana—B

Maine—E

Massachusetts—C, D, G

Michigan—C, E, L

Minnesota—C, E, M

Mississippi—C, I, N

Missouri—G, J

Montana—C, E, O, P

Nebraska—D (exception: if a body is placed in a metal or metal-lined sealed container immediately after death, it may be considered the same as an embalmed body), G, J

Nevada—Q

New Hampshire—R

New Jersey—C, E, I, N

New Mexico—A, C

North Carolina—G, J

North Dakota—A, C, E, M

Oklahoma—B, C

Oregon—C, D, E, F

Pennsylvania—H

Puerto Rico—E, I, K

Rhode Island—E, J

South Carolina—E

Texas—D

Utah—C, D, E

Washington—B, C, E

West Virginia—A, C, E

Wisconsin—C, E

Wyoming—B

—Adapted from *Funerals: Consumers' Last Rights* (Mount Vernon, NY: Consumers Union, 1977), pp. 260–68.

Purposes for which anatomical gifts may be made

To a hospital, surgeon, or physician for medical or dental education, research, advancement of medical and dental science, therapy, or transplantation

To any accredited medical school or dental school, college, or university for education, research, advancement of science, therapy, or transplantation

To any **bank** or storage facility for education, research, advancement of science, therapy, or transplantation

To any specified individual for therapy or transplantation needed

---

bank *A facility licensed, accredited, or approved under state law for storage of human bodies or parts.*

Of Interest

Most states now have anatomical donor forms on the back of driver's licenses. These should be used in addition to Uniform Donor wallet cards that may be obtained from various organ banks.

Of Interest

The Church considers the donation of organs to be an act of Christian charity.

The Uniform Anatomical Gift Act

The Uniform Anatomical Gift Act says that any individual of sound mind and 18 years of age or older may give all or any part of his or her body after death for one or more of the purposes listed in the chart above. This act has been adopted as law by the District of Columbia and all states, except Delaware, Massachusetts, Mississippi, Nebraska, Ohio, Rhode Island, and West Virginia.

The anatomical gift is usually made in a person's will, donor card, or recorded message, and may be taken immediately after death. The recipient may accept or reject the gift.

A person may donate one, several, or all of the following vital organs:

- *Eyes.* In the United States alone, the sight of 30,000 people could be restored if enough corneas were available. Corneal transplant operations are now effective in restoring sight in 90 percent of all patients. (At the present time, it is not possible to transplant the entire eye.) Corneas must be removed within two to four hours after death. Airlines will fly them to their destinations without charge.
- *Ears.* More than 18 million people in the United States suffer partial or total deafness. Persons with hearing problems or other ear disorders are urged to bequeath their inner ears to temporal bone banks for research.
- *Kidneys.* Severe diabetics and people suffering from renal failure desperately need kidneys. While kidney transplant operations are becoming more successful, not enough kidneys are available for all those who need them.
- *Tissues.* Body tissues, such as bone, ear, eye, heart, heart valve, and arteries are needed by regional tissue banks for transplantation.
- *Pituitary Glands.* An estimated 10,000 children in the United States suffer from serious pituitary deficiency that retards growth. Donated pituitary glands can help produce the hormones these children need.
- *Skin.* A donation of skin can be extremely valuable to persons suffering from serious burns.

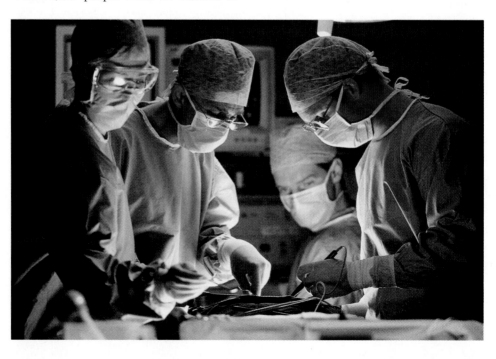

Writing a Will

Most people spend their entire lives accumulating possessions, real estate, and bank accounts. But in the end, the popular saying "You can't take it with you" holds true for everyone. A legal will is a way of dispersing one's possessions according to one's wishes.

The person who makes out the will is called the *legator*, or *settlor*. The person or charitable organization that receives the benefits is called the *beneficiary*. When a person dies, his or her lawyer should be contacted for a reading of the will. The administrator or **executor** sees that the will is carried out. Before the beneficiaries can receive their inheritance, the **probate court** makes sure that the deceased's funeral expenses and all outstanding bills are paid.

Everyone should write a will. The will can be changed and updated at any time, either with an entire new document or with **codicils**. Waiting until you are old or ill to write a will is not a good idea. As you have learned, death can strike anyone at any time. By procrastinating, you may end up dying **intestate**, or without a will.

What happens if you die without a will? Then the state will write your will for you. Your possessions and money will be distributed in accordance with the laws of your state. The probate court will appoint an administrator to see that the state's laws are carried out. If the person is a married adult, most state laws stipulate that one-third to one-half of the person's estate goes to his or her spouse and two-thirds to the children. If the person is a single adult or child, the law stipulates that the entire estate goes to the deceased's parents.

The probate process is both time-consuming and costly. It takes an average of six months to a year to process an estate. Probate fees can range anywhere between 8$\frac{1}{2}$ percent to 20 percent of the entire estate. This means your beneficiaries will receive significantly less than you may have intended. If this is not the way you want your possessions and money to be distributed, then you need to make out a will.

Writing a will is more than a legal procedure. It is also a psychological challenge to the writer to accept, rather than to deny, the reality of death. Furthermore, it is an expression of love for one's spouse, relatives, charitable organizations, and friends.

Church Law

When the *Code of Canon Law* was revised in 1983, it reduced the forty previous canons (from 1917) dealing with death and burial to ten. As you will see, these laws allow local bishops a great deal of latitude.

Canon 1176

§1: The Christian faithful departed are to be given ecclesiastical funeral rites according to the norm of law.

§2: Through ecclesiastical funeral rites the Church asks spiritual assistance for the departed, honors their bodies, and at the same time brings the solace of hope to the living; such rites are to be celebrated according to the norm of liturgical laws.

§3: The Church earnestly recommends that the pious custom of burying the bodies of the dead be observed; it does not, however, forbid cremation unless it has been chosen for reasons which are contrary to Christian teaching.

Canon 1177

§1: As a rule the funeral rites for any of the faithful departed must be celebrated in his or her own parish church.

§2: However, any member of the Christian faithful or those commissioned to arrange for his or her funeral may choose another church for the funeral rites with the consent of its rector and after informing the departed person's pastor.

§3: If death has occurred outside the person's own parish, and the corpse has not been transferred to that parish and another church has not been legitimately chosen for the funeral, the funeral rites are to be celebrated in the church of the parish where the death occurred unless another church has been designated by particular law.

---

legator *Person who makes the will; another term for a legator is* settlor.

beneficiary *An individual or group that is named as an heir in a legal will.*

executor, executrix *Person (male or female) who carries out the wishes of the person who made the will.*

probate court *The legal institution that is responsible for overseeing the handling of a will and the payment of all debts belonging to a person who has died.*

codicil *A change or revision of an original will.*

intestate *The situation of dying without leaving a will.*

Of Interest

When President Franklin D. Roosevelt died, the probate lawyers and administrator took 11 percent of his estate.

notorious *An action that is publicly known or has been committed in such circumstances that it is entirely impossible to conceal it or offer any legal justification for it.*

apostate *Baptized person who totally repudiates Christianity.*

heretic *A baptized Catholic who obstinately denies or doubts some truth believed to be part of the faith.*

schismatic *A baptized Catholic who refuses to obey the Holy Father or refuses communion with the members of the Church.*

manifest sin *A sin for which there are eyewitnesses who can give testimony about it. If there is no public scandal, the right of burial is not to be denied even to manifest sinners.*

Of Interest

Canon 1264 states that the bishop should fix the amount or set a limit on the amount to be given on these occasions. No one is to be denied Christian burial because of lack of money.

Of Interest

At one time in Church history, criminals, strangers, the illegitimate, and those who committed suicide could not receive ecclesiastical burial.

Canon 1178

The funeral rites of a diocesan bishop are to be celebrated in his own cathedral church unless he has chosen another church.

Canon 1179

As a rule the funeral rites of religious or members of societies of apostolic life are to be celebrated in their own church or oratory by their superior if it is a clerical institute or society, otherwise by the chaplain.

Canon 1180

§1: If a parish has its own cemetery, the faithful departed are to be interred in it unless another cemetery has been legitimately chosen either by the departed person or by those who are responsible to arrange for his or her interment.

§2: However, everyone, unless prohibited by law, is permitted to choose a cemetery for burial.

Canon 1181

The prescriptions of can. 1264 are to be observed in regard to the offerings given on the occasion of funerals; precautions are nevertheless to be taken in funeral rites against any favoritism toward persons and against depriving the poor of the funeral rites which are their due.

Canon 1182

After the interment an entry is to be made in the (parish) death register in accord with the norm of particular law.

Canon 1183

§1: As regards funeral rites catechumens are to be considered members of the Christian faithful.

§2: The local ordinary can permit children to be given ecclesiastical funeral rites if their parents intended to baptize them but they died before their baptism.

§3: In the prudent judgment of the local ordinary, ecclesiastical funeral rites can be granted to baptized members of some non-Catholic church or ecclesial community unless it is evidently contrary to their will and provided their own minister is unavailable.

Canon 1184

§1: Unless they have given some signs of repentance before their death, the following are to be deprived of ecclesiastical funeral rites:

1° **notorious apostates**, **heretics**, and **schismatics**;

2° persons who had chosen the cremation of their own bodies for reasons opposed to the Christian faith;

3° other **manifest sinners** for whom ecclesiastical funeral rites cannot be granted without public scandal to the faithful.

§2: If some doubt should arise, the local ordinary is to be consulted; and his judgment is to be followed.

Canon 1185

Any funeral Mass whatsoever is also to be denied a person excluded from ecclesiastical funeral rites.

—*Code of Canon Law, Latin-English Edition* (Washington, DC: Canon Law Society of America, 1983).

In addition to these canons, the Church says that major amputated members (arm, leg, and so forth) that maintain some recognizable human quality are to be disposed of in consecrated ground by burial or by cremation. With proper consent, the amputated member may be used by medical schools for purposes of study and dissection.

Your Will

Many state laws require a person to be 21 years of age in order to execute a legal will. This age requirement may differ in the same state with regard to real property and personal property. Real property is land and buildings (house, commercial building). Personal property includes clothes, automobiles, furniture, mortgages, promissory notes, stocks and bonds. Generally the minimum age is lower for personal property than it is for real property. The minimum age may also differ, depending on one's gender.

Many people consult a lawyer to write their will. It is also possible, however, to write one without a lawyer. Books and computer software are available to assist people who wish to do this. It is important that the person making a will be of sound mind, good memory, and under no coercion from others. There are other considerations as well.

Ordinarily a will is drafted with a typewriter, computer, or pen. Some states even allow a will to be in the form of an audiotape or videotape. A will written in pencil is not legally binding. The final copy needs to be perfect, with no erasing or crossing out. No special form is needed, as long as the intentions of the person are clear. The will, however, does need to be dated and signed in the presence of two or three witnesses and notarized.

Unless all of your possessions are to go to one person or charity, your will should list all properties (real or personal) by name (leather jacket, gold watch, and so forth) or by categories (jewelry, books, record collection). The will should also clearly specify the name of the person or charity that is to inherit each item. It is not enough to omit the name of a family member if the intention is to disinherit that person. The family member must be mentioned in the will, along with the express statement that he or she will inherit nothing.

Write a false draft of your will. Indicate on the page that you are not writing an actual will. Use the outline below to help you.

Of Interest

The following states, as well as the Philippines and Puerto Rico, require a person to have three witnesses to a will: Connecticut, Georgia, Louisiana, Maine, Massachusetts, New Hampshire, South Carolina, and Vermont.

Of Interest

In Louisiana, a parent is prohibited from disinheriting any child.

Last Will and Testament (false draft)

I, _____, a resident of _____,
　　　　　　(your legal name)　　　　　　　　　　　　　　　(city)　　　　(county)　　　　(state)

declare that this is my last will. I hereby revoke all wills and codicils that I have previously made.

I make the following cash gifts:　　　　　Amount　　　　　　　　　　Beneficiary

I make the following gifts of personal property:　　　Property　　　　　　　Beneficiary

I give the rest of my estate to _____.

I nominate _____ as executor. If he/she shall for any reason fail to qualify or cease to act as

executor, I nominate _____ as executor.

I subscribe my name this _____ day of _____, 19 ____, at _____,
　　　　　　　　　　　　　　　　　　　　　　　　　　　　　　(city)　　　　(county)　　　　(state)

and do hereby declare that I am of sound mind and that I voluntarily sign this instrument as my last will.

_____
(your signature)

Witnesses (signed names and addresses):

_____　　　_____

_____　　　_____

Of Interest

full couch A style of casket in which the whole lid opens or lifts off so that the entire body may be viewed.

half couch A style of casket in which half of the lid opens or lifts off, so that the body may be viewed from the waist up.

Appendix B:
Financial Aspects of Death

Traditional Funeral Costs

A traditional funeral includes embalming, a casket, a funeral service, and burial in a cemetery. In 1997, the National Funeral Directors Association reported that the average cost of a traditional adult funeral was $4,783. This amount, however, did not include other expenses, such as cemetery plot, marker or monument, floral expenses, or unpaid medical bills, which tended to push the total cost to $8,000.

Most funeral homes offer package plans that cover everything for a traditional funeral except the casket. The price of the entire plan is roughly five times that of the price of the casket. One disadvantage to purchasing a package plan is that you may pay for services you don't want or choose not to have. One advantage is that package plans are often 15 percent less than the cost of buying each item separately. Today, all funeral homes must also provide customers with itemized plans. In these plans, you pay only for the services you actually need and want.

The services you must pay for in a traditional funeral include the funeral director's services, the casket, embalming, transportation, cemetery expenses, the grave marker or tombstone, and miscellaneous expenses. We will look at each service individually.

The Funeral Director's Services

Each funeral home charges a fee for its role in arranging and supervising the funeral. Because these fees vary widely, it is important to comparison shop between several funeral homes before selecting one. The funeral home fees include the following services:

- consultation with the funeral director

- use of funeral home facilities for storage of the body, visitation (optional), wake (optional), and funeral services (optional)
- death certificates (usually ten copies are needed for legal purposes) and other required permits
- six hired pallbearers (unless the family will provide them)
- thank-you cards and a guest registry book
- cosmetics and hairstyling of corpse
- hearse and driver
- ushers for funeral
- bier upon which to rest the casket
- burial clothing or shroud (unless provided by the family)

Casket

The casket is the largest single expense of a funeral. Most funeral homes have selection rooms where caskets are displayed. The price will vary greatly, depending upon style and construction materials. Caskets come in three main styles, or types. On a **full couch** casket, the entire lid opens or comes off so that the entire body may be viewed. On a **half couch** casket, only the top half opens so that the body

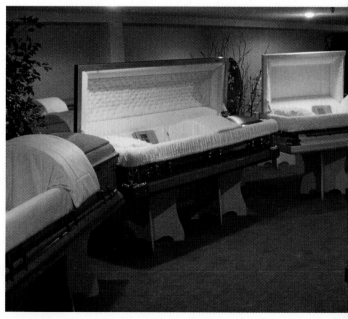

may be viewed from the waist up. A **hinge cap** casket is similar to the half couch, except for the placement of hinges.

The least expensive casket is a plain pine box. The next upgrades include caskets made of chestnut, cypress, or red cedar. These are usually covered with cloth. Caskets in the intermediate price range include the more expensive hardwoods: mahogany, walnut, oak, birch, maple, or cherry. They are treated with clear natural finish. The most expensive caskets are made of metal—specially treated iron, steel, copper, bronze, fiberglass, stainless steel, and zinc. Such caskets may come with inner-spring mattresses and satin or velvet lining. If you don't see a casket in the funeral showroom in your price range or desired color, it is a good idea to ask.

Embalming

Two processes are involved in embalming: arterial embalming and cavity embalming. In arterial embalming, the body is drained of blood. Then the blood vessels are filled with **formalin**. In cavity embalming, fluids are removed from the thoracic cavity and abdominal cavity, then replaced with a preservative fluid.

State laws vary regarding whether the corpse needs to be embalmed or not. (See Appendix A.) If embalming is not performed, the funeral home may charge for refrigerating the body.

Transportation

These fees include the cost of transporting the body in a hearse or ambulance from the place of death to the funeral home, to the church for the funeral service, and to the cemetery. Extra fees will be charged for limousines to transport family members from the church to the cemetery, for transporting the body to another city or state for interment, and for motorcycle police escorts.

Transportation fees include transporting the body in a hearse or ambulance from the place of death to the funeral home, to the church for the funeral service, and to the cemetery.

Cemetery Expenses

A cemetery may either be a traditional one or a **memorial park**. Traditional cemeteries allow grave markers or monuments to be put on a grave provided they meet size limitations. Memorial parks require uniform markers that are level with the grass. As a general rule, cemeteries operated by non-profit organizations, such as cities, states, or churches, are less expensive than privately owned cemeteries or memorial parks. Again, comparison shopping for a cemetery is a good idea if you want to keep funeral expenses down.

Basically, cemetery expenses include four things: the plot or mausoleum space, opening and closing a grave, the vault or grave liner, and **perpetual care**.

- *Plot or mausoleum space.* A ground plot is less expensive than above-ground burial in individual, family, or community mausoleums. Many cemeteries allow people to buy a plot on a time-payment plan. Again, comparison shopping is a good idea. Some cemeteries charge no interest on their plans; others charge up to 20 percent per year. In some cases, it may be less expensive to get a bank loan than to accept the cemetery's financing.

Of Interest

Some casket manufacturers offer a thirty-year or even a fifty-year warranty on their metal coffins and say they will replace those that prove defective during that time.

---

hinge cap *A style of casket similar to the half couch, except for variations in the placement of the lid hinges.*

formalin *A solution of formaldehyde and water that is used in embalming.*

memorial park *A private cemetery that requires uniform grave markers level with the grass.*

perpetual care *A contract between a grave owner and cemetery to maintain the grave forever.*

Of Interest

---

grave liner *A concrete vault surrounding a casket that has been buried.*

Most cemeteries require that a casket be placed inside a concrete or metal vault when it is placed in the ground.

- *Opening and closing a grave.* Grave diggers and cemetery workers belong to a union, with strict rules regarding their hours and pay. For this reason, the cemetery will charge more to open and close a grave on weekends or holidays.

- *Vault or grave liner.* Most cemeteries require that a casket be placed inside a concrete or metal container when it is placed in the ground. This container keeps the ground from caving in when the casket and body decompose. Usually, the container is simply called a *vault*. But sometimes a concrete enclosure is called a **grave liner** and a metal enclosure is called a *vault.* Concrete vaults are less costly than solid steel or copper ones that form an airtight seal. Vaults sold by cemeteries are less costly than those sold by funeral homes.

- *Perpetual care.* Future maintenance of the cemetery may be an optional expense or part of the cost of the plot. If perpetual care is optional, you might ask to see graves that have it and those without it, for comparison. In some states, the money

for perpetual care must be placed in a trust fund. The earnings from the fund are used to maintain the cemetery's grounds.

Grave Markers or Monuments

Some cemeteries require that you purchase their own markers or monuments. Others allow you to purchase them from independent monument companies. The cost will depend on size, material, design, and craftsmanship. Bronze markers are less expensive than granite markers. Markers are less expensive than monuments. Elaborate monuments can run into thousands of dollars, depending upon the type of stone, the size, and the amount of engraving to be done. There may also be an extra installation fee.

Miscellaneous Expenses

Numerous other expenses can contribute to the cost of the funeral. Among these are the following:

- attorney's fees regarding the will and estate taxes
- airline tickets, rental cars, and hotels, if family members have to travel to get to the funeral
- dry cleaning, if needed, for burial clothing
- newspaper death notices and obituaries
- honorarium for officiating minister or priest (It is usual for the minister to be given a fee for his services. Sometimes this fee is included in the funeral home's charge. More often, it is sent by a member of the family, along with a thank-you note.)
- music for the funeral service (Check with the minister or priest about appropriate fees for the organist, vocalist, and any other musicians you may have.)
- flowers
- the post-funeral meal (In rural communities, neighbors may prepare food for the reception after the funeral. In cities, food will often be catered by a restaurant, at the family's expense.)
- postage for thank-you notes (Survivors should always send written notes of thanks for flowers, Mass cards, food, and

donations to charity, and to the priest, pallbearers, ushers, and musicians. If hundreds of cards need to be written, the family may wish to pay the added expense of having cards printed or engraved.)

Financial Resources

Now that you have an idea of the costs involved in a traditional funeral, another consideration emerges: how to pay for it all. Fortunately there are certain resources you can tap, death benefits that will help defray funeral expenses. Survivors must apply for almost all of these benefits; they are not sent automatically when someone dies.

Here are some resources for you to look into:

- *Social Security*. Death benefits are available under some conditions to the survivors of persons who were covered by Social Security. Consult your local social security office for more details about the benefits and how to apply for them.

- *Trade Unions and Fraternal Organizations*. Many trade unions and fraternal organizations provide death benefits to the families of their members. Also, there are benefits for the survivors of anyone who has ever been a railroad employee.

- *Life and Casualty Insurance*. If the deceased had life insurance, this money may be used by beneficiaries to pay for the funeral. Other possibilities include automobile club insurance, accidental death insurance (available through some credit cards), and liability insurance.

- *Employee's Benefits*. Depending on the nature of the death, survivors may be entitled to Workman's Compensation benefits. The families of state employees in some states are entitled to survivor benefits. Burial expenses for indigent families are commonly paid by the county.

- *Veterans Administration*. Veterans are eligible for death benefits if they served in the United States Armed Forces during the Spanish-American War, World War I, World War II, Korean War, Vietnam conflict, Persian Gulf War, and certain peacetime service, provided they have not been dishonorably discharged. For more information, contact the Veterans Administration.

The above resources are available in the United States. Canadian death benefits include the Canada Pension Plan (the equivalent of the Social Security System in the United States), which pays a lump sum death benefit to the estate of any person who has contributed to the plan for at least three calendar years. Veteran benefits in Canada are not guaranteed. The Last Post Fund is a private organization that arranges funerals and burial for veterans who die without the means to do so for themselves.

Of Interest

When someone dies, it is important to notify insurance companies, including automobile insurance, for immediate cancellation and available refund. Survivors should also check promptly on all credit card payments. Some cards carry insurance clauses that will cancel debts in the event of death.

Some Alternatives

One way to cut costs is not to have a traditional funeral and burial. Three of the most common alternatives are cremation, direct cremation or direct burial, and donation of one's body to science.

If cremation is chosen, the body is still laid out in a funeral home and there may still be a funeral. Cremation costs include fees for embalming, a casket, and transportation charges from the place of death to the funeral home and then to the crematory. There will also be an additional fee for the container the body must be placed in when cremated (usually a hardboard or cardboard box).

The advantage of cremation is that it eliminates the need for a cemetery plot, a vault or grave liner, opening and closing a grave, and a marker or monument. Total expenses for cremation will vary, depending upon the disposal of the cremains. Here are some options and their cost considerations:

- Ashes are stored at home (cost of urn only).

- Ashes are stored in a niche in a columbarium. (The price of a niche depends on its size, location, and quality. Perpetual care costs may or may not be included in the niche price.)

- Ashes are buried on private property, in a cemetery plot, or in an urn garden. (No urn is necessary; the cremains can be buried in the container provided by the crematory. But there will be a cost for opening and closing the plot, perpetual care, and a memorial plaque.)

- Ashes are scattered over land or sea, according to state law. (You will probably have to hire the services of a commercial pilot or boat.)

In direct cremation or direct burial, the funeral director removes the body from the place of death (transportation cost), provides a container (for cremation) or plain coffin (for burial), and transports the body directly to the crematory or cemetery (transportation cost again), all within a matter of hours. Memorial services are usually arranged at a later date (fees for minister or priest, music, flowers, food). Because this type of disposal is not very profitable, funeral homes may charge more for transportation. Other funeral homes that specialize in direct burial or cremation provide the same services at less cost.

People who wish to donate their body to science should make arrangements in advance with the chosen medical school, dental school, or research center. Thousands of **cadavers** are needed each year for the training of future doctors and dentists. Many schools require special embalming and will pay for the cost of transporting the body to the school. Transportation may take place either after visitation and funeral services or immediately after death. After the school has finished with the body, it has a moral responsibility to see that it is disposed of by Christian burial or cremation.

cadaver A dead body intended for dissection.

Thousands of cadavers are needed each year for the training of future doctors and dentists.

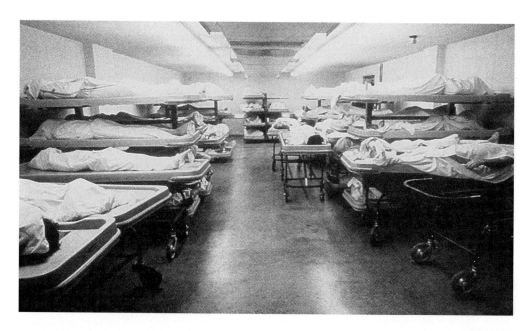

Pre-Planning

What do you do if you want a traditional funeral but you also want to keep expenses down? The most logical answer is to plan and pay for your funeral before you die. Today, 25 percent of funerals are paid with **pre-need** contracts. Far from being a morbid exercise, pre-planning has a number of advantages. First, since you have already taken care of the details, family members know exactly what you want and how much it will cost. They won't have to make uninformed decisions or negotiate for a funeral during their time of grieving. Second, planning ahead helps you and your family accept death. And finally, paying for the funeral in advance freezes the cost at today's prices.

Among the types of pre-need plans available are the following:

- *Funeral Insurance.* Many families carry a small insurance policy (usually $10,000) on each member for the specific purpose of covering burial expenses. This is a term life policy, with premiums paid either all at once or in installments. The funeral director is the beneficiary of the policy.

- *Protection Through a Credit Union.* Many credit unions have an arrangement whereby deposits made before age 55 are doubled (not to exceed $1,000 to $2,000) at the time of death. Check with your credit union to see what type of plan it offers.

- *Pre-Need Trusts.* The family funds a trust with a bank or savings institution. The trust's principal and interest pays for funeral expenses.

- *Mutual Aid Plans.* Some groups, including a number of Quakers and Mennonites, care for their dead without the assistance of a funeral director. Member families authorize the church burial committee to act on their behalf to get the death certificate from the doctor and record it in the county courthouse, to get a transportation permit (if needed), and to get a **burial permit** or authorization to cremate. Following the disposition of the body, a memorial meeting is planned, to suit the needs of the family and community.

In addition to these church groups, there are now over 170 funeral or **memorial societies** in the United States, with over a million members. These societies are consumer groups organized to minimize funeral costs and to stress simplicity, dignity, and economy when dealing with death. Memorial and funeral societies are effective. They can save up to 50 percent in funeral costs, no matter what type of disposal is preferred, because they have the ability to bargain with funeral homes for reduced rates. Some societies even help non-members plan funerals on short notice.

Memorial societies were first formed in 1939. In 1963, the Continental Association of Funeral and Memorial Societies was formed in the United States. In 1971, a separate Memorial Society Association of Canada was formed. Membership in a memorial society is open to anyone for a small one-time family fee.

Because wills are usually not read until after the funeral service, it is important for anyone who has done pre-planning to let family members know about his or her intentions and wishes. Every person should have a computer file or paper file marked "In Case of Death." A family member should be told the location of the file so it will be available when needed.

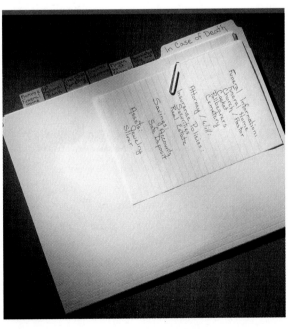

pre-need planning Funeral and burial arrangements that are made before death by an individual. These arrangements may or may not include financial payment.

burial permit A permit issued according to state law regarding the interment, disinterment, removal, reinterment, or transportation of human remains.

memorial society Consumer group organized to ensure a dignified funeral at low cost.

Of Interest

A file marked "In Case of Death" should contain the following information:

- Location of will
- Name and address of attorney
- List of bank accounts
- List of all securities and properties owned and their whereabouts
- Insurance policies
- Location of safe deposit box and key
- Name of preferred funeral home
- Information regarding burial plot
- Place where funeral should be held
- Choice of casket
- List of pallbearers
- Location of all silver and jewelry
- Choice of burial or cremation
- Note about organ or body donation

Before You Go

You can help your survivors handle the business details of your death by doing some research and making some decisions now. Use this first page to find out how much different options cost. Then, on the next page, write down your preferences. Finally, discuss your preferences with your family.

Itemized Funeral Costs	Price Range
Funeral director's basic fees	
1) Funeral home #1	
2) Funeral home #2	
3) Funeral home #3	
Moving the remains to the funeral home	
Embalming	
Cosmetology and burial clothes	
Refrigeration (per day)	
Casket	
1) pine box or other soft woods	
2) hardwood types	
3) metal casket	
Visitation room	
Coordination of funeral service	
Chapel	
Hearse	
Limousine(s)	
Flowers	
Motorcycle escorts	
Clergy	
Music	
Cemetery plot	
Vault or grave liner	
Opening/Closing of grave	
Perpetual care	
Food	
Alternatives	**Price Range**
Cremation	
1) columbarium niche	
2) commercial boat or pilot	
Direct cremation or burial	
Memorial society plan	

My Funeral Preferences

My funeral home preference is: _____

I want my body to be: buried _____ cremated _____ donated to science _____

(state where) _____

I want my remains placed in: cemetery plot _____ mausoleum crypt _____ urn _____ elsewhere _____

(describe) _____

If I die in another state or country, I want (circle one):

    a) my body/remains shipped to: _____

    b) to be interred there

I would like an autopsy: yes _____ no _____ undecided _____

If undecided, under what conditions would you want an autopsy performed? _____

_____

I would like my body embalmed: yes _____ no _____

I would like to have special cosmetics: no _____ yes _____ (specify) _____

_____

I would like my hair arranged in the following way: _____

Clothing I would like: _____

Accessories I would like to be viewed with (jewelry, glasses, watch): _____

_____

Accessories I would like to be buried with: _____

The type of casket I would like:

    a) pine box _____ other softwood (specify) _____

    b) hardwood (specify) _____

    c) metal (specify) _____

    full couch _____ half couch _____ hinge cap _____

    sealed? yes _____ no _____

Expressions of sympathy I would prefer: flowers _____ Mass cards _____ memorial fund or charity _____

(specify) _____

My cemetery preference is: _____

The type of vault I would like: concrete _____ metal _____ sealed _____ unsealed _____

Glossary

abolitionists People who oppose the practice of capital punishment.

abortion The spontaneous or induced expulsion of a fetus from the womb.

acceptance The last stage of dying, in which a person accepts death and looks forward to future life after death.

acute Sharp, severe pain that has a sudden onset and lasts only a short time.

afterlife Continued life or new life after death.

agape meal A memorial meal of love, sometimes celebrated with a funeral.

altruistic death A form of self-sacrifice in which an individual gives up his or her life for a noble cause, a sense of patriotic duty, or a religious ideal.

angels Pure spirits with intelligence and free will who act as messengers of God.

anger One of the stages of dying, in which a person is indignant about his or her approaching death and may seek someone else to blame.

Anointing of the Sick One of the seven sacraments of the Catholic Church, to be received by a sick or elderly person or by someone who is dying. The three parts of the sacrament include the prayer of the faithful for all the sick, the laying on of hands, and the anointing with the Oil of the Sick.

apocalypse Term that refers to the end of the world, with a general resurrection and final judgment as well as the events leading up to it. Christians refer to this event as the last judgment or the second coming of Christ.

apostate Baptized person who totally repudiates Christianity.

arms control An agreement between countries to limit the development, testing, deployment, or use of nuclear weapons.

arms limitation An agreement to limit the number of nuclear weapons.

Ars Moriendi Latin for "the art of dying." This art is thought to be acquired by the practice of right living.

Ascension Catholic belief that Jesus returned to heaven in his glorified body after the resurrection.

Assumption Catholic belief that Mary was taken body and soul into heaven after her death.

autopsy The examination and dissection of a dead body in order to determine the cause of death.

bank A facility licensed, accredited, or approved under state law for storage of human bodies or parts.

bargaining One of the stages of dying, in which a person tries to buy more time by making a deal with God.

beatific vision The intuitive, immediate, and direct experience of God enjoyed by the blessed in heaven.

beneficiary An individual or group that is named as an heir in a legal will.

bereavement The entire grieving process, especially experienced by someone who has lost a loved one to death.

bier A movable platform or framework upon which a casket is placed for easy movement.

bigots People who are intolerant of the different opinions and lifestyles of others. Bigots usually think their own views are the only correct ones.

bioethics The discipline that deals with the moral implications of biological research and applications to humans, especially in medicine.

burial Placement of human remains in a grave.

burial park A track of land intended for ground burial of human remains.

burial permit A permit issued according to state law regarding the interment, disinterment, removal, reinterment, or transportation of human remains.

cadaver A dead body intended for dissection.

canonization The process by which the Church officially declares a dead person to be a saint. If the Church can prove that the person led a life of heroic virtue, it confers the title "venerable." If one miracle is worked through the person's intercession, the Church confers the title "blessed." If two miracles are worked through the person's intercession, the Church confers the title "saint."

capital punishment The killing of a criminal for particular crimes committed.

capital sins Evil tendencies within us that predispose us to sin. The seven capital sins—pride, covetous, lust, anger, gluttony, envy, and sloth—are the root causes of most sins. They also cause a great deal of suffering in this world.

casket A receptacle in which the dead body is placed during the funeral and for burial.

catacombs Underground burial sites of many early Christians, especially around Rome.

catafalque An immovable platform upon which a casket is placed. A catafalque is usually used for the public visitation of a deceased government official, as in a capitol rotunda.

catechumens People who are studying about the Catholic faith with the intention of being baptized.

cemetery A word that means "land of those who are sleeping." According to the law, a cemetery is any place that contains six or more human bodies. It may include a burial park for earth interments, a mausoleum for crypt or vault interments, or a crematory and columbarium for cinerary interment.

chrism Holy oil (olive or vegetable mixed with balm), forms of which are used at Baptism, Confirmation, and Holy Orders.

chronic Long-term pain; suffering that may not ever be relieved.

ciborium Container for the consecrated Hosts at Mass. The ciborium is usually made of gold or silver.

codicil A change or revision of an original will.

coffin An obsolete term for a casket.

columbarium A building, room, or other space containing niches for inurnment of cremated remains.

committal The act of disposing of human remains by earth burial, mausoleum entombment, or columbarium inurnment.

communion of saints The union of all people of God—living, dead, in heaven, or in purgatory—with Christ and one another in faith, grace, prayer, and good works.

compassion To suffer with others; to be moved by the suffering of others in such a way that we try to alleviate that suffering.

coroner Public official delegated with the responsibility of determining the cause of death in cases where death is not from a natural or apparent reason. The coroner is also responsible for the disposition of unclaimed bodies.

cortege A funeral procession with the casket.

cremains Human remains after incineration.

cremation Burning the body of a deceased person; reducing the body of a deceased person to ashes.

crematory, crematorium A building or structure containing a furnace to incinerate the bodies of deceased persons.

cryonics The practice of freezing the body of a person who has died of a disease with the hope of bringing him or her back to life in the future when a cure for the disease has been developed.

crypt A space in a mausoleum in which casketed remains may be placed and sealed; the lower part of a church used for worship and/or burial.

death The permanent cessation of all vital bodily functions: (1) total brain function, (2) spontaneous function of the respiratory system, and (3) spontaneous function of the circulatory system.

death certificate A legal document certifying the time, place, and cause of death.

death notice A paid notice in a newspaper announcing the death and funeral arrangements of a person.

deceased A person who has died.

decedent A dead person, stillborn infant, or fetus.

denial One of the stages of dying, in which a person refuses to admit the truth of his or her condition.

depression One of the stages of dying, in which a person becomes sad about approaching death and begins to assess his or her life.

dignity The belief that all people have an intrinsic worth because they are made in the image and likeness of God. Because of human dignity, all people have a right to respect and to whatever is needed for life (shelter, food, clothing, medical care).

disarmament The actual destruction or reduction of nuclear weapons.

disinterment To dig up a grave for the purposes of identifying or moving human remains; to exhume.

dispensary A place where medical aid is given to people who need it.

donor Individual who makes a gift of all or part of his or her body after death (organs, tissues, eyes, bones, arteries, blood, other body fluids, and any other parts of the human body).

durable power of attorney for health care A legal document authorizing someone else to make medical decisions in the patient's best interest if he or she is unable to make such decisions. The authorized person (agent) has the same legal force as if it were the patient speaking on his or her own behalf.

Easter The first Sunday after the first full moon following the spring equinox. On this day, Catholic and Protestant Christians celebrate in a special way the resurrection of Christ.

Easter Triduum The Christian celebration of Christ's passing from death to life; the Easter Triduum begins on Holy Thursday with evening Mass of the Lord's Supper, includes the Good Friday service, the Easter Vigil service, and Masses on Easter Sunday, and ends with evening prayer on Easter Sunday.

ecclesiastical burial Interment according to the rites of the Church. All Catholics in good standing have the right to ecclesiastical burial, as do catechumens, unbaptized children whose parents intended to have them baptized, and baptized non-Catholics, unless it would be considered against their will.

embalming The process of preparing a dead body for burial. During the embalming process, body fluids are replaced with preserving chemicals.

entombment Placement of human remains in a crypt or vault.

epitaph The inscription on a tombstone or grave marker.

eschatology The branch of theology that deals with the four last things: death, judgment, heaven, and hell, as well as the final state of perfection of the people and of the kingdom of God at the end of time.

eulogy A speech that praises an individual who has died.

euthanasia The painless putting to death of someone who is hopelessly ill; sometimes called *mercy killing*. In voluntary active euthanasia, the physician not only provides the means of death but actually administers the lethal injection at the patient's request. The Church considers euthanasia to be murder and thus to be immoral.

executor, executrix Person (male or female) who carries out the wishes of the person who made the will.

exorcism A rite in which evil spirits are driven out of a person or place by the authority of God and with the prayer of the Church.

faith A theological virtue that enables us to believe that God exists and loves us. Faith also enables us to have a personal relationship with God and to live by gospel values, despite situations of suffering and pain.

flower car A convertible or other specially designed car that transports funeral flowers to and from the church and to the cemetery.

formalin A solution of formaldehyde and water that is used in embalming.

fratricide The killing of one's brother.

full couch A style of casket in which the whole lid opens or lifts off so that the entire body may be viewed.

funeral director Person who is licensed in the state in which he or she practices to arrange and conduct funeral ceremonies, rites, and rituals. Other terms for a funeral director are *mortician* and *undertaker* (obsolete).

funeral home A building designed for preparation of the dead, the observance of wakes, visitations, and funerals. Another name for a funeral home is a *mortuary*.

gerontology The study of aging.

Good Friday The Friday before Easter Sunday. Christians remember in a special way on this day the Paschal mystery, especially the passion and death of Jesus.

grace A sharing in God's life, love, and light. Grace is God's free gift to us.

grave Space of ground in a burial park, used for burial.

grave liner A concrete vault surrounding a casket that has been buried.

grave marker A wood plank, heap of stones, or boulder used to mark the site of a grave.

grief Deep and poignant distress, usually accompanied by sorrow.

half couch A style of casket in which half of the lid opens or lifts off so that the body may be viewed from the waist up.

hearse A vehicle for transporting the casket and remains.

heaven The Christian belief that those who have achieved salvation are in the eternal presence of God.

hell A state of eternal punishment and alienation from God.

Hemlock Society USA A modern-day society that believes each person should have the right to choose the time of his or her death. The society advocates suicide, especially in circumstances of advanced age and terminal illness.

heretic A baptized Catholic who obstinately denies or doubts some truth believed to be part of the faith.

hinge cap A style of casket similar to the half couch, except for variations in the placement of the lid hinges.

holiness The perfect state of goodness and righteousness. God alone is perfectly holy, but God calls all people to become holy.

Holy Thursday The Thursday before Easter Sunday, on which the Church begins its celebration of the Easter Triduum, focusing particularly on the institution of the Eucharist.

homicide The intentional killing of a human being.

hope The theological virtue that enables us to trust that God is always working for our good and will someday bring us eternal happiness.

hospice A care facility for individuals who are terminally ill.

hospital An institution staffed and equipped for the diagnosis and treatment of the sick or injured. Most hospitals today have both inpatient and outpatient facilities.

immortality The survival and continuing existence of the human soul after death.

indulgence The remission before God of temporal punishment due for sins that a person (with the right attitude and actions) acquires through the intervention of the Church.

infanticide The practice of killing sick or unwanted infants and children.

infirmary A place where the sick are lodged for care and treatment.

integrity Acting according to the values we hold true. Integrity means being faithful to our values and beliefs. Our actions match what we say.

interment A disposition of human remains by inurnment, entombment, earth burial, or burial at sea.

interment plot A space in a cemetery, intended for burial of human remains. A single plot may include more than one grave, crypt, or vault.

intestate The situation of dying without leaving a will.

inurnment Placing cremated remains in an urn and placing it in a niche.

just war theory A moral position that states that war may be justified if it meets six criteria.

last judgment Final judgment by Christ at the end of the world and the general resurrection from the dead.

legator Person who makes the will; another term for a legator is *settlor*.

leprosarium A hospital for leprosy patients.

living will A legal document in which people make known their wishes about what medical or health care treatment they would or would not want if they became seriously ill. The purpose of the document is to ask that one's dying not be unreasonably prolonged.

love (a) The theological virtue that enables us to worship, praise, and value God above anything or anyone else. (b) The moral virtue that enables us to relate unselfishly to others, with sincere concern, understanding, and forgiveness.

magisterium The highest teaching authority in the Catholic Church. The magisterium is composed of the bishops in union with the pope. The magisterium has the responsibility of teaching and defending the principles of Catholic faith and morality.

manifest sin A sin for which there are eyewitnesses who can give testimony about it. If there is no public scandal, the right of burial is not to be denied even to manifest sinners.

martyr A Greek word that means "witness;" one who voluntarily dies for the faith or some Christian virtue.

masochism An unhealthy desire to inflict pain, humiliation, abuse, or suffering on oneself.

Mass stipend A monetary offering given to a priest to celebrate Mass for a certain intention. People frequently request that Masses be celebrated for and in memory of deceased family members.

matricide The killing of one's mother.

mausoleum A structure or building for entombment of casketed human remains in crypts or vaults.

memorial A contribution that is made to a charitable organization or public cause in the memory of someone who has died.

memorial park A private cemetery that requires uniform grave markers level with the grass.

memorial society Consumer group organized to ensure a dignified funeral at low cost.

morgue A place to which human remains are removed pending proper identification and release to relatives; a morgue may be a special building in more populous areas or a special section in a hospital.

mortality Death; the end of human life.

mourning A process by which people express their grief after the death of a loved one.

necromancy Supposed communication with the dead.

neophytes The newly baptized.

nerve Fibers of nervous tissue that connect the central nervous system (brain and spinal chord) with neurons throughout the body.

neuron A nerve cell; cell that has the ability to receive and transmit electrical and chemical impulses related to motion and sensory perception.

neurosis An unhealthy mental condition in which one is trapped within an endlessly recurring pattern of emotional suffering—anxiety, obsession, self-centeredness, paranoia, fatalism, and so on.

niche A space in a columbarium used for inurnment of cremated human remains.

nirvana A blissful state of perfect happiness, in which there is no suffering or death.

notorious An action that is publicly known or has been committed in such circumstances that it is entirely impossible to conceal it or offer any legal justification for it.

nuclear winter Environmental devastation that would probably result from explosions in a nuclear war.

obituary A newspaper column containing a biographical sketch of someone who has recently died.

Oil of the Sick Oil blessed by the bishop at the chrism Mass on Holy Thursday. This is usually olive oil, unless it cannot be obtained. Then another oil derived from plants may be substituted. The oil is used to anoint people in the Sacrament of the Anointing of the Sick.

omniscient The ability of God to know everything—past, present, and future. God can read human hearts and know what we need before we say the words.

original sin The sin of Adam and Eve; the lack in humans of the original holiness and justice that the first humans had, resulting in concupiscence, which is the inherited tendency within all humans to be attracted to evil and to choose sin over virtuous living, even after Baptism.

ossuary A container for the bones of the dead.

pacifism Opposition to all war or violence as a means of settling disputes.

pall A large white cloth that is placed over a casket as a reminder of Baptism and the white garment the person received at Baptism.

pallbearer A person who helps carry the casket to and from its place in church and at the cemetery. An honorary pallbearer escorts the casket but does not actually carry it.

paradise A perfect world; a heaven on earth in which people walk and talk with God.

parousia The second coming of Christ, which will mark the final judgment and the perfection of God's kingdom at the end of the world.

parricide The killing of either or both parents.

particular judgment Judgment that occurs at the moment of death, when each person goes either to heaven, hell, or purgatory.

passion A word that means "to suffer." To be passionate means to experience intense, driving, overwhelming emotion and feeling. It also means having a strong liking toward, desire for, or ardent devotion to something or someone else.

Passover (1) A Jewish feast held each spring to celebrate the Exodus event. (2) A term used to describe the Paschal mystery, Jesus' passing from death to new life.

patricide The killing of one's father.

perpetual care A contract between a grave owner and cemetery to maintain the grave forever.

pharmacy A place where medicine is dispensed.

physician-assisted suicide A type of mercy killing in which a physician or family member assists a person in committing suicide. The physician provides the means of death but does not administer the lethal injection or dose. The Catholic Church considers physician-assisted suicide to be murder and thus to be immoral.

prayer The raising of the mind and heart to the Blessed Trinity in praise, thanksgiving, contrition, and petition. Prayer may be vocal or silent, solitary or with others.

pre-need planning Funeral and burial arrangements that are made before death by an individual. These arrangements may or may not include financial payment.

probate court The legal institution that is responsible for overseeing the handling of a will and the payment of all debts belonging to a person who has died.

prognosis A doctor's estimate of the amount of time a patient may have left before death.

purgatory A Christian belief regarding the state of those who die in grace but with some attachment to sin. Purgatory is a state of passive suffering and purification for venial sins before admittance into heaven.

purity of heart Single-minded focus on goodness and the things of God. Single-heartedness; having motives that are free from moral fault or guilt.

relic A sacred object associated with a saint. A first-class relic is the saint's body or part of the saint's body. A second-class relic is a part of clothing or an article used by a saint. A third-class relic is any object touched to a first-class relic.

religion The praise and service of the Trinity as expressed in divine worship and in daily life. A person's total response to the demands of faith; religion is a living faith, a personal relationship with and a self-commitment to God.

reliquary A container for safeguarding and exhibiting the relics of saints.

resilience The ability to handle whatever life deals us. Resilient people do not just cope with pain and suffering by merely surviving; they thrive despite the problems they are having.

resurrection Jesus' Passover from death to life in and through the power of God. People who die believing in Jesus will rise, as he did, to new life.

retributionists People who favor the use of the death penalty.

retributive justice The type of justice in which good people are rewarded and evil people are punished.

sadism An unhealthy desire to inflict pain, humiliation, abuse, or suffering on someone else.

sanctoral cycle A Church calendar of saints' feast days. Commemorations on these days are intended to illustrate how the saint followed Christ, to honor the saint as a hero of holiness, and to appeal for the saint's help.

sarcophagus An ornate and elaborate outer casket, usually made of granite, marble, or heavy metal. The body may be placed directly inside it, or the entire casket may be placed inside the sarcophagus.

schismatic A baptized Catholic who refuses to obey the Holy Father or refuses communion with the members of the Church.

sepulcher A place of burial; tomb.

shroud A white sheet or robe-like garment that may be worn by the deceased.

single-heartedness The virtue that enables us to envision a goal and keep our attention and energy focused on reaching it. The ability to want just one thing with all our hearts.

sororicide The killing of one's sister.

spiritualism Attempts to communicate with spirits and departed souls by means of seances, table-tapping, Ouija boards, and other methods. Spiritualistic practices, which often involve fraud, are considered a violation of the virtue of religion because they give spirits Godlike powers over the present and the future.

suffering An unpleasant sensory and emotional experience associated with being alive. To suffer means to "to endure death, pain, or distress, to sustain loss or damage, to be subject to disability or handicap."

suicide The intentional killing of oneself.

superstition The non-Christian belief that bad luck has irrational causes—magic or certain actions, such as walking under a ladder, crossing the path of a black cat, stepping on a crack in the sidewalk, breaking a mirror, or traveling on Friday the 13th.

terminal sedation An ethical course of treatment intended to relieve the pain of a dying patient rather than intentionally kill the patient. In terminal sedation, a physician gives the dying patient medications (usually barbiturates or benzodiazepine) that cause unconsciousness. Life supports are removed, including intravenous food and water, while the disease runs its final course. The patient usually dies in a few days or a week.

thanatology The study of death.

theodicy The problem of trying to reconcile God's justice with the fact of unjust evil and suffering in the world. In other words, how could a good God allow bad things to happen to good people?

tomb A grave or space for the burial of the dead.

tombstone A grave marker containing the name of the deceased, dates of birth and death, and perhaps an epitaph. A grave marker that is placed over a person's head is called a headstone; a grave marker placed over the feet is called a footstone.

union with God A state of eternal happiness, life, and oneness with God.

utopia A perfect, or ideal, society.

uxoricide The killing of a wife by her husband.

vault A metal receptacle to receive the casketed remains, which provides protection against the elements of the earth and prevents the ground above a casket from sinking after decomposition has taken place.

viaticum A word that means "food for the journey." Viaticum refers to the Eucharist that is received by a dying person, in preparation for death and eternal life.

visitation Specified hours when friends and acquaintances pay their respects to the deceased and his or her family.

voluntary stopping of eating and drinking (a) A situation in which a dying patient voluntarily decides not to eat or drink. Death eventually is caused by dehydration or starvation. (b) A situation in which a dying patient (who has previously given his or her consent) is taken off life-support and disconnected from feeding tubes.

wake A watch kept over the dead, which may take the form of visitation, calling hours, or *shiva*. The revised *Order of Christian Funerals* calls for a vigil service as part of the wake, including prayers and Scripture readings.

will A legal document that states what a person wants done with his or her possessions after death.

works of mercy Charitable actions directed toward meeting the physical and spiritual needs of others. The corporal works of mercy are: (1) Feed the hungry. (2) Give drink to the thirsty. (3) Clothe the naked. (4) Visit the imprisoned. (5) Shelter the homeless. (6) Visit the sick. (7) Bury the dead. The spiritual works of mercy are: (1) Admonish the sinner. (2) Instruct the ignorant. (3) Counsel the doubtful. (4) Comfort the sorrowful. (5) Bear wrongs patiently. (6) Forgive all injuries. (7) Pray for the living and the dead.

Index